Butterfly, the Bride

Law, Meaning, and Violence

The scope of Law, Meaning, and Violence is defined by the wide-ranging scholarly debates signaled by each of the words in the title. Those debates have taken place among and between lawyers, anthropologists, political theorists, sociologists, and historians, as well as literary and cultural critics. This series is intended to recognize the importance of such ongoing conversations about law, meaning, and violence as well as to encourage and further them.

Series Editors:

Martha Minow, Harvard Law School
Elaine Scarry, Harvard University
Austin Sarat, Amherst College

Butterfly, the Bride

Essays on Law, Narrative, and the Family

Carol Weisbrod

Ann Arbor

THE UNIVERSITY OF MICHIGAN PRESS

Copyright © by the University of Michigan 1999
All rights reserved
Published in the United States of America by
The University of Michigan Press
Manufactured in the United States of America
⊗ Printed on acid-free paper

2002   2001   2000   1999   4   3   2   1

A CIP catalog record for this book is available from the British Library.

Library of Congress Cataloging-in-Publication Data

Weisbrod, Carol.
    Butterfly, the bride : essays on law, narrative, and the family
/ Carol Weisbrod.
        p.   cm. — (Law, meaning, and violence)
    Includes bibliographical references and index.
    ISBN 0-472-10921-9 (cloth : acid-free paper)
        1. Law and literature.   2. Long, John Luther, 1861–1927.—Madame
Butterfly.   3. Loti, Pierre, 1850–1923. Madame Chrysantheme.
4. Narration (Rhetoric)   5. Family in literature.   6. Marriage in
literature.   7. Family law and legislation.   8. Contracts.
9. Violence (Law).   10. Effectiveness and validity of law.   I. Title.
II. Series.
PN56.L33   W396   1998
809'.93355—dc21   98-25389
                                                                                CIP

We always believe ourselves without further ado until we learn to consider the objections of others and to internalize such discussions in the form of reflection.

Jean Piaget, *Six Psychological Studies*

Acknowledgments

The work on this book was done over some years and I was helped at many points by many people. I would like particularly to thank Milner Ball, Mark Janis, Carolyn Jones, Richard Kay, Martha Minow, Thomas Morawetz, Carl Schneider, Pamela Sheingorn, Aviam Soifer, Lee Teitelbaum, Eva Weisbrod, and Larry Yackle for assistance of various kinds.

Institutional support from the University of Connecticut has been generous through the years that I have been on that faculty. The law school's present Dean, Hugh Macgill, is to be specially thanked for his encouragement.

Almost all of the material in this book was discussed, to my great profit, with the late Leon Lipson.

Others who are not named here have also contributed to this work, among them family, friends, and colleagues, as well as participants in the meetings at which a number of these papers were presented. Conversations and encounters in different times and places have made this book possible. I am grateful for them.

Portions of this work were published, in a different form, in the following journals:

"The Way We Live Now: A Discussion of Contracts and Domestic Arrangements," *Utah Law Review* 777 (1994).

"Family Governance: A Reading of Kafka's Letter to his Father," 24 *University of Toledo Law Review* 689 (1993). Reprinted by permission of the University of Toledo Law Review.

"Divorce Stories: Readings, Comments and Questions on Law and Narrative," *Brigham Young Law Review* 143 (1991).

"On the Expressive Functions of Family Law," 22 *U.C. Davis Law Review* 991 (1989). Copyright 1989 by The Regents of the University of California. Reprinted with permission.

Contents

Introduction

This book consists of a set of discussions that look at law, and particularly family law, in light of works commonly classified as narrative or literature. The objective is to enrich our understanding of marriage and the family, and the role of law in dealing with and shaping these institutions and our ideas of these institutions. The narratives discussed here are of different kinds, some biographical, some fictional. The featured story—best known through Puccini's opera—concerns a young woman named Butterfly who becomes a bride, and each chapter begins with a brief discussion of the legal implications of a piece of that story. These sections on Madame Butterfly are used as short introductory expositions of the issues considered in the chapter that follows. The questions raised are not so much answered as developed, illustrated by a variety of textual material. The range of images and ideas in the butterfly story and in the other narratives—the biblical account of Vashti, who refused to obey her husband's summons, the diary of Miriam Donaven, a modern woman who killed her lover and herself, Kafka's letter to his father, among others—are used to evoke a complex reality. In its largest meaning, the butterfly is an image of this reality, the totality of things.

This reading of the butterfly is not the most common one. One conventional definition sees the butterfly as the symbol of the soul and the transformation of the butterfly—caterpillar, chrysalis, butterfly—as tracking the idea of the soul leaving the body at death. In Christian art, the butterfly and its life cycle come to represent life, death, and resurrection.[1]

The butterfly is also associated with beauty. However, as Primo Levi notes, the transformation of the butterfly must mean that it represents more than beauty. In the caterpillar stage, it is also associated with all that we tend to find ugly. "Just as butterflies are beautiful by definition, so caterpillars are by definition ugly: clumsy, slow, bumbling, voracious, hairy, obtuse; they are in turn symbolic, the symbol of what is crude, unfinished, an unattained perfection." As to the beauty of the butterfly, "We would not think them so beautiful if they did not fly, or if they flew straight and briskly like bees or, above all, if they did not enact the perturbing mystery of metamorphosis."[2]

If the butterfly is about contradictories and about metamorphosis and transformation, we can see the idea that the butterfly is a symbol of life, rather than a state after death. For example, we have Cirlot's description of an illustration in Lehner's *Dictionary of Symbols:* "The Angel of Death was represented by the Gnostics as a winged foot crushing a butterfly, from which we may deduce that the butterfly was equated with life rather than with the soul."[3] Another definition sees the butterfly as representing the totality of things: "the butterfly contains within itself all its previous incarnations and the promise of future generations."[4]

The argument of this book offers the butterfly as life, and law as something associated with violence.[5] This reading altogether minimizes the positive aspects of the legal system in ordinary understanding, its associations with order, the facilitation of aspirations to the good life, and shared moral ideas. Cicero's *De Legibus* is a positive description: "Law is the highest reason, implanted in Nature, which commands what ought to be done and forbids the opposite."[6] The present emphasis stresses the violence in the command and in the definition of the substantive imperatives. The law's violence, as it is understood here, goes beyond direct coercion. We see the relationship between law's violence and the butterfly in a form suggested by Alexander Pope: He attacks someone who would "break a butterfly upon a wheel."[7] This broad reading of the butterfly, as broad perhaps as the idea that "butterflies are free,"[8] is made concrete here by a story in which Butterfly is the name of a young girl, the fifteen-year-old Cho-Cho-San, whose life takes the shape of one particular legal form, a bride.

The use of Madame Butterfly as a structural device is not inevitable. *Madame Butterfly*—and more particularly the libretto of this highly theatrical, very accessible opera—is simply useful as a way of introducing to a general reader some questions with which readers of law reviews (the original audience of much of this work) are already familiar. The larger idea of the butterfly as a symbol of life, shaped or even crushed by law's violence, is one way of saying something that others have said without invoking butterflies.[9]

Puccini's opera, first performed in 1904,[10] is the story of a young geisha who marries an American naval officer and is abandoned by him when he returns to America and marries a "real" wife. In the opera, the story ends with her suicide. The narrative is often taken to be about the betrayal of the constant lover by the casual seducer. For modern readers, it may also be about the stereotyping of Asian women as compliant to the point of suicide. In outline, the narrative is based on the story by the American lawyer John Luther Long, who published his "Madame Butterfly" in the *Century* magazine in 1898.[11] A play by David Belasco built on the Long story was seen in London by Puccini, who did not understand the language but saw the dramatic possibilities.[12] Cho-Cho-San is seventeen years old in Long, fifteen in Puccini. In Long, Madame Butterfly does not die.

There are other significant butterfly narratives. *M. Butterfly*, David Hwang's deconstruction of the Madame Butterfly story, involves the love affair between a French diplomat and an actress in the Chinese theater who is in fact not only a male but also a spy.[13] Another relevant narrative is *Madame Chrysanthemum*, the 1887 novel by Pierre Loti, presumably an indirect source of the John Luther Long story.[14] In *Madame Chrysanthemum*, the temporary marriage is a commercial transaction throughout and not necessarily the first such marriage for Madame Chrysanthemum. At the end, the French narrator asks to be washed clean of his "little marriage" for payment. The bride, at the end, is testing coins as possible counterfeits.[15]

Another butterfly story is offered by Tolkien in his poem "Errantry": "he begged a pretty butterfly that fluttered by to marry him."[16] Tolkien tells us that the butterfly was caught and taken to the bridal bed. Later, however, there was quarreling (suggested to be her fault), and the husband continued wandering. Any pain or regret in this story is concealed by the lightness of the meter and the wordplay. It is perhaps Tolkien's butterfly who is most like our culture's picture of the bride in her long gown and weightless lace veil. We see her in a young woman described as "the prettiest, silliest, most affected, husband-hunting butterfly."[17]

The idea of narrative here is broad, along the lines of a recent definition: *Narrative* is "a telling of some true or fictitious event or connected sequence of events, recounted by a narrator to a narratee (although there may be more than one of each)." Narrative "includes both the shortest account of events (e.g. *the cat sat on the mat*, or a brief news item) and the longest historical or biographical works, diaries, travelogues, etc., as well as novels, ballads, epics, short stories, and other fictional forms."[18]

My perspective stresses issues of law, social structure, and institutional shapings—and individual understandings and responses. Inevitably, issues of violence are basic, the law's violence and the law's response to the violence of individuals.

The general method involved, that of looking at law from the outside and through something else, has been used systematically for some time, from a variety of points of view. Thus we have law and economics, law and history (as against legal history, which tends to focus on the history of legal doctrines and institutions), and law and psychology. In the present enterprise, the law is explored through the analysis of particular texts, loosely classified as literary or narrative, though not all are works of fiction.

I do not analyze these texts in the way that a professional literary critic or academic theorist would tend to do. There is in general little concern here with some of the questions that concern them. The context of the narratives, for example, the writer's and his or her time's attitudes toward class, gender, and race are of minimal interest. Rather, the narrative or literary text is the vehicle for the exploration of certain questions that are prominent in a contemporary legal and social conversation. The texts are sometimes read idiosyncratically, with a stress on the point that variant texts are always possible. (Even the story of the Prisoner's Dilemma, standard fare in the law-and-economics movement—where one might have expected more standardization and certainty—exists in various forms.)[19]

Law has various relationships to narrative. Sometimes a narrative is the foundational story of the giving of the law, providing legitimacy and authority (and its coercive power) to the law itself. But it is common nonetheless to distinguish between the social significance of law and that of narrative or literature. Law and literature are both cultural artifacts, products of the values and orientations of the societies that produce and consume them. Their characteristics as cultural artifacts are, however, quite different. It may be argued that literature or art influences society. But it is also true that this influence is fairly remote and quite speculative compared to legally enforced punishment. Law's effects are direct, while the social effects of literature are indirect. Law is linked directly to authority, power, and violence: judges, Robert

Cover says, are people of violence.[20] This is not generally true of narrative, though it is often born out of violence and oppression.

The book has three major thematic emphases. One is the idea of legal pluralism, which stresses that multiple sovereignties interact with each other in society. This idea is explored most directly in chapter 4, on Kafka. Another is the idea of contract, seen as a legal and political instrument that has transformative potential, and addressed directly in chapter 3, which uses materials from Trollope to illustrate contractual themes. The third theme might be described as the idea of intellectual reticence. That is, there are limits on what we can know in any perfect way and limits on what we can expect the law to do. Narratives may suggest the further point that the problem is less the law than the social meaning of the legal act.

Relationships between these themes could be structured in different ways. Taking contract as the largest idea, one could say that contract is a way to include pluralist ideas in the official system, and that limits on law's power or efficacy suggest a restriction on the transformative potential of official contract. Taking limits of law as the largest idea, one could say that law as order, certainty, and authority is undercut by legal pluralism—the existence in fact of competing normative orders—and the idea of contract (within law) is something that "limits" official law by introducing the idea of private ordering. Taking legal pluralism as the largest idea, we could see contract as a vehicle for pluralism and limits of law as a fact made inevitable by the existence of competing sovereignties.

My emphasis on limits of law, while certainly not new, needs some comment, given that normative values and improvement in the law are taken as prime values in legal scholarship. It is typically urged that some very specific reform is desirable, necessary, and even possibly sufficient to accomplish some general good. Some academic writing exhausts much of its energy at a fairly high level of theory and then—under the impact of a demand for normative proposals—reduces itself to the advocacy of a limited straightforward legislative or judicial solution, a change of the standard of review by the Supreme Court, an expanded definition of state action, or the introduction of waiting periods for divorce. In general, a proposal for reform is considered basic to the scholarly enterprise in law.

This is not the approach taken here. There is no obvious law reform that comes from the perspective suggested in the following essays. To the extent that reform is the goal and these essays are directed to institutional questions, they involve a call for a study commission more than a call for a statute. One reason is that narratives may suggest varying reforms. Another is that we may not yet know how to evaluate narratives for these purposes.

For all the questions, however, narrative has a function in law reform; it gives access to material and understanding at a level that social science does not reach. This function is of considerable importance in the case of family law, where we deal with a particularly intense form of storytelling that involves the shaping of personal history and private life. In the end, because we live with others in a social order, our conversations with others and with ourselves assume visible institutional forms. As George Steiner has written, "There is language, there is art, because there is 'the other.' We do address ourselves in constant soliloquy. But the medium of that soliloquy is that of public speech."[21] In this context, public speech includes law.

This book explores the relationships between the inner and the public worlds through an examination of what is ordinarily classified as the sphere of "private" life, the world of family relationships. A basic proposition of the sociology of law that informs this work can be offered in a single sentence, written by Eugen Ehrlich in 1912: "At the present, as well as at any other time, the center of gravity of legal development lies not in legislation, nor in juristic science, nor in judicial decision, but in society itself."[22] But "society" is not a monolith. The "itself" must be opened, to reveal the complex interior life. Narrative allows that possibility.

Chapter One

The Bride

There is no dispute as to the facts. In 1897 John Luther Long wrote a novel entitled "Madame Butterfly," which was published in the Century Magazine and copyrighted by the Century Company.
                                        Ricordi v Paramount, 189 F2d 469 (1951)

It is possible that the story of Cho-Cho-San and Pinkerton is true, in the sense that it is based on real events that happened a hundred years ago to real people. It may be as suggested, that Long's sister, the wife of a missionary, heard this true story in Japan and told her brother.[1] Or it may be true at one level removed, based not on a tragic anecdote but on an earlier, possibly autobiographical, work, Pierre Loti's Madame Chrysanthemum. *Or it may be true in some other sense, as a fiction that speaks more deeply than fact.*

Law and literature have very different approaches to the idea of fact. While in some contexts law may stress its own complexities and pluralism, it seems that, at least by contrast to literature or, more expansively, narrative, law stresses a single, integrated, hierarchical vision and a single authoritative voice. Law and narrative are always in tension to the extent that law emphasizes clarity and reduction to a single vision, while a major point in narrative, both the telling and the questions we ask about the telling, is ambiguity and complexity. Law's idea of truth is captured in the oath for witnesses: "Do you swear to tell the truth, the whole truth and nothing but the truth?"[2] Narrative has a different sense: "Is this true? Is this the whole story? I think not."[3]

At the same time we know that the law is not always concerned with literal truth. The clear, but perhaps debatable, statement of the facts in the litigation over the copyright to "Madame Butterfly" evokes law's general approach. The established facts are facts for the purposes of a lawsuit. An eighteen-page story becomes a novel. We say that the work was written in 1897, when it seems that what we really know is that it was published in 1898. We have found facts on which to build.

Is Long's Madame Butterfly though told by an omniscient narrator to be understood as Cho-Cho-San's narrative? If so, how reliable is it? Do we perceive her as deceived or, perhaps, deluded, "wilfully blind"?[4] If deluded—misunderstanding the nature of marriage—does her choice count? Would her choice count in any case given her subordinate role?

The first section of this opening chapter uses the biblical story of Vashti to raise methodological issues of truth and partiality in narrative, important questions if we want to use narratives to ground law reform. Feminist dimensions are explored separately, in the second part of the chapter, which considers issues of autonomy in relation to women as well as questions of the different voice. The concluding section of the chapter deals with the utility of narrative for law, official and unofficial, and places the story of the bride in the context of the family law.

Some Problems of Narrative

Vashti

On the seventh day, when the king was merry with wine, he ordered Mehuman, Bizzetha, Harbona, Bigtha, Abagtha, Zethar, and Carcas, the seven eunuchs in attendance on King Ahasuerus, to bring Queen Vashti before the king wearing a royal diadem, to display her beauty to the peoples and the officials; for she was a beautiful woman. But Queen Vashti refused to come at the king's command conveyed by the eunuchs. The king was greatly incensed, and his fury burned within him.

Then the king consulted the sages learned in procedure. (For it was the royal practice [to turn] to all who were versed in law and precedent. His closest advisers were Carshena, Shethar, Admatha, Tarshish, Meres, Marsena, and Memucan, the seven ministers of Persia and Media who had access to the royal presence and occupied the first place in the kingdom.) "What, [he asked,] "shall be done, according to law, to Queen Vashti for failing to obey the command of King Ahasuerus conveyed by the eunuchs?"

Thereupon Memucan declared in the presence of the king and the ministers: "Queen Vashti has committed an offense not only against Your Majesty but also against all the officials and against all the peoples in all the provinces of King Ahasuerus. For the queen's behavior will make all wives despise their husbands, as they reflect that King Ahasuerus himself ordered Queen Vashti to be brought before him, but she would not come. This very day the ladies of Persia and Media, who have heard of the queen's behavior, will cite it to all Your Majesty's officials, and there will be no end of scorn and provocation!

"If it please Your Majesty, let a royal edict be issued by you, and let it be written into the laws of Persia and Media, so that it cannot be abrogated, that Vashti shall never enter the presence upon another who is more worthy than she. Then will the judgment executed by Your Majesty resound throughout your realm, vast though it is; and all wives will treat their husbands with respect, high and low alike."

The proposal was approved by the king and the ministers, and the king did as Memucan proposed. Dispatches were sent to all the provinces of the king, to every province in its own language of his own people.[5]

The story of Vashti is told in the Book of Esther, which does not use God's name, and a book about which it might be said that no one, including Esther, is above criticism.[6] The Book of Esther and the celebration of Purim concentrate on Esther, the girl who saves her people. Another reading of the Book of Esther might focus on Vashti.

What can be said about Vashti? To begin with, she does not tell her own story. The narrative is told by someone much more interested in the processes of men than of women. Vashti's story is not only told from the outside, but told without empathy. The narrator does not suggest that he knows Vashti's thoughts or motives in refusing to obey the king's command.

Thus, there have been many discussions of Vashti's motives, attempts by centuries of commentators to deal with the text's failure to give a reason for Vashti's conduct. One suggestion is that Vashti did not come because it was contrary to Persian custom for her to be present. However, "It was not Persian custom to seclude the women as in the modern Orient. The Queen could be present at banquets. . . . that Vashti refused to come because it was contrary to Persian custom is therefore untenable."[7] Another idea is that Vashti was commanded to appear naked, a version that assimilates this story to the account in Herodotus of Candaulas, King of Lydia.[8] The text, however, makes no reference to this. Moreover, if this were true, it would give Vashti a

good reason, or even an excuse, for not coming. Thus, the nakedness
explanation had to also be rejected, at least within the rabbinic tradition. The rabbis "could not see why such a shameless creature as Vashti
was painted by tradition should be unwilling to come even in this condition."[9] Paton cites other explanations that have been offered. Perhaps
Vashti "had a disfigurement which she was unwilling to reveal." Perhaps "she refused because she thought her feast as good as that of
[Ahasuerus] and was unwilling to depreciate hers by gracing his." Others thought "that the refusal was due to the fact that the men were
drunk, and that Vashti feared to be insulted by them. However, the
women were guarded by eunuchs when they attended banquets . . . ;
and surely a Persian queen must have been accustomed to the spectacle
of drunkenness." Paton concludes that the author of Esther apparently
regards the refusal as "merely a whim, for which he offers no explanation."[10]

Feminist readings of Vashti have assumed that, whatever the reason for Vashti's refusal, it was heroic. As a result, Elizabeth Cady Stanton included Vashti among the positive female images in her discussion of the Bible.[11] She writes: "The Bible cannot be accepted or rejected
as a whole, its teachings are varied and its lessons differ widely from
each other. In criticizing [sic] the peccadilloes of Sarah, Rebecca and
Rachel, we would not shadow the virtues of Deborah, Huldah and
Vashti."[12] Stanton saw Vashti's refusal as having a reason. Vashti, who
is said in the Woman's Bible to have refused to come with "dignity," is
the model of the woman Stanton argued for all her life—the woman
who refused to countenance the drunkenness of men.[13] Stanton inter-
polates this sentence in the Vashti story. Vashti said: "Go tell the king I
will not come; dignity and modesty alike forbid."[14] Stanton then quotes
Tennyson.

> Oh, Vashti! noble Vashti!
> Summoned forth, she kept her state,
> And left the drunken king to brawl
> In Shushan underneath his palms.[15]

A second commentator in the Woman's Bible offers a different reason for Vashti's behavior. Here it is as if Vashti's refusal was noble in
itself; Vashti was the "woman who dared" to disobey her husband.[16] In
fact, she may have known his condition, but the real point seems to be

that "she had a higher idea of womanly dignity than placing herself on exhibition as one of the king's possessions."[17]

Vashti McCollum,[18] in the tradition of the nineteenth-century feminists, writes of her namesake that she "was a spirited woman who refused to exhibit her beauty before the king's drinking companions on the seventh day of a party when 'royal wine in abundance' had made the king hilarious. It was a man's world in those days," writes McCollum, "and Vashti was banished for her successor, Esther. My mother was fond of saying that Vashti was the first exponent of woman's rights. Perhaps it was for that reason that I have always liked and been proud of my name."[19]

Ultimately, in Vashti's case, we know what she did, but we do not know why. It is clear that she paid a high price, but just how high a price is unclear. In one version of the story, Vashti is not only put aside and banished,[20] but in fact killed.

> In consequence of all this, Daniel advised, not only that Vashti should be cast off, but that she should be made harmless forever by the hangman's hand. His advice was endorsed by his colleagues, and approved by the king. That the king might not delay the execution of the death sentence, and Daniel himself thus incur danger to his own life, he made Ahasuerus swear the most solemn oath known to the Persians, that it would be carried out forthwith.[21]

Stanton writes: "I have always regretted that the historian allowed Vashti to drop out of sight so suddenly. Perhaps she was doomed to some menial service, or to entire sequestration in her own apartments." The *Woman's Bible* also suggests that the king's judgment might have been "modified . . . when his wrath abated."[22]

What would Vashti have said if she had told her own story? We would assume that, as a human being, she would narrate her account to serve her own ends. She quite possibly would have identified herself as a victim. We would also assume—unless we thought her a straight-out liar—that her account would have some relation to the actual events, the raw facts of the world. But the relation of the account to the raw facts would be seen as an issue to be explored. Vashti's account would be subject to the observations made by sociologist Ernest Mowrer concerning the use of personal narratives in connection with a woman's diary. "Even a document such as [the wife's diary is] incomplete in many respects," he writes, "written too much in the spirit of the martyr who desires sympathy from the reader to contain always a candid account of the attitudes of the husband."[23] Mowrer also notes the more basic problem, that "where the chief interest is in the conflict between husband and wife, a more complete account is needed to bring into relief the attitudes of the husband."[24]

We would have to think about how we could ever know the objective reality against which to measure Vashti's version of the events.[25] We would not take the version of the king, the Jewish commentators, or the twentieth-century Christian scholar as that reality. We would not assume these accounts to be truer than Vashti's own. This is not bias against them or against Vashti. It is simply systematic skepticism. A certain consonance between Vashti's version and the king's or minister's version would have been needed for communication between them, and we might take as true points on which they agreed. But they might all be wrong, or the various accounts taken together might merely be parts of a whole.[26] If we are fortunate, the parts will fit: but we may still be mistaken as to the whole, not knowing just how many parts there are. The various parts might not fit. Or the principals might simply never have communicated at all. Vashti might say to the king "Wanting me to show myself to the ministers, you never saw me." To which the king might respond—obliquely—"I married you."

As to Vashti's own story, we would consider whether it was told in the heat of the events, or recast later; rethought, reexamined, and finally recreated to fit her later sense of herself. "I thought I was happy with him," Vashti might have written, "but of course I see now that I was not, and so finally when he told me to come and show myself, that was the end of it." She, as she is in her later now, could not have been happy as that earlier self.[27] Her present narrative might tell of her [assumed suppressed] prior anger. The motivations of the later self explain the acts of the earlier self. We as readers may be more sympathetic with the new Vashti and less willing to credit the values of the old Vashti. Alternatively, we may find the new Vashti brainwashed, a new convert, more royalist than the king, and the old Vashti authentic—true to her inner voices, her essential nature, or her social responsibilities.

Yet Vashti's narrative would be important. And it is important that we do not have it, since we can see in Vashti the issue of the silence of women (or other groups). It is the silence of the often-cited sister of

Shakespeare and the hardly remembered sister of Mozart.[28] Vashti's narrative would have been a text for us to work on, where now we have only the texts of others looking at her story.[29] And it is worth noting that on one reading, it may be exactly the point that we do not have Vashti's narratives and that we do not understand Vashti's reasons for refusing to show herself. Vashti's silence and her refusal to explain may be more a key to Vashti than the fact of the refusal and certainly more than the contextual aspects of the king being merry. The point about the refusal may not be that it was based on a "whim," but that it was based on a secret. And the point of secrets is that they are not told. On this reading, Vashti stands as one of the great noncommunicators, in the line of Cordelia and Bartleby, and we can never have Vashti's narrative.

The problem arising out of the fact that the women's narrative is missing is just the beginning. We now have women's narratives that we read and interpret as we do all narratives—with particular questions and purposes. For some, the questions go to issues of self-expression or to a fuller sense of the facts. It is another version of thick description. We need all voices to get a fuller sense of what is real. Thus, Patricia Williams writes about her great-great grandmother to reach a hidden story "which had been overlooked and underseen."[30] Through such "overlooked stories," women may write to educate men.[31] For others, the emphasis is on narratives as a vehicle for self-expression, publicly or privately. We use narratives as readers, and perhaps as writers, to locate ourselves, to clarify our own story, to test alternative realities in our minds, without taking the risks of learning through actual experience. "It is the precise role of narrative to offer us a way of experiencing those effects [consequent on behavior] without experimenting with our own lives as well."[32] But this emphasis seems to involve as much what we bring to narrative, as what we get from it.

What, after all, does Vashti's story teach us? That if we disobey authority we are put away? Divorced? Banished? Killed? That if we disobey authority future generations may look at things differently and think that we were heroic? That, for the sake of X, Y and Z, we might be justified in doing A or B?[33] That the law ought to be changed? And, if so, how? And to strengthen which position? These lessons are not intrinsic to Vashti's story. They are in us, reading it.

The use of Vashti's story conceals a significant problem. We do not have to defend an interest in the Book of Esther; a text that has been read and written about for many centuries may safely be considered worthy of current attention. We say of such texts that if it was worth their time, it is probably worth ours. Such texts are of interest for themselves, ends not means. Modern texts—novels, poetry, legal scholarship—often require some additional justification. As to these narrative texts—which are not read primarily for information or argument— sometimes we say that they are art, and as good as anything ever done. But the narrative products of legal scholars do not usually suggest that they should be held to this standard. Our interest in them is not defended as primarily artistic. They are seen as neither data nor art, while being generally both, and they are seen as especially important in relation to law and legal institutions. One relationship that might be possible between law and narrative: a law/society relationship in which narratives are used as evidence of societal standards that are also reflected in state law.

"Pulling a Butterfly"

David Henry Hwang says that Asians may say an Asian woman is "pulling a Butterfly" when she is assuming the role of a submissive oriental woman.[34]

Hwang's play raises the problem by having a man love a submissive oriental woman (playing a Pinkerton to her Butterfly), only to find that she was the strong one and he was Butterfly.

Vashti, after all, is a woman who said no, in a context in which the social situation demanded another answer. How, given women's subordination, was she able to do so? Why was she not reduced either to submission or at least the appearance of submission?

The dominance perspective in feminist theory, at least in its most extreme form, invites a generalized attack on female capacity. Liberal theory recognizes participation only by competent actors. Children, the insane, and other incompetents cannot participate because they cannot, or cannot be permitted to, choose.[35] Only if the consequences of subordination or suppression are viewed as essentially moderate—as a remediable injustice rather than a total annihilation of the autonomous self (a phenomenon is sometimes discussed in the psychological context without special emphasis on social or cultural factors)[36]—can one go in the direction of immediate public participation by women within liberalism,[37] and if the consequences of subordination are merely moderate, the evil cannot be so great as is sometimes suggested. We may start with the idea that the evil is that great, however, and that female consciousness is almost entirely controlled. Catherine MacKinnon, who stresses this view, concedes that female consciousness is nonetheless not entirely conditioned and notes that this point requires explanation. She does not, however, seem to believe that it makes any difference. Olsen suggests that MacKinnon's focus on dominance rather than (limited) freedom may be strategic.[38]

MacKinnon realizes, of course, that under her view, feminism could not have happened. She writes,

> Feminism criticizes this male totality without an account of women's capacity to do so or imagine or realize a more whole truth. Feminism affirms women's point of view, in large part, by revealing, criticizing and explaining its impossibility. This is not a dialectical paradox. It is a methodological expression of women's situation.[39]

On this theory, serious issues exist as to women and choice. Why should sexual activity initiated by women, for example, be any more voluntary than that initiated by men and consented to by women? "A person is not required to deal with another unless he so desires, and, ordinarily, a person should not be required to become an obligor unless he so desires." So speaks the Restatement of Restitution § 2 comment a (1936). The Restatement does not describe the world of necessity, which is to say it does not describe the real world. There is a flatness and formalism in the legal treatment of consent that parallels the treatment of consent in some feminist jurisprudence, particularly those arguments about taking "yes" and "no" seriously. In context, these are necessary and important arguments. In general, they offer a simpler view of human interaction and communication than that to which we are (otherwise) committed. One commentator, for example, notes, "Implicit in [Susan Estrich's] position is a model of how people should conduct their sexual relations, a model which is quite intellectualized and verbal."[40] Why should the "I do" of the marriage ceremony count? Why, as Carole Pateman formulates it, should a woman's "yes" be any more privileged, or any less open to invalidation, than her "no"?[41] If everything becomes a matter of false consciousness, a serious issue, as Jean Bethke Elshtain noted, is that we have no way to deal with the specifics of false consciousness—to determine, as she put it, what is altogether false and ascribed, what is partly true but distorted, and what is altogether true.[42]

Feminine behavior may for example be seen as "tact" and a question of meeting expectations rather than subordination.[43]

Some feminists' writing does acknowledge the impact of culture on men. Lucinda M. Finley notes, "Men, of course, are forced into masculine roles by the process of socialization and the obligations of social and economic dominance.[44] Goffman quotes a description by Simone de Beauvoir of the culturally induced artifice of women and indicates that it is a universal problem. "Through social discipline, then, a mask of manner can be held in place from within. But as Simone de Beauvoir suggests, we are helped in keeping this pose by clamps that are tightened directly on the body, some hidden, some showing."[45] If everything becomes a false consciousness problem—but somehow exclusively for women and not for men—we would seem to be in deep trouble.[46]

Some writing presented in the specific context of consent to sexual intercourse is, in effect, about taking women's consent (or lack of consent) seriously.[47] *No* means *no.* Other writing, however, suggests, in effect, that women in this society are unable to consent freely, having been so molded by the culture that it is impossible for them to refuse certain options. Under this view, the problem is nothing so limited as, for example, how women who value X are to function in a Y professional world; the answer to that might well be to change the professional world, and indeed some feminist writing is addressed exactly to that issue.[48] That these choices are complex and difficult is given. Embry provides one example of the reality behind the yes and no of the franchise. As part of the antipolygamy campaign, the federal government insisted that the Woodruff Manifesto, renouncing polygamy, be ratified by the church membership. One plural wife said,

> I was there in the Tabernacle the day of the Manifesto and I tell you it was an awful feeling. There President Woodruff read the Manifesto that made me no longer a wife and might make me homeless. I sat there by my mother and she looked at me and said, "How can you stand this?" But I voted for it because it was the only thing to do. I raised my hand and voted a thing that would make me a unlawful wife.[49]

The current version of this view suggests that women are molded to be what they are; early political theorists believed that women fit this model naturally. Against this, Mill argued it is impossible in present state of society to obtain "complete and correct knowledge" of natural differences between the sexes.[50] Whatever its basis, however, the point here is that the dominance views—in effect an explanation of women's condition rather than a rejection of the traditional descriptions—are drawn so sharply that they seem to echo earlier debates over, for example, whether women had souls (a subject that Keith Thomas tells us was "Half frivolously, half seriously" debated by theologians for many centuries)[51] or could be held to full criminal accountability.[52] The question sometimes seems to be once again the one Dorothy Sayers saw: Are women human?[53]

Women's most critical yes/no answer historically has been to a proposal of marriage or marriage and divorce. The law of divorce, and the changing idea of marriage and divorce that formed the background of women's choices, are the subject of the next chapter.

Narratives and Official and Unofficial Law

What is the utility of narrative for reform of official law? Somehow we must move from individual narrative to a specific legal proposal. This raises some difficult general questions.

This book outlines some narratives and some law, suggesting a correspondence, over time, between narrative and the evolution of the official law of divorce. It does not, however, conclude which came first.[54] It is simply noted that certain legal regimes concerning divorce are associated with, that is, their values can be evidenced by, certain themes in personal narrative. The power of narrative lies in its capacity to awaken us, and then change us.[55] Often we want to say that the narrative shapes attitudes that shape the law. If so, this carries a heavy responsibility.[56] Because we are appealing to something complex and polyphonic,[57] something whose emotional content is understood to be high (and thus a problem for rational decision-makers), our standards for narrative as a source of any particular law reform must be clear.

What is gained from the narratives that summaries would not provide? Here, as an exercise, are summaries of material in chapter 2.

In the early nineteenth century Eunice Chapman, in a histrionic public account, tells how (for assorted grounds some of which are related, as she sees it, to the crimes of the Shakers) she obtained a divorce and managed to recover her children from the Shakers. Included in this narrative is incidental information about the state of travel in the early decades of the nineteenth century. Elizabeth Cady Stanton, in speech that reflects her personal pain and disgust, describes how a young friend of hers endured a desperately unhappy marriage to a chronic drunkard and lost him and all her children.[58] Miriam Donaven's early-twentieth-century diary records, in overwrought language, her disappointments in marriage. It demonstrates her lack of serious interests, her infantile vocabulary, and her neurotic need for affection.

Certainly, we could, in the manner of the historian, add a few selected quotations and paraphrase the narratives. It would not be necessary to abstract, as was done above. Yet something would still be missing. Clearly, if we are to evoke serious empathy—and this is repeatedly stated to be the goal of narrative—we require something more than exposure to the simple outline of the narrative. Indeed, the entire movement to narrative is resisting the tendency to abstract, to give the gist, the point, the argument. As Aviam Soifer puts the issue: "[L]iterature seems to thrive upon empathetic emanations from the characters portrayed; law's propensity is to reduce people to stock figures, jammed into the narrow confines of a legal classification system too often concerned only with those facts readily containable within preexisting phrases, articulated by using a standardized vocabulary."[59]

This brings us to the justification typically raised; narratives are not merely art, they tell us something. This something is not, as Milner Ball indicates, "a matter of simply conveying information. It is rather a question of moving us into other worlds."[60] The suggestion is made that narratives are a kind of testimony; they reveal things previously hidden or rejected, truths denied by the main system, or perspectives ignored by the dominant discourse. Frequently, what we find is those other worlds is pain. But what is the relation between this pain and law reform? First, of course, law is seen as a generalized and institutionalized source of the injury. Then there is the assumption that by feeling another's pain (as against simply saying that there is in the abstract somebody somewhere in pain) we—as readers turned reformers—get closer to eliminating that pain. This may be true. It may also be true, however, that if we can in any sense forget our own pain, we can forget the pain of others.

Moreover, simply talking about pain—our own or that felt by another—is not itself a painkiller, though in certain processes it is considered a precondition to ending pain.[61] And we are not often encouraged to admit that there is pain in the world with which we choose not to identify. Presumably the king in the account of Vashti felt a certain pain when he was embarrassed in front of his friends, but this is discarded as, in effect, the pain of the slaveholder whose slaves are freed. And there are also female victim stories with which we tend not to identify.[62] When we say that no-fault requires this result, do we fail to recognize their pain? Our sympathy is with the abandoned or the newly impoverished individual, but not necessarily with the claim to preservation of the marital status or possible law reforms based on that idea. As to this, our view, in common with that of much of society, is that relationships are private, that marriages must be allowed to end freely (which is to say finally and unilaterally), and that the problem for the law is limited to an equitable rearrangement of property and a reasonable guarantee of continued economic security for (typically) the homemaker wife. If the women's pain is a necessary cost, then we must explain why some pain is held to be necessary while other pain is considered avoidable. Narrative will not do this work itself.

There are also questions about the narrative of pain itself. Its prime value is apparently that of testimony. There seem to be questions, however, that we are not supposed to ask[63] because these questions, at least at certain times and in certain contexts, are seen to blame the victim or demonstrate that one is in the wrong, or that one has a serious failure of understanding. It seems that we are sometimes asked to accept not only the fact of pain, but also the account of etiology and the suggestion for cure.

Do we assume that narratives have some relationship to truth? Are they to be understood as testimony, and examined by the conventional approaches, for example, of the legal rules of evidence?[64] Or is the appropriate standard more like the standard for truth in art? With reference to *Black Rain* by Masuji Ibuse, a novel about the bombing of Hiroshima, a reviewer observed: "[W]e do not know whether Ibuse imagined this or whether it is truth; or rather, we know that it is true in the sense that Ibuse convinced us in every word he writes that this is how it was and this is how people endure."[65] We accept this in art. We might accept it in certain scholarship.[66] It is an issue we cannot ignore.

The argument for narrative work assumes that narrative is not only not trivial,[67] but is even useful for law reform. This is viable, however, only if the use of narrative (and particularly narrative scholarship) is susceptible to analysis and judgment.[68]

This, however, presents a variety of problems. For example, it is clear that in a field dominated by language, we must deal with the issues raised by modern critical techniques that reject the notion of objective truth.[69] One answer is that the proposition that all stories are partial is different from such propositions as all stories are false and no story is more reliable than another.[70] But it seems that narrative scholarship itself rarely discusses how to make these determinations. We tend to avoid the issues by assuming the greater validity of the later story[71] and by granting the victim's story the status of an expert's testimony.[72]

The issues of the normative implications of narrative—even when they are explicit[73]—raise other issues about the relation between the idea and the speaker. One tradition insists that the idea and the work stand apart from the speaker.[74] Another emphasis is on the speaker, an emphasis that, in effect, insists on narrative as a preliminary to normative conversation or debate.

For example: why comment on Stanton's life and its influence on her ideas about divorce? For some, her life might be used to test the validity of her ideas.[75] For others, her life might suggest the existence or nonexistence of expert status in writing about some ideas. In the political context, it might tell us something about the underlying biases at work. It has been noted that "much (all?) scholarly work is at some level about ourselves."[76] But why do we assume that where we are coming from is defined socially by race, class, or gender rather than some highly individualized response to issues like race, class, or gender?[77] The point is not that life and work are unrelated. Particularly within feminist theories, with their heavy emphasis on the experiential aspects of feminist thinking, we assume that Stanton's experiences and choices in her private life reflect in some way the program she argued for in her political career. The point is that that reflection could cover many relationships, most of them unknown to us and some perhaps hardly known to her. One may argue for a range of public choices that one has no intention of making oneself; as one may condemn behavior in which one engages in privately, or even publicly. Finally, the work or idea stands or falls by itself.[78] A bad person can have a good idea, and a good person a bad one. Our favorite poets may have been unpleasant people.

The insistence that we tell where we are coming from before we offer our beliefs suggests that our beliefs are shaped by our situations in a more direct and linear way than is likely to be the case.[79] If we get to the point of saying that whatever we do is shaped entirely by our individual backgrounds, directly or by opposition, transformation or creative refining, ultimately we have not said much. Race, class, gender, religion, psychological history are blended in the individual in ways beyond calculation. But it may be that if we choose to tell our life story, it is not because we see the telling as a validation of the ideas so much as that we believe the narration provides a credential. We were there. (Though sometimes people who weren't see the truth more clearly.)[80] At other times, the telling of the life seems to have something to do with bias and self-interest.[81] But *self-serving* is, again, a dimension apart from *right* or even *interesting*.[82] And again, reduction of the relevant categories to race, class, and gender is clearly inadequate.[83]

These, it seems, are generic problems about narrative and law reform. But narrative has a specific utility—in the context of legal pluralist approaches—again in the context of divorce.

In discussing narrative and law reform to this point, it is worth noting as a significant aside that we have been using too narrow a definition of law. Narratives suggest that other unofficial legal systems, for example, religious legal systems, operate in people's lives and deserve attention. Typically, we think of these legal systems as "law" in the sense that they are formal and emanate from an authority (albeit not the state). Religious legal systems are the model of such alternative systems.

Immigrants brought with them not only traditions of food, clothing, and music, but also traditions of law. Some of this law was religious, ancient and well articulated. Religious legal systems coexisted and were used by adherents of particular religious groups within the American legal system. Some of these systems involved institutions foreign to the main system.[84] Conditional divorce in Jewish law is one example. The *New York Times* in 1905 published this story.

> NEWARK, Jan. 15.—Following an ancient Jewish custom, Mrs. Hattie Sobel has received a conditional divorce from Samuel Sobel, a member of the Anshe Israel Congregation, who is dangerously ill with paralysis at his home, at Morton and Prince Streets. In the event of Sobel's death Mrs. Sobel will be at liberty to remarry, but if he recovers the divorce will become void.

The ceremony of divorce was performed in the presence of two rabbis and several other witnesses, and was intended to serve as a relief to Mrs. Sobel, if she becomes a widow, from certain religious requirements to which she would otherwise be subjected, among them a divorce from her husband's brother. The ceremony was performed at Sobel's request. His brother lives in Brooklyn.[85]

The Jewish law of marriage and divorce is different from the state law in several respects. To begin with, religious law permits divorce without specific fault grounds. Then, it assumes levirate marriage. (Note the reference to divorce from her husband's brother.)[86] Finally, it includes the idea of conditionality in a divorce decree. The *New York Times* includes the story in its pages as a piece of ethnography, as it might report some other odd event or ritual. The Sobel divorce indicates that particular groups within American society live in a domestic system operating within the official state system. Some efforts at law reform may therefore be directed at that system.

The subgroups that think about divorce in their own way vary from each other.[87] They may be religious minorities in the sense that they are not mainstream Protestant, or they may indeed reflect mainstream Protestants as a minority. A nineteenth-century writer saw Christians as one such group, paralleled by another group, skeptics, who used civil divorce.

Marriage is, among Christians, a contract for life, involving a vow before God. The law has no authority to annul this compact. Let it stand guarded by the command, "Those whom God hath joined together let no man put asunder." Let the skeptics have their own system. A civil contract, elastic as necessary, could be drawn by each State.[88]

The group subplot is not, however, the only subplot visible in American family law in the sense that normative ideas about family life are not only derived from religious or minority legal systems. It is possible that in the United States the traditional conception of family law as mandatory (like the criminal law) has been broken down,[89] and that family law is understood, not as the instrument of enforcement of the norm of the good life, but rather as the vehicle for exploration of the question what is the good life.[90] Not knowing how to shape marriage collectively, we return to the notion of marriage as a contract, governed by its own law. But this emphasis first on the individual and the good life, and second on contract—the law of the parties—may raise more general questions regarding narrative and law.

The proposals for reforming the law typically assume that we know what the law is; yet this may not be the case in divorce law. The internal orderings of marriage are such that the rules for their dissolution are in one dimension not really known.

Thus, we reach the use of narrative urged by Leon Petrazycki, who said that we should use stories as tests of our own legal experiences so that we would better know our own sense of duty or obligation and our own sense of when another party had a claim on us.[91] In Petrazycki's version of law, we would be comparing our own individual law with the law of the outside society or of any subgroup.

The first point is that each marriage has its own rules.[92] Thus Sumner writes,

> The definition of marriage consists in stating what, at any time and place, the mores have imposed as regulations on the [timeless] relation's existence and the reproduction of the species. . . . It has no structure. Each pair, or other marital combination, has always chosen his own "ways" of living within the limit set by the mores.[93]

Translating this idea into legal terms, it could be said that each marriage has its own individual grounds for divorce within the official state law of divorce. This is not a new perspective. In 1911, Ellen Key wrote, "In the ideas of the Church, the incapacity for marriage of one party freed the other from the duty of fidelity." Along parallel lines,

> it will be equally evident that the same right exists to dissolve a marriage which has remained unconsummated in a spiritual sense; and there may be just as many possibilities in the capacity to fulfill the spiritual claims of marriage as there are men and women; therefore also just as many causes of divorce.[94]

This approach is also suggested by Petrazycki's description of each family as its own legal field.

> [F]rom the point of view of the psychological theory of law as imperative-attributive experiences, family and intimate domestic

life (regardless of whether or not there are between those participants any bonds officially recognized) is a broad and peculiar legal
world which is awaiting investigation: a legal world with innumerable legal norms, obligations, and rights independent of what
is written in the statutes, and solving thousands of questions
unforeseen therein.[95]

Where each marriage has its own grounds for divorce, and each
individual has his or her own sense of the proper grounds for divorce,
the corresponding umbrella of state law is no-fault divorce.[96]
   "The individual does not go about merely going about his business,"[97] Goffman once wrote. "Rather, he individually goes about trying to sustain a viable image of himself in the eyes of others."[98] Our
identities—constructed in so many ways and of so many affiliations—
often include "married" or "unmarried" as a critical part.[99] A spouse,
and even a particular kind of spouse (e.g., a status wife), has critical
importance in the social and contextual aspects of marriage, which is a
highly public and, in varying degrees, a private relationship.[100] To the
extent that it is public, it has a clear relation to official law, which deals
with public relationships and their social implications.[101] We increasingly see the social cost of divorce[102] in the way we, as a culture, have
structured it, and a new interest in "commitment" is evident in the law
reviews and in the culture.[103] We see divorce now more the way Euro-
peans did.

> [W]here a European regards the rupture of a marriage as produc-
> ing social disorder and the loss of a capital of joining recollections
> and experiences, an American has rather the impression that "he is
> putting his life straight," and opening up for himself a fresh future.
> The economy of saving is once again opposed to that of squander-
> ing, as the concern to preserve the past is opposed to the concern to
> make a clean sweep in order to build something tidy, without com-
> promise.[104]

That discussion, however, has tended to neglect the issue of rethinking
the institution to which we are seeking commitment.[105] Changes in the
social and legal definitions of marriage and divorce, illustrated by a
variety of narratives, are the subject of the next chapter.

Chapter Two

The Couple

Marriage is a serious thing in America, not a temporary affair as it often is here.

Sharpless, the American consul, in David Belasco,
Madame Butterfly

Long's Butterfly story can be seen as juxtaposing two institutions of marriage, the lifelong Christian marriage of the West, to which Cho-Cho-San adheres (though the Westerner Pinkerton does not) and the temporary marriage of Japan, used for their own purposes by Pinkerton, Yamadori, and the narrator of Madame Chrysanthemum.[1]

The legal issues involved, including the conflict of laws,[2] are of considerable complexity. Butterfly marries Pinkerton in a country where a husband who abandoned his wife was taken to have divorced her under traditional customary law. The wife had no corresponding right to divorce her husband.[3]

The civil code of 1898 introduced a fault-based system available to either party. These changes in the marriage law, whatever significance they may have had in real-life Japan, do not show much in the world of Madame Butterfly, Pinkerton, and Yamadori. The legal background provided by Long makes it possible that Pinkerton assumed he was operating under the older legal regime. The accounts offered seem often to describe customary law before 1898. Thus Long writes: "If Pinkerton had told her to go home, even though she had no home to go to, she would have been divorced without more ado."[4]

Puccini's opera invokes the law of Japan and of the United States. The descriptions of American law come largely from Butterfly, who has presumably been informed (or misinformed) by Pinkerton. She stresses that in America, unlike Japan, one cannot simply tell one's wife to go home. In the United States, she thinks, there is a proceeding involving a judge and possibly jail.

The contrast is between the system of sequential marriages (represented at its fullest by Yamadori) and the system that Butterfly believes to be operative in the United States, in which marriage is for life, although divorce is in

*some cases, and with great difficulty, a legal possibility. Butterfly takes this
law as controlling her own marriage to the American sailor, Pinkerton.*

*The story by John Luther Long can be read as a comment on the "serial
polygamy" that was becoming common in the United States, through the freer
divorce law increasingly found in the American statutes. Cho-Cho-San's version of American divorce law—distorted and in pidgin English[5]—describes a
law where one could not simply walk away from a marriage. Even "jail" was
visible in the background. But she is describing an institution under attack—a
process that reached its high point finally in the twentieth century with no-fault
divorce and a revised set of expectations of marriage. The historical change was
one not only in the facility of divorce but in the meaning of marriage.*

*This chapter reviews the history of marriage and divorce in America,
using women's narratives to illustrate that history. The emphasis falls on the
relation between the social institution and state regulation of it. Ordinary use
of the term* marriage *conceals major changes in the social institution of marriage that have parallels in changes in the law of divorce.* Marriage *does not
mean one thing, and the law's understanding both influences and is influenced
by the social meanings. Where an institution is understood (as now, in the
United States) to be designed for the private happiness of the couple, it is
almost necessary that it be regulated by a system of free and even unilateral
divorce.*

Marriage and Divorce: Doctrines and Understandings

The following narratives come from different historical periods. They
were produced for different purposes and against different legal backgrounds. This chapter uses them to stress a consonance between the
law of the state and the actual social sense of the marital institution.
This social sense of marriage is not derived from the narratives used,
but is taken from the work of historians. The narratives are used to support the historians' work, providing evidence of a social meaning as
well as testimony about an inner meaning.[6]

Initially, this chapter provides an overview of the law of marriage
and divorce together with the present understanding of substantive
changes in those institutions. In effect, the narratives are used to illustrate conventional understandings. The narratives are selected and
read to support the point—a point implied in historical and social-

science approaches to the history of divorce—that state divorce law is built on a particular model of marriage.[7]

Marriage

Marriage, even in monogamous societies, clearly is not one thing. It is therefore initially an error to conceive of the history of divorce as if it concerns changing ways of dissolving the same institution. As tempting as it is to assume a universal quality in human emotions and institutions, it is more useful to start with the critical sense that emotions and institutions are historically variable to a considerable degree. We are misled in this respect by the fact that we use the same words to describe certain institutions, for example, marriage. As to ancient Greece, Finley tells us that "Odysseus was fond of Penelope, beyond a doubt, and he found her sexually desirable. She was part of what he meant by 'home.'" Monogamy was the rule, but this form of monogamy did not "impose monogamous sexuality on the male nor did it place the small family at the centre of a man's emotional life." Indeed, Finley notes, "the language had no word for the small family, in the sense in which one might say, 'I want to go back to live with my family.'"[8]

We have reached quite a different point. Historians and anthropologists have attempted to convey both the range of marital institutions[9] and, particularly important for present purposes, the growth of the affective aspects of the institution we currently call marriage.[10] It is now conventional to link the demands of that particular institution to free legal divorce and the increased social acceptance of divorce. The view that, in effect, divorce makes modern family life possible has many echoes.[11]

The contrast here is between an earlier and a later view of marriage as it relates to obligation. Bishop's definition of marriage suggests the traditional nineteenth-century focus on duties and the community: "Marriage . . . is a civil status of one man and one woman united in law for life, for the discharge, to each other and the community, of the duties legally incumbent on those whose association is founded on the distinction of sex."[12] This definition has been expanded in our time to include personal fulfillment.[13] Historian Elaine May contrasts the earlier understanding with the contemporary.

[M]arriage was part of an effort to establish a tranquil domestic environment. Violations of familial ethics which culminated in divorce were an affront to the community as well as the aggrieved spouse. Husbands and wives neither expected nor hoped that their spouse would provide them with ultimate fulfillment in life, or that the home would be a self-contained private domain geared toward the personal happiness of individual family members.[14]

This limited-expectation form of marriage changed over time.

By 1920, we find that the ideal of marriage had evolved somewhat ambiguously. Matrimony was intended to promote the happiness of the spouses. A certain amount of fun and amusement was expected as part of the bargain. At the same time, children were anticipated and the familial responsibilities of both husbands and wives remained virtually unchallenged.[15]

This meant that wives "wanted their mates to be good providers as well as funloving pals; men desired wives who were exciting as well as virtuous." The idea was that "marriage would include fewer sacrifices and more satisfactions. When combined with persistent Victorian holdovers, new expectations could lead to new tensions."[16]

Sociologists provide additional descriptions of present expectations. They offer insight into the content of what is ordinarily called "companionate marriage"[17] that goes beyond the judicial suggestion that it historically relates to some sort of idea of equality and companionship. Peter and Brigitte Berger write,

Bourgeois marriage is designed to provide a "haven" of stable identity and meaning in a social situation where these are very scarce commodities. Here there is the norm of mutual concern for all aspects of the individual's life. Further, it is here that two individuals are in a position to construct a "world of their own," again something that is not easy to do elsewhere amid the complexities of modern life.[18]

The Bergers stress that marriage serves as a source of meaning.

It is here that the individual will seek power, intelligibility, and, quite literally a name—the apparent power to fashion a world, however Lilliputian, that will reflect his own being. . . . This idea has immense consequences. It is not an aspiration that one gives up easily. And thus those who have found it unrealizable in one marriage, in large numbers try again—and if necessary, again once more.[19]

Like others, the Bergers see the high divorce rate as the idealization of marriage.

In this sense, we would contend, the high divorce rates indicate the opposite of what conventional wisdom holds: People divorce in such numbers not because they are turned off by marriage but, rather, because their expectations of marriage are so high that they will not settle for unsatisfactory approximations. In other words, divorce is mainly a backhanded compliment to the ideal of modern marriage, as well as a testimony to its difficulties.[20]

The Bergers conclude, "Bourgeois marriage, among those who continue to live within its normative boundaries, continues to provide the stable identity and meaning it was originally designed to provide."[21]

Brigitte Bodenheimer, writing from the perspective of a family law teacher and scholar, offers this description of marriage:

The meaning of marriage has undergone profound changes within the last few generations, as has been pointed out by many writers. Husband and wife, often uprooted from their home communities, are facing each other in isolation as never before. The wife's subordination has ended. True, equal partnership is the goal, with a highly personal bond, a commitment in depth and complexity, between the spouses. This refined and lofty ideal imposes much higher demands and therefore carries in itself the seeds of more failures than the older, more down-to-earth idea of matrimony.[22]

The idea of the companionate marriage had to do with the idea that marriages (assumed now to be built on ideas of family planning) ought to be focused on companionship. As Nancy Cott formulates the point, family life in the early twentieth century was "a specialized site for emotional intimacy, personal and sexual expression and nurture among husband, wife and a small number of children."[23] The idea of companionate marriage modified a traditional position of feminism.

Where feminism had once attacked bourgeois marriage, the "sexual pattern advanced in social science (and popular culture) of the 1920s confirmed bourgeois marriage as women's destination."[24] An emphasis on psychological needs and increased psychological sophistication meant that the demands for intimacy became greater and greater.[25] Marriage was the basis of the family, and marriage created a new nomos. This nomos, at least in theory, made a claim of exclusiveness so total that all nonmarital intimacy of any quality could be seen as in derogation of marriage.[26]

In effect, what we have seen is the triumph of the liberals in the nineteenth-century debate over marriage and divorce. "Nothing so divided liberals and conservatives as the relationship of happiness to [the divorce question]."[27] As the traditional functions of marriage and the family have been increasingly taken over by other institutions,[28] the emphasis on marriage and the family as vehicle for happiness has increased. O'Neill notes that "conservatives invariably felt that happiness, if it came at all, was a bonus which no one had a right to expect. . . . Nothing was more revolutionary about the liberals' defense of divorce than their insistence that happiness was a necessary condition of marriage."[29]

Marriage is an issue for both men and women, though there is a dimension to it that relates particularly to changes in the status of women. Companionate marriage, as it was understood until very recently, coexisted with extreme gender role division and a general context of male dominance.[30] Options became available in the twentieth century, however, that were largely unavailable earlier. In nineteenth-century America, marriage for women was effectively an economic necessity. On this issue, Susan B. Anthony saw the change in her lifetime: "Woman is no longer compelled to marry for support, but may herself make her own home and earn her own financial independence."[31] But, as Nancy Cott has noted, while there is less reason to marry for economic reasons, "[T]he model of companionate marriage with its emphasis on female heterosexual desires made marriage a sexual necessity, for 'normal satisfaction.'"[32] The word "normal" here suggests an entire sanctioning system outside the legal system, one based on norms of health and well-being, and one that took as its basic position an opposition to difference.

The history of women following the end of the period of legal restriction of women's public rights is in a way incomprehensible—

Why did so few women go to school, enter professions, or seek lives outside the home?—without the understanding that conformity, or at least avoidance of excessive deviance, rather than conformity to any particular ideal, is the goal of most of the people most of the time.[33] The normal may itself create problems. Thus, the ideal of normal sexuality conceals a fair number of questions about the meaning of sexuality for women, and particularly the use of sexuality as a substitute, as Susan Sontag wrote, "for genuine freedom and for so many other pleasures (intimacy, intensity, feeling of belonging, blasphemy) which this society frustrates."[34] But whatever the difficulties with the ideas of normal sex and normal marriage in American culture, these ideas were in fact the norm. Marriage was a significant way by which to express one's integration into the larger social community and make public the fact that one had met the demands of that community, enforced by the legal system, by the social system, and by the immediate demands of one's own family.

Divorce

The history of divorce involves various strands, of which two are commonly discussed. The first is the free divorce of the Roman Empire, in which it was possible for men and women to marry and divorce many times. The second is the highly restrictive divorce of Christianity, which conceived of marriage as not only for life, but indeed beyond,[35] in that some theologians rejected the idea that one could remarry after the death of a spouse.

While the conflict between these approaches went on for some time, the Anglo-American tradition formally derives from the second. For example, there was no divorce except legislative divorce in England for some time,[36] and the American colonies began with a fairly restrictive approach to divorce derived from the Protestant adaptation of the Catholic position. By the early nineteenth century, legislative divorce in the United States began to yield to the institution of judicial divorce.

As Roscoe Pound indicates in his discussion "Justice according to Law,"[37] legislative divorce is an aspect of legislative justice, and, along with other illustrations of this process, it "all but came to an end" in the nineteenth century. It should be noted, however, that while the constitutionality of legislative divorce was debated, a divorce granted by a territorial legislature was upheld by the Supreme Court as late as 1887.[38]

Divorce was granted only for specific reasons. Expansion of these grounds was one basis for the controversies over divorce in the nineteenth century. The development of divorce law became a notable illustration of the difference between the law on the books and the law in action. Pound wrote,

> What would the average community do to a [man] convicted judicially of extreme cruelty to a [woman]? Yet there are coming to be respected persons of high standing in all communities against whom there are such records. We know that in many parts of the country, at least extreme cruelty has become a convenient fiction to cover up that incompatibility of temper that may not unreasonably exist between a respected [man and his wife]. The . . . judge-made rule against collusion remains in the books. But husband and wife agree upon a settlement of property out of court, they agree that she shall aver and prove cruelty unopposed. . . . [In those communities], public thought and feeling have changed, and whatever the law in the books, the law in action is changing with them.[39]

This, then, is the late fault period, a period in which collusive divorce in the old categories becomes consensual divorce in the new ones. To the extent that modern no-fault divorce is read as having merely eliminated the fiction of the late fault divorce, it may also be read as doing little new. But it did more in fact than simply facilitate consensual divorces; it moved essentially to a system of unilateral divorce.[40]

Friedman and Percival have summarized the history of divorce.

> In the first stage, divorce is *difficult* and *rare*. Only a few grounds are available. There is social pressure against divorce, and divorce bears a heavy stigma. Women are generally subservient to men. Middle-class women on the whole rarely take part in the work force. A divorced woman has an awkward role in society. Divorce is confined, as a practical matter, to a few people, mostly upper class. As far as we can tell, the grounds alleged in court are grounded in reality. That is, if adultery is the complaint, the defendant really was an adulterer or adulteress, and adultery was either the cause or at least the excuse for the plaintiffs case.[41]

They describe the increased expectations of marriage and the democratization of divorce.

> [P]eople expected more out of marriage than in traditional eras; a wife was to be more than sex partner, servant, and nursemaid; a husband was to be more than a breadwinner and protector. Marriage was supposed to be a partnership of love. This was presumably a minority view, which slowly percolated downward and outward in society. As it spread, divorce was no longer restricted to the upper class. Divorce was democratized.[42]

Friedman and Percival also add a new dimension focusing on legitimization of status.

> New demands on marriage increased the demand for easier divorce. But changing expectations cannot alone account for loose divorce laws. No doubt Italy too felt the pull of modern marriage, at least to a degree; but divorce remained stubbornly outlawed. What was strongly felt in the United States was a demand for *legitimization of status.* . . . In the first place, divorce was probably less stigmatic than sex outside of marriage. Men and women who had left their old partners wanted to form new families, have children, live normal economic and social lives. They saw no reason why the law should not let them do so, legitimately.[43]

Narratives and Divorce Law

Our information about early American divorce is often based on divorce records themselves.[44] As Nancy Cott suggests, the "history of divorce practice documents sex-role expectations [and] permits comparison between the obligation and freedom of husbands and wives."[45] Lawrence Friedman tells us about southern legislatures that "granted divorces by passing private statutes, dissolving the marriages of specific persons. The statute books contain hundreds of these private divorces. They are usually short, stereotyped, and tell little or nothing about what led to the divorce."[46] He cites, as an example, an 1839 Virginia law[47] declaring that the marriage between Mary Cloud and William Cloud "is hereby dissolved, the said Mary forever divorced from her husband . . . and the power and authority of the said William over the person and property of the said Mary, shall henceforth cease and determine."[48]

Nineteenth-Century Divorce Narratives
Legislative divorce in the early nineteenth century. Notwithstanding the stereotypical nature of legislative divorces, perhaps we can use a narrative of the legislative divorce in a particularly extreme case to project an image of nineteenth-century marriage. The narrative relates to the controversy between a married woman and her husband, against the background of the early-nineteenth-century Shaker communities.[49] The narrative illustrates the grounds thought appropriate for a legislative divorce and permits the inference that the law believed marriage could be dissolved only for factually grave cause. The grounds presented to the system in the petition for divorce are in fact the reasons as presented in the narratives.[50]

The author of the narrative is Eunice Chapman, the daughter of a man from Bridgeport, Connecticut. She had married James Chapman, a merchant from New Durham, New York, and they had three children.

> From the year 1804 until about the year 1809, I lived with him in the most cordial harmony, stupid and insensible to his faults—vigilant to make his life comfortable and happy, when he, about this time, had several interviews with the Shaking Quakers, after which he gave himself up to a continual intoxication and vice. When in his sober hours, I, with eyes dissolved in tears, entreated of him for the sake of the dear pledges of our mutual love, to refrain from dissipation, lest it would result in the misery of his family. With a conscience awakened to horror and despair, he would hurry to the haunts of vice to get a draught to drown his senses and to stir his conscience. He would frequently return home at a late hour of the night with such a very menacing countenance and conduct, that I often felt in imminent danger of my life.[51]

In 1811, Chapman left his wife, leaving her with no furniture (according to her account) except her bed, and generally failing to provide for her maintenance.[52] He joined the Shakers in 1812.[53] Passing over the events of the intervening period, we are told that Chapman finally indicated to his wife that the Shakers had a house for her and the children.

In 1814, she went to the Shaker village to see the house but found none. When she returned home, her children were gone.[54]

The rest of the story is an account of Mrs. Chapman's efforts to persuade the New York legislature to give her a divorce. Her grievances ranged from desertion, neglect, non-support, and drunkenness, to cruelty and adultery. In 1818, the legislature gave Eunice Chapman a divorce,[55] and, in 1819, she received a court order giving her custody of the children.

The tone of Mrs. Chapman's narrative[56] is clear from the following extract, focused not on the divorce itself, but on the problem of retrieving the children from the Shaker community after the divorce. She is a heroine more than a victim.

> After the [divorce] bill had become a law, and I could protect and defend myself, I resolved to go in pursuit of my children. In a remarkable manner I was informed where they were carried when taken from Niskeyuna. I first sent my books to Enfield, and then dismissed my school. On the 9th of May, 1819, I entered the stage, in a dismal thunder storm, under a fictitious name, to avoid being traced by the Shakers. After a perilous journey, caused by the state of the roads at that season, I arrived at Brattleboro, 76 miles from Albany, at 2 o'clock in the morning, having been 24 hours in coming that distance. On the 10th, there fell torrents of rain, and with a crowded stage, which coming near upsetting, I fainted through fear. At evening, I arrived in Hanover. On the 13th, I took the stage to Enfield, and stepped at the stage house, two miles beyond the Shaker Village.
>
> I complained of being unwell, and much fatigued, and unable to travel; thus made an excuse to stop a few days to rest. I soon found I had landed in one of the best of families, who, suspecting my business, privately sent for Mary Dyer,[57] who hastened to my apartment, and introduced herself by exclaiming, "Mrs. Chapman, can this be you?" We met like two unfortunate sisters.[58]

Mrs. Chapman's narrative suggests that an individual's complaint,[59] if given sufficient time, could result in the solution of the particular problem. Blake writes that the New York legislature devoted more of its time and energy to a single private divorce bill than it ever

did to any general marriage law proposal referring to the period
1815–18, when the legislative divorce in the Chapman case was finally
granted.[60] The particular solution also could enter the statutes as a formal grounds for divorce.[61] The entire story suggests that an element
considered to justify the dissolution was the intensity of the difficulty
with the marriage. Divorce with full rights to remarry for both parties
was not the only legal solution in such cases. Both the legislatures and
the individuals involved might well have considered separation as an
alternative. A narrative quoted by Nancy Cott sounds the theme of separation: "I persuaded myself, that if he would do what was right, relative to our property, and would go to some distant place, where we
should be afflicted with him no more, it might be sufficient."[62] Separation was seen as an appropriate remedy in a case involving incest and
adultery. The standards involved—that the presence of the husband
afflicted the wife and children—can be read as the general standard for
divorce in low-expectation marriages.

A narrative of late nineteenth century feminism. Elizabeth Cady
Stanton's interest in the problem of divorce is well known. She
addressed the question for many years, and her last published article
before her death dealt with the issue. We can begin the discussion with
a story told by Stanton concerning a victim of an unhappy marriage.

Traveling, not long since, I noticed in the seat near me a sweet, girl-
ish looking woman, dressed in deep black. She looked so sad and
lonely that I went to her and proposed a walk on the platform
while the cars were stopping. We were soon friends, and she gave
me her sorrowful experiences. Married at sixteen to a young man
of wealth, education and good family, but of intemperate habits,
which she thought his affection for her would enable her to control; the mother of three sons before she was twenty, all sickly, ner-
vous, restless; her own health broken down with anxiety, and
watching not only the children, night after night, but the father;
friends, thinking it best to get him out of New York from the many
temptations of a city, with active business in the country, sent him
to the oil regions in Pennsylvania, and there this delicate, pure,
refined young child spent six years of her life trying to win a besot-
ted man to the paths of virtue and peace. Night after night, when
the babies were asleep, she would go alone through sleet, and rain,
and snow, all round one of those rough pioneer settlements, into

every den of vice, looking for the father of her children [sic] that she might get him home. "One thing," said she, "he would always do—lay down his cards and glass and follow me, but on our way home he would say: 'Mary, such places are not fit for you.' 'Then,' I replied, 'a man who frequents such places is not a fit companion for me.' But these," said she "were six long years of useless struggle. He became cross and irritable, loathsome, bloated, disgusting, turned my love to hate, and after a fearful attack of delirium tremens, the grave covered my shame and misfortunes, and my three children lie by his side. And when, with aching heart, I buried them all there, you may wonder to hear me say so, but it was with a sorrowful thankfulness, for I remembered that warning in the second commandment, given mid the thunders of Sinai: 'The sins of the fathers shall be visited upon the children.' Now, said I, I shall be saved the unspeakable sorrow of ever seeing my own sons come reeling home to me with that silly, sensual leer that is worse than abuse and profanity." What a chapter of experience for a girl not twenty-five! And multitudes are following in her wake!![63]

Stanton concluded that liberal divorce laws were necessary to save women from the slavery of marriage. The precise shape of the divorce laws proposed by Stanton varied, sometimes focusing on expansion of the fault grounds, and sometimes focusing on free divorce parallel to free marriage. In 1884, she argued (perhaps strategically) that we were still in an "experimental stage" with reference to divorce and that it was too soon to formulate a national law.[64] But the victim of an unhappy marriage was equally a victim of a system in which women were not educated for their self-support.[65] Better divorce laws—though a significant focus of Stanton's activities—were logically only one part of the solution.

Stanton's narrative is in the tradition of horror stories designed to move political audiences.[66] Apparently it did.[67] But the moral of the story, and its normative message, is not necessarily free divorce. Rather, at the time, the point might have been that women should not have to stay married to drunkards.[68] An expansion of the fault grounds provides an adequate remedy. The theory is that, in effect, divorce is permissible, even important, for particular reasons.[69]

What is the relationship between these ideas and Stanton's own marriage? The Stantons, we are told, had an unusual marriage. Griffith says that Henry Stanton was absent as much as ten months a year for twenty years, and that when he died in 1887 the couple "were apparently at odds and had not lived in the same place for twenty years."[70] She was never divorced and apparently never tried to be.

Griffith tells us that "she built her argument against 'manmade marriage' between 1840 and 1863, the first half of her own forty-seven-year marriage, and used as evidence 'from my own life, observation, thought, feeling and reason.'"[71]

Perhaps Stanton's own description of her marriage can help us get the life and the ideas into relation.[72] Thus, Stanton writes that her own wedding day was delayed.

> This delay compelled us to be married on Friday, which is commonly supposed to be a most unlucky day. But as we lived together, without more than the usual matrimonial friction, for nearly a half a century, had seven children, all but one of whom are still living, and have been well sheltered, clothed, and fed, enjoying sound minds in sound bodies, no one need be afraid of going through the marriage ceremony on Friday for fear of bad luck.[73]

Among the possible reasons for her failure to divorce are loyalty to her spouse (as father of her children), fear of injury to herself or her children if she did divorce, and no need to divorce, nor desire to remarry. Apparently, economic reasons were not a consideration.[74] But it is also worth noting that our interest in the relationship between Elizabeth and Henry Stanton and their unusual marriage relates as much to our expectations of marriage as to hers. We identify the unexcused absence of her husband as an indicator of a violation of marital norms, but this may have been much less true of a society that considered separation more appropriate than divorce. We appreciate Stanton's comments, which indicate a commitment to romantic love and a highly idealized version of a marital relationship.[75] But her well-known essay *Solitude of Self* indicates that she may well have viewed marriage as an institution whose importance was focused on children, and whose meaning for adults might be various, but which was not finally a solution to the issue of the human condition in its largest sense.

The early narratives may be read as consistent with the view that the purpose of marriage was delineated by various functions and roles, and that divorce was a solution when difficulties were so acute that the performance of those functions, or the living in those roles, was impossible. Thus, the language is intense and extreme; one talks of cruelty and misery. Situations are intolerable. But we see also in the late nineteenth century the proposition that marriage had something first to do with happiness, and second with romantic love, not only in its creation, but as a condition for its continued existence. This proposition underlies our current ideas of marriage.

Twentieth-Century Divorce Narratives
In 1956 William Goode noted, "All societies recognize that there are occasional violent, emotional attachments between persons of opposite sex, but our present American culture is practically the only one which has attempted to capitalize these, and make them the basis for marriage."[76] More recently, in a discussion of the models of family life, Herbert Jacobs noted that not only has the companionate marriage become dominant, but that "[t]he romantic ideal not only rules courtship but it also governs the criteria for continuing marriages."[77]

The work on divorce published early in the twentieth century emphasized a distinction between the legal grounds for divorce and the true reasons for the breakup of a marriage. For example, in 1924 Mowrer wrote,

> The purpose of this article is to show that the law does not recognize as causes for divorce the natural causes of family disintegration. Thus our divorce laws become molds into which the discord arising in family relations must be made to fit before the state will sanction a discontinuance of that relationship.[78]

The legal grounds were typically a camouflage or a fiction because the true grounds must, of necessity, be specific to a relationship. The actual grounds might be the legal grounds, but it was not at all necessary that this should be true.[79] Finally, in the no-fault divorce system the fiction was eliminated, so we are allowed to keep to ourselves the true reasons without the need for a mask of legal grounds. The true reasons, as some works suggest, may be violations of the norms of companionate marriage: intimacy, companionship, and sexual fulfillment.[80]

The narratives of the period of expanded expectations of marriage see fault not in the specific evils identified by the fault grounds, but in the failure of the love relationship. The diary of Miriam Donaven, apparently a product of the 1920s, is a story of romantic love,[81] but without the complexities introduced by modern feminism, that is, women in the market competing with their spouses. Miriam Donaven is prepared to base her life on the love of her husband, but she cannot.

The diary of Miriam Donaven: an early twentieth-century companion-ate marriage. Eight years after her marriage, Miriam Donaven, then divorced, killed her lover and herself. Her diary was found in her apartment, the scene of the murder-suicide. Mowrer writes, "The diary opens during the seventh week of married life, December 1, 19——. Miriam Donaven is already beginning to find disillusionment in marriage."[82]

> December 1. —The past month has been one of happiness to us both, and I would not write of what I did. Just a month ago today I have been living in this dear flat. . . . Every night for over a week he has come home dead tired, crawled right into bed and after kissing me dutifully, goes to sleep with my head on his arm. One night there was no arm for my head to rest on, and not even a good-night kiss, so I turned over and cried myself to sleep. [Oh, I wish my husband knew how much I want to be loved]. I tell him, but he does not realize what I mean all the time, every minute he is with me. . . .
>
> Oh God, how will our life end? What are we coming to? Last night Alfred was kind to me when I cried. I could not hold in any longer and he quieted me and put my head on his bare breast and kissed me. Oh, how thankful I was for that attention and of how I needed it and do now. He told me he wants a pal, his little girl, and wife back again and misses her oh so bad. Oh, God, when has that part of me gone? Is the fault mine, his or ours? He says I have changed the last three weeks in what way I can't understand because I feel right toward my boy. Last week one night when he came home I cried and told him I had been lonely all day and the Saturday before Easter Sunday we kneeled and prayed to God to make us happy and Easter he said would be Little Girl's day and every Sunday thereafter. All that was less than three weeks ago, was his ideal gone then? Well, while I was crying my heart out to God I asked Alfred what he wished to do, if we could go on and he suggested separation. All of a sudden I seemed to really know what that would mean for me and I thought I would go mad. I cer-

tainly am an unhappy woman with him now sometimes, how should I feel without him?[83]

Mowrer analyzes Donaven's expectations of marriage.

Dominating the life of Miriam Donaven was the wish for response. A husband to her was a man who loved one, caressed one, and was attentive at all times. As a value he was the product of romanticism. One went to him for response. But to Alfred a wife was one who gave herself to him sexually, and who played the conventional role—cooked, kept house, mended his clothes, etc. This conflict in attitudes seems to have been the basis of the discord throughout their married life.[84]

Mowrer considers the issue of Donaven's lack of a vocation.

One writer, in commenting on the diary, has made a great deal of the fact that Miriam had no vocational qualifications. Her career in life was dependent upon her sex appeal—a dependence which became more marked, of course, after her separation than during her life with Alfred. She did not like housework. She could not see how Alfred could respect her when she had to clean the bathtub after him with her own hands. She seems to have known little about cooking when they were first married. Miriam tried several kinds of work; folding circulars, working in department stores, china-painting, posing for a corset company, etc. In none of these occupations was she particularly adept, nor did she like any of them very well. She spent considerable time drawing, but that did not give her response. She was ambitious to become a motion-picture actress. But she never really developed a vocation. As a result, much of her effort was expended in restless attempts to realize her romantic ideal, to be loved all the time, fiercely, passionately.[85]

The reasons for divorce, as Mowrer analyzes them, are different from the legal grounds. Mowrer writes that, finally, "Alfred agrees to give her cause of divorce."[86] Later Miriam and her husband separate and are finally divorced. The pattern is being repeated with another man. Finally Miriam Donaven kills herself and her lover.

Donaven's diary does not deal extensively with children, an issue of importance in modern marital situations. Writing in the 1960s,

Goode noted the conflict between two norms in marriage.

> [M]uch of the verbal approval of the mother's working is likely to
> be hollow in actuality. That is to say, within almost every social
> group the working mother is under strong pressures to take care of
> her children and to leave the job market. Her claim that the extra
> salary is absolutely needed for survival is viewed with consider-
> able skepticism, even when the claim is not openly rejected. This
> general disapproval becomes relatively strong in precisely those
> middle-class strata where the egalitarian notions are held most
> strongly, because in such strata and groups the recent psychody-
> namic justifications for child freedom, child affection, breast feed-
> ing, security in mother love, etc. have become most fully
> accepted.[87]

Goode suggests that "all other role obligations are residual, compared
to this, and must wait until those of mother are satisfied." Clearly both
men and women occupy several statuses. However, "Compared with
other major statuses, that of mother is more likely to be viewed as
exclusive, other roles as residual." This means that "the legitimacy of
nonmaternal responsibilities is questioned unless it can be shown that
the maternal responsibilities themselves are being properly met; and
the clarity and moral force of this prescription are greater than for her
other statuses."[88]

All of this may still be true.

Even aside from motherhood, issues of competition between the
spouses are far from resolved. The problem of multiple loyalties, to individuals, work, and home, suggests that the tensions between marriage
and friendship, or marriage and families, may be as great as the tension
between marital and nonmarital sexual relations. The reasons for this are
clear. The present definition of marriage as a norm does not permit the
possibility of other orderings of equal intensity.[89] The model requires
that even the demands of work, friendship, and the extended family
must yield—at the normative if not the practical level—to the demands
of the marriage and the world it creates. Certainly this is true for mothers, usually for wives and even at times for fathers and husbands. To say
of someone that he or she is married to work states a violation of a marital norm. The spouse has a grievance. The norm of marriage can understand "[t]he exclusion of all others"[90] in a fairly large way.

A fictional narrative. Contemporary feminism, with its emphasis on the problem of an autonomous being within marriage, signals a problem with the idea of companionate marriage itself. This problem can be further illustrated by a fictional narrative by Doris Lessing.[91] Like Stanton, Lessing suggests that marriage cannot answer all questions. Lessing's story describes the perfect marriage of the Rawlings, an intelligent couple that does things correctly. They are not too young or inexperienced when they marry. They have the right number and kind of children. The wife devotes herself to the family for twelve years, only to find that she sees herself as having put herself on hold, in cold storage, in bondage to others. She now requires time and space to herself. She therefore rents a hotel room in which to be alone. (Her husband thinks—he almost prefers, as against other possibilities—that the room is to be used for a lover, so that the husband and wife with their respective friends can make a civilized foursome). In that room, she kills herself.

This narrative describes what we see as the humanely intelligent contemporary marriage and its inability to solve the problem of ultimate meaning. Infidelity seems unimportant in the sense that in its very normalcy it is preferred to other kinds of estrangement. While earlier narratives were focused on personal, individual experience, the Lessing story is a comment on the costs of companionate marriage in general.[92]

Lessing suggests that the failure of companionate marriage is not about a failure of individuals, but rather about a failure of the world companionate marriage creates. The Rawlings have everything. That everything, for the wife at least, is destructive to her core. The view of marriage is suggested in the nightmare figure of a man Susan Rawling projects. He "wants to get into me and take me over."[93] It was her inner experience of companionate marriage, based on intelligence, good planning, and apparently perfect understanding.

> Their life seemed to be like a snake biting its tail. Matthew's job for the sake of Susan, children, house, and garden—which Caravanserai needed a well-paid job to maintain it. And Susan's practical intelligence for the sake of Matthew, the children, the house and the garden—which unit would have collapsed in a week without her. But there was no point about which either could say: "For the sake of this is all the rest." Children? But children can't be a

centre of life and a reason for being. . . . Matthew's job? Ridiculous. It was an interesting job, but scarcely a reason for living. . . .

Their love for each other? Well, that was nearest it. If this wasn't a centre, what was? Yes, it was around this point, their love, that the whole extraordinary structure revolved. For extraordinary it certainly was. Both Susan and Matthew had moments of thinking so, of looking in secret disbelief at this thing they had created: marriage, four children, big house, garden, charwomen, friends, cars . . . and this thing, this entity, all of it had come into existence, been blown into being out of nowhere, because Susan loved Matthew and Matthew loved Susan. Extraordinary. So that was the central point, the wellspring.

And if one felt that it simply was not strong enough, important enough, to support it all, well whose fault was that? Certainly neither Susan's nor Matthew's. It was in the nature of things. And they sensibly blamed neither themselves nor each other.[94]

The sense of individual isolation, an isolation that cannot be relieved by a social institution like marriage, is reminiscent of late Stanton. Stanton had said, "No matter how much women prefer to lean, to be protected and supported, nor how much men desire to have them do so, they must make the voyage of life alone, and for safety in an emergency, they must know something of the laws of navigation."[95] For Stanton, it did not matter "whether the solitary voyager is man or woman; nature, having endowed them equally, leaves them to their own skill and judgment in the hour of danger, and, if not equal to the occasion, alike they perish."[96]

Women's narratives of divorce describe personal or existential pain.[97] There are, of course, other possible narratives: of husbands, children, and extended family. That marriage involves more than the couple, and more even than the couple and their children, is plain. We see it best in the history of parental consent, but we can also see its survival in the public nature of the marriage ceremony and the sanction that one's presence at the ceremonies gives to the marriage.

The marriage is one basis of the family. One issue here is whether the family is a unit or an entity, or, an aggregate.[98] How shall we look at it? This question is opened in chapter 4. Chapter 3 continues the treatment of marriage itself, using contract theory to press the issue of whether marriage is more than one thing.[99]

Chapter Three

Contracts

I will give a solemn writing.
Yamadori, in John Luther Long, "Madame Butterfly"

The wealthy Prince Yamadori appears in the three versions of the Madame Butterfly story as the Japanese suitor who, through a marriage broker, wants to marry Cho-Cho-San after Pinkerton has returned to the United States. In the short story by John Luther Long, Yamadori is of an "august family" and a man "bred to the Law." In the play by David Belasco, Yamadori is a "citizen of New York," temporarily in his native country.

Perhaps on the basis of customary law, Yamadori understands Pinkerton to have divorced Madame Butterfly.¹ Yamadori has had some experience of marriage. In the Long story, Yamadori has been married and divorced twice. In the Belasco play, he has been married and divorced eight times. Yamadori says that Madame Butterfly is different from his other wives. She will have a palace to live in, a thousand servants, and, finally, she will be buried with his ancestors.

Because she considers herself the wife of Pinkerton, Cho-Cho-San refuses Yamadori, against the advice of the American consul, Sharpless. Seeing, later, that Pinkerton has taken an American wife,² Butterfly resolves upon suicide.

The relationship between the traditional Japanese conception of a contract of marriage and a contract for a house is stressed at the opening of the Long story. "With the aid of a marriage broker, [Pinkerton] found both a wife and a house in which to keep her."³ He leases the house for 999 years but does not tell Cho-Cho-San that the lease can be canceled at the end of any month by simple failure to pay the rent. He marries her but does not say that his commitment is problematic.

Pinkerton's bargains for the house and wife reinforce the point that contract theory underlies both economic and family arrangements. The implication of Yamadori's proposal is that two kinds of marriage are possible for his wives, a temporary marriage under a customary system in which a man's desertion constitutes divorce, and something approaching Western marriage for life, achieved through contractual promises. This approach to marriage is the subject of the present chapter. Not only does marriage *mean different things over time, but several kinds of marriage can exist in one society.*

This chapter invokes narrative to examine the utility of contract and con-tract theory in reordering domestic arrangements. It examines marital and other domestic relations in terms of the contract theory of another generation (focusing particularly on the work of the leading legal realist, Karl Llewellyn, and a less well known figure, Nathan Isaacs) and explores problems that might arise in adapting their thinking, largely based on applications to commercial undertakings, to the area of intimate and family relations. The novels of Anthony Trollope (together with some other literary material) are used to illustrate.

Contracts and Domestic Relations

Law means so pitifully little to life. Life is so terrifyingly dependent on the law.

> Karl N. Llewellyn, *What Price Contract?*

There is currently great interest in the subject of contracts and the fam-ily, particularly among those who apply principles of law and econom-ics to marriage contracts.[4] Works discussing marriage and contracts sometimes treat contracts issues generally as they relate to the creation of lives-in-common and sometimes target specific contractual solutions to problems of family law, such as support after divorce[5] or surrogacy contracts.

There is also great skepticism about contracts and family law, par-ticularly as the contracts involve long-term, ongoing, typically marital, relationships.[6] The skeptical view resists the "commercial" version of marriage such as that described by George Bernard Shaw in 1903: "[N]othing is more certain," Shaw wrote, "than that in both [England and America] the progressive modification of the marriage contract will be continued until it is no more onerous nor irrevocable than any ordinary commercial deed of partnership."[7] Under one standard Anglo-American view, marriage must be more than an ordinary com-mercial arrangement and is weakened by comparison with such arrangements.

A broad version of the skeptical position rests in part on a view that associates contract law with individualism in the sense of selfishness, and with the well-known idea that one party has the right to break a contract so long as that breaching party pays damages.[8] This approach—perform or pay damages, it does not matter which—is not, it is thought, an appropriate one to use in the domestic and particularly marital context, in which there is so much reliance on the idea of a permanent association.[9] In the end, the proposition of the skeptics is that there are radical and finally insurmountable tensions between the ideas represented by contract and family, both in the state of mind necessary to enter the structures, and in the sorts of values that the two are said to encourage.

The tensions between the ideas of contract and the ideas invoked by the words *marriage* and *family* can be stated in different vocabularies. Tönnies's distinction between gemeinschaft and gesellschaft and Hegel's comment that rights in the family do not exist until the family dissolves both suggest the current idiom.[10] The contrast is often between a liberal, individualistic, rights emphasis and a communitarian emphasis, or between "contract" representing individual wills and "status" representing a collective judgment and a limit on individual choice. We know that the state of mind that the law of contracts generally requires focuses on arms-length bargaining, and a relationship of economic exchange. How could we even imagine that this would work within family relationships?

Indeed, there is a long history of opposition to the idea of marriage as a contract, even when its contractual aspects are noted. The late-nineteenth-century Supreme Court, in *Maynard v. Hill*,[11] stressed how different marriage is from ordinary contracts. The Court noted, in regularly quoted language, that "whilst marriage is often termed [a civil contract]—to indicate that it must be founded upon the agreement of the parties, and does not require any religious ceremony for its solemnization—it is something more than a mere contract."[12] There were many ways in which the marriage contract was different from other contracts. To begin with, "The consent of the parties is of course essential to its existence, but when the contract to marry is executed by the marriage, a relation between the parties is created which they cannot change."[13] By contrast, "Other contracts may be modified, restricted, or enlarged, or entirely released upon the consent of the parties."[14] In the end, the focus was on the larger social meaning of marriage. Marriage, the Court said, "is an institution, in the maintenance of which in its purity the public is deeply interested, for it is the foundation of the family and of society, without which there would be neither civilization nor progress."[15]

The largest issue here would seem to be the relation between the family and the state, and the role of the state in marriage and other domestic arrangements. Traditionally, the issue of law and the collective decision represented by law is conceded to be very large in the context of the regulation of marriage—despite the paradoxical point that the family is often said to be "autonomous" and in the "private" sphere.[16] The state, it has been said, is the third party to the marriage contract. Yet of course, from one point of view, the state is a kind of third party to all contracts. The role of the state is, finally, what distinguishes contracts from unenforceable understandings or agreements. Thus the different role of the state in relation to marriage and ordinary contracts is a difference in degree and not in kind. It remains true, however, that one way of talking about this difference in degree is to insist that it is, finally, a difference in kind. One can also say that while marriage itself is a contract, the contract is executed with the marriage, and that afterward marriage is a status in which the judgment of the community, through law, controls the situation.[17]

An argument based on the special character of marriage might also stress that marital promises are too vague to be truly contractual.[18] Alternatively, it might be argued that in long-standing relationships in which there are constant adjustments and readjustments to be made,[19] there is no point in talking about enforceable contracts. Indeed, as a general matter, one might do better thinking in terms of obligations.[20]

As to these observations, certain specific answers may be proposed. First, the traditional marriage contract may be more precise than is sometimes suggested. In 1939, Max Radin gave a clear outline of this view of the contractual aspects of marriage.[21] He noted the unusual character of marriage as a contract: "The contract of marriage, even as a consensual contract, is not treated in law as other contracts are treated."[22] But then Radin gave depth to the promises of mutual love and support. The reciprocal duties owed, he said, are these: "(1) cohabitation, (2) sexual access, (3) sexual fidelity, (4) conjugal kindness. In addition, (5) the husband owes the wife maintenance and support and (6) the wife owes the husband the duty of household management."[23]

As to long-range readjustment issues, we may note Ian Macneil's work on relational contracts suggests that the emphasis in contract law on one-shot transactions mischaracterizes the many commercial transactions that are long term.[24] This approach almost necessarily suggests an interest in problems of ongoing action and readjustment, and thus one might look for affinities between contract issues in family law and commercial law.

On the issue of "rights" versus "obligations," one might remember that promises, including contractual promises, are a way of creating obligations.[25] If a discussion insists on looking at contract in terms of rights rather than obligations, this seems to reflect a cultural overlay more than the contractual idea itself. One might also note that there are contracts (such as church covenants) that do not have economic transactions as their prime focus.[26] There may be no legal difference between a contractual promise, a legal agreement, a covenant, and a vow. The history of contracts is a history of different contracts in different contexts, and marriage is one of these. Thus it misconceives the issue to ask now whether marriage is appropriately part of a unified theory of contracts understood (at the moment) to be focused on economic relationships of one particular kind.

On the issue of hedonistic individualism, one might recall the quite different values associated with the individualism of Thoreau, who went to the woods because he wished to "live deliberately,"[27] or the Hasidic rabbi who said that he would not be asked, in the coming world, why he had not been Moses but rather why he had not been himself.[28] This, one might say, is the high ground of individualism, the "Here I stand, I can do no other" sort of individualism that ordinarily commands a certain respect.[29]

This discussion does not so much offer detailed responses to detailed questions as suggest that an emphasis on the status or collective-judgment aspect of marriage to the point of the rejection of contractual themes (or possible contractual solutions to certain problems) cuts us off from some interesting ideas in the traditional contract literature. These ideas are particularly important in a time of significant social uncertainty, much of it arising out of the impact of the current changes in the situation of women. The skeptical position on the use of contracts tends to a conclusion that an official state attitude toward such contracts must begin with a presumptive negative, based on the view that the law and theory of contract is most likely to be irrelevant. Analysis of these issues from within the field of contracts suggests that the state stance can often be more open to individual variation without sacrifice of collective judgment.

This chapter returns to some ideas about contract common in the first half of the twentieth century. Scholarship of that era sometimes viewed contracts in relation to general questions of law and society and did not restrict its inquiry to the incentive-based bargaining of individuals. Contracts material was founded on issues of law and social change, although the change was often in commercial practice rather than, for example, social relations.

The presentation here adopts a stance in which everything is discussable in contract terms. This is done not because everything *is* contracts, but because this exercise is useful in bringing to the surface a variety of interactions between individual and official behavior. The chapter addresses in this manner some arguments rejecting connections between contracts and family law and supports some material suggesting that there are in fact certain connections between these fields.

The second part of this chapter considers the idea of domestic contracts within the contract theory of another generation, discussing Karl Llewellyn's views of contracts and group life, including his comments on marriage and divorce. As background to that discussion, there is an exposition, following some suggestions in the work of Nathan Isaacs, of the relationship of standardized or default contracts[30] to status/contract questions in a time of social change.

Addressing the argument that there is some fundamental incompatibility between the exchange ideas underlying contracts and the substance of domestic arrangements, the third part of the chapter offers fictional examples of negotiation in domestic relationships.[31] These fictional contracts often relate not merely to issues of economic arrangements on dissolution of the relationship, but also to the substance of the arrangement itself. Within the context of particular ideas about the role of women, specific contracting for domestic arrangements was apparently not foreign to, for example, the nineteenth-century English mentality and may not be as foreign to our own as is sometimes suggested.

The fourth part of this chapter discusses domestic agreements as legally enforceable contracts, using the general framework of article 2 of the Uniform Commercial Code (UCC) as a point of departure. Article 2 was developed to solve a problem in the field of sales that has an analogue in the present discussion of domestic arrangements. The problem was that the law recognized one model while the social fact revealed many models. This is our situation as to domestic arrangements. It seems clear that one answer will not do for everyone. Some, for example, still want "traditional marriages, while others insist that only economic independence can give anyone a basis for equality in any domestic relationship.[32] As to each group, there will be some who want to apply their understandings universally, and some who, while believing that their mode is in some sense more valid, will be concerned about the methods available that will allow others to live out their versions of the good life.

The relationship of this discussion to general issues of pluralism and tolerance is obvious. While many methods are available in different contexts to achieve a pluralist goal,[33] in the context of domestic arrangements, it seems clear that explicit contracts are a possible way of both achieving individualized solutions and, ultimately, of perhaps changing the substance of the default contract or contractual options. The limits on the idea of contract—limits found in the law of contracts itself, in policing doctrines, and in nonvariable default provisions—are ways of accommodating the various state interests involved.

Marriage as an Institution: Some Older Theory on Private Ordering of Marriage and Divorce

"The nub of the situation," Llewellyn wrote, "is the persistence of old patterns side by side with new. . . . This side-by-sideness is found inside single marriages, and as between different couples. Here, as in business and industry, the old is far from dying because, or as soon as, the new has come. While law still purports to seek a single way for all."[34] In *The Death of Contract*, Grant Gilmore indicated that if asked to "locate the law of contract on the legal spectrum," most people would place it in the field of commercial law. It is true, he writes, "that our unitary contract theory has always had an uncomfortable way of spilling over into distinctly non-commercial situations." Thus, "what may be good for General Motors does not always make sense when applied to charitable subscriptions, ante nuptial agreements and promises to convey the family farm provided the children will support the old people for life." Still, he concluded, "we feel instinctively that commercial law is the heart of the matter and that, the need arising, the commercial rules can be applied over, with whatever degree of disingenuity may be required, to fit, for example, the case of King Lear and his unruly daughters."[35]

Not surprisingly, the present contractual discussion in the field of family law focuses on the problem of marriage and, more particularly, marital dissolution in an era of no-fault divorce. The contracts discussion has been approached with various objectives. Sometimes the idea has been to provide a new wife with contractual incentives (promises to support on divorce) to live within a traditional model.[36] Sometimes the idea has been that alternative models could be developed through contract. As to both, it would seem that the older work in commercial law may have some relevance.

As already noted, the current discussion of contracts and the family, like much of the writing on contracts generally, uses the insights of an economic discussion and focuses on incentives and individual bargaining behavior. An earlier literature dealt with different questions. Some of it, understood broadly, considered the problem of the law of contracts and "life," "society," or "social change." As to such issues, one view of contracts and social life might stress issues of inequality of bargaining power. Legal realists presented another, more positive, view, stressing the potential of the law of contracts for autonomy and the structuring of institutions.[37]

While law and social change is a subject of continuing interest, it is frequently addressed today, and has been for some time, in terms of public law and legislation, clearly a major mechanism through which law addresses the world. It is also, of course, implicated in the discussion—the preoccupation of American legal theory for decades—of judicial decision-making and was addressed in the 1920s and 1930s by Karl Llewellyn in his work on contracts and sales. Llewellyn worked in the fields of contracts and commercial law. He was interested in the "role of contract in the social order, the part that contract plays in the life of men."[38] He produced writing that related these areas to more general issues of group theory and, at least once, directly wrote on issues of the family in the context of divorce.[39] Related questions were addressed somewhat earlier by Nathan Isaacs,[40] again often using contracts as the basic material. When Llewellyn used an idea like the "standardized contract" of marriage, he invoked a contracts literature on the subject that can be represented by Isaacs,[41] who worked both on issues of standardization and on status to contract ideas, well known in their formulation by Sir Henry Maine. The stance adopted here as to both

Llewellyn and Isaacs stresses connections between their perceptions of family law and contract law. Of course, neither devoted primary intellectual attention to issues of family law.

In *The Standardizing of Contracts,* Isaacs proposed that "status-to-contract" was about differences in degree rather than kind and that these differences were reflected in cycles of change.[42] An adhesion contract that was now a status relation might once have been an individualized contract relation.[43] He saw an advantage to adhesion contracts as they related to issues of oppression in bargaining, suggesting that there was much to be gained by standardization in freeing people from the "accident of power in individual bargaining."[44]

Isaacs entered the conversation on adhesion contracts through a discussion of the soundness and universality of Sir Henry Maine's familiar sentence to the effect that "the movement of progressive societies [was] a movement from status to contract."[45] Roscoe Pound had responded in part by noting that whatever may have been true of Roman law, this was not an accurate statement about Anglo-American law. Isaacs suggested that perhaps we might think about the whole thing somewhat differently. "After all," he wrote, "the question is not so much one of status and contract as it is of a broader classification that embraces these concepts: standardized relations and individualized relations." Maine, he said, labeled as status those relations, including "ancient family relations, or caste," that were "thoroughly standardized." In such relations, the "peculiarities of the individual agreement of individual members of society were irrelevant." But this was true, he continued, "of [many] peculiarities of . . . agreement . . . in later stages of society, where a formal contract of this or that type results in a more or less standardized relation." Among these relations, of standardized contract, he included not only early Roman forms of sale and English conveyances of land, but also marriage. For Isaacs, it is worth noting, "In origin, these relations are . . . contractual." It is in their workings that they "recall the *regime* of status."[46] Status-to-contract is a difference of degree, not of kind, and Isaacs saw in his own time a distinct "veering back to status" via standardized contracts.[47]

Taking the view of a legal historian writing very broadly about cycles of legal history over millennia, Isaacs noted that it might be that "if we were able to go back to what we accept as standard family relations, we should find their basis, too, in the hardening of individual practices into rules." It might even be that behind the idea of caste "there was a progress from the individual non-standardized conduct to the standardized." The point was that one should get away from an idea of legal history progress as movement on this point in one direction or another, and see "a kind of pendulum movement back and forth between periods of standardization and periods of individualization."[48] Codification, Isaacs suggested, was associated with the freezing of patterns and equity with the individualized contract.[49]

Isaacs commented on adhesion contracts again in 1939 in a way that included the idea of standard default contracts and the problem of nonstandardized categories of transactions. He first considered transactions at the bank, post office, department store, doctor, and insurance company. The standardized categories and relations "are not necessarily simple, but they are standardized to such a degree that, when nothing is said, the law is able to supply the necessary details." There would, however, be a problem when the social situation was changing: "It is only when one uses the method of silence in such odd and outlandish relations as hiring a personal publicity man, campaign manager, travel companion, or ghost writer, that the whole scheme breaks down because the law has no guide for filling in the blanks."[50]

Two points are important here. First, the idea of the law filling in contract terms from a presumed intent based on a standard transaction is very different from law telling people what to do based on an imposed norm. Second, in a time of radical social change, the method of silence in which an underlying default contract is assumed by both parties will often be inadequate. If there was a judicially approved default pattern, a problem would arise where a recognized form no longer fit diverse facts.[51]

For present purposes, the significance of Isaacs's historical perspective is not his version of the great cycles of legal history, but the suggestion that the social rule has its ultimate origin in the practice of individuals. The individualized contract might historically—and, by extrapolation, for the future—be itself the source of the legal norm.

Related ideas in contracts and variation of rules of contract—whether or not Isaacs is the precise source[52]—were discussed by Karl Llewellyn in his work on contracts and, with particular application to the family, on divorce.[53]

Llewellyn's work on divorce, as he indicated in the first of his articles, was not well received by his colleagues, one of whom suggested that its defects of style were exceeded only by its defects of substance.[54] Still, the work is of continuing interest.

Llewellyn sees not only the "main story" of the history of marriage[55] but also the variant patterns and finally the individual stories and the individually negotiated arrangements within the general patterns. "[T]oo much is thought and written," he said, "as if we had a pattern of ways that made up marriage."[56] Recently divorced, and distressed to some degree about the speed with which it was possible to be divorced, Llewellyn nonetheless emphasized the critical point that, in the divorce crisis of the 1930s, only one form of marriage was actually in decay, the preindustrial limited-expectation form, and that "[n]ew institutions of marriage, adjusted to new times, are in the building."[57] The motives and concerns of those entering were, of course, not the same. For example, as Llewellyn pointed out, "Those who marry at twenty search in the main with other and less economic eyes than suitors ten or twenty years their seniors."[58] Llewellyn indicated that this work on divorce related to his other work on law and society and on contracts.[59] He was throughout the essay concerned with the relations between law and society: "Society moulds and makes the individual; but individuals are and mould society. Law is a going whole we are born into; but law is a changing something we help remodel. Law decides cases, but cases make law. Law deflects society, but society is reflected in the law."[60]

Llewellyn was, as Gilmore noted, a particularizer rather than an abstractor.[61] These details, however, were not simply laid out, but were reconfigured, juxtaposed with constant footnote asides, unsystematically, and to many people irritatingly without order or clarity.[62] But Llewellyn's descriptions of the human situation generally, whether in the context of family law or contracts or commercial law, have a striking richness and immediacy.[63] He saw, for example, that the issue of marital stability, in which he was interested, had more fundamentally to do with marriage than with divorce itself. "[D]iscussion of divorce has too often started from the premise that divorce was an evil in itself, as if it was *divorce* that mattered. Whereas what matters is wedlock."[64] He saw the extreme diversity of institutions that even the United States of his time revealed. "Our society shows not a marriage institution, but a goodly number of such, overlapping, contradictory, both in needs and in effects."[65] He saw the impact of parents on children,[66] as well as a more general social pressure on young couples. "Not all folk are born parents" he wrote, "indeed I suspect that considerably less than half of the existing stock would accept that job, and that even of women not so hugely many would 'want children' if social patterns had not taught them that children were a thing to want."[67] He saw that marriage norms might vary by region, class, and culture and stressed that he was dealing with bourgeois marriage.[68]

While is it sometimes suggested that his interest in the family, and particularly his articles on divorce, have their origin in his particular biography—and especially his divorce from his first wife—it is equally important to see that Llewellyn's intellectual map included families as among the significant groups in society. The transactions he saw included family transactions. Among them was use of an engagement ring as one of the unambiguous tokens of a "definitive intent to change the existing situation—and to be relied on, the overt sign of utter intent to assume obligation."[69]

In the context of divorce, Llewellyn had specific institutional concerns and was, by present standards, moderate or even conservative in his proposals, as was also true of his work on article 2 of the UCC.[70] (In the commercial context, what concerned Llewellyn was the way in which the law sometimes dealt with commercial life, and "commercial men.") The problem was not merely the abstractions A and B of the Restatements.[71] The bloodlessness of those hypotheticals, and the abstract reading of laws with which they are associated, are still criticized by some concerned with individual personality.[72] He seemed concerned with protecting individuals[73] and creating a system that would permit the growth of various forms of the marital institution. For if the underlying idea was "[n]ew institutions adjusted to new times,"[74] it was not likely that the process would somehow end.

In general, Llewellyn wrote on marriage and the family against the background of his understanding that social life was based on groups, not individuals.[75] The marriage contract built an institution, not a relationship. The domestic arrangement—the family and the household— was in some ways a group like other groups.

But "group" ideas were not to be seen abstractly, and specificity marks Llewellyn's work on divorce as well as his work in contracts. When Llewellyn attempted to redo Williston's Sales Act,[76] he was sensitive to the problems of internal differentiation. The common example of this is the distinction in the UCC between merchants and nonmerchants.[77] For present purposes, the important thing is that Llewellyn's idea was not that there was a single mercantile community distinct from the rest of society. Rather, the merchant community was made up of many kinds of merchants, and transactions took many different forms. Llewellyn admired the English judge Scrutton because he really knew the timber trade.[78] Llewellyn's casebook on sales had an index of commodities.[79] So too, in his work on divorce, the point was that there were many kinds of marriages. Here, just as in the Sales Act, the law recognized only one. The interest in the social side of the law, the underlying human pattern, is a constant in Llewellyn's work. "I love the law of sales," he wrote; "the material grows in fascination for me from year to year; nowhere does one come closer to life or to the observable impact of lawmen on laymen and of laymen on law's ways."[80] Nowhere except, perhaps, the law of divorce, "the major area of interaction between the social institution and the legal."[81]

In relation to contract law, family cases appeared to Llewellyn as trouble spots in a field largely focused on the problems of business. But the area of family contract law did exist. "[I]t includes the promise made and relied on, but which did not bargain for reliance, and in the case of promises to provide it laps over into the third party beneficiary problems."[82] Still, he cautioned, precedents on consideration, for example, could not be carried over unthinkingly from family cases to professional dealing among commercial parties.[83] Llewellyn included marriage and family as two among many of society's "going concerns." Presumably in all cases, going concerns "are not apples to be plucked from trees."[84] Despite attacks on the idea of viewing parties to contracts as individuals,[85] in the context of the ongoing concern of marriage, perhaps inevitably, he stressed the role of individual work and individual action.[86]

In his work on divorce, Llewellyn was perhaps more explicitly normative than we expect from the writer who insisted on at least the temporary separation of *is* and *ought*.[87] He saw as a particular concern the older woman.[88] He feared that divorce was already in his generation too easy and thought that there might be special rules for marriages of long standing.[89] He was doubtful about special rules for marriages with children, largely because he believed that whatever binding force the children have would already have operated.[90] Throughout, he worried about the question whether law had any useful role in maintaining some particular value or whether the social sanctions could stand on their own.[91] But he did not seem prepared to simply follow society or facilitate existing practice. Writing in 1931, Llewellyn addressed two kinds of law, one mandatory and based on public policy, the other "yielding."[92] Both of these are "law,"[93] and both have something to do with law's channeling of human behavior.[94] Default contracts, or presumptive contracts, also channel behavior and expectations.

The application of these ideas to the present situation in domestic arrangements would look something like this. Our sense of the relative rights and obligations of married couples, nonmarried couples, and roommates—all arguably kinds of families—differ substantially. This fact suggests that social context dictates different kinds of default contracts to which the individuals in these relationships may be presumed to have adhered. Recognition of this point is concealed first by an emphasis on romantic love and second by what are taken to be the individualistic aspects of romantic love. These default ideas seem to exist, however, and are available to the legal system as the basis for implied terms in a contract and are also available in dealing with the issue of whether it is likely that in fact a certain sort of contract was made.

Of course, one would have to define the relevant community to see what expectations might be in fact at any time. In general, however, we seem often to have such expectations, some of which may be uncomfortable for us to acknowledge. This is why, when a woman who has been a mistress, rather than a wife, indicates that a man promised her lifetime support, we may consider his promise mere pillow talk. It seems to be an analogue of seller's puffing, something not seriously understood as contractual talk. Thus, when Llewellyn thought that nonmarital sexual arrangements were "specialized" and did not involve property or inheritance, he was simply reflecting a general social view.[95] We may not think the same way about a relationship we consider a "trial marriage," or a "pre-marital" or "non-marital" partnership. A "star boarder" may not be involved in the same sort of deal as a nonmarital domestic partner. The descriptive language communicates our outside sense of the "deal" when we distinguish between a "live-in companion"—the apartment belongs to the one whose companion he or she is—and two people living together under a more egalitarian arrangement, whose property implications are less certain.

Of course, the contract can be express or implied, but this does not free us from the underlying problem of knowing what a contract "means" or when or how to imply a contract. The classic formulation of the doctrine of implied contracts is that of Holmes: "You always can imply a term in a contract." The question is why you do it. It might be "because of some belief as to the practice of the community or of a class, or because of some opinion as to policy."[96] Whether contracts are express or implied, the policies involved relate to the appropriate relations between men and women generally. These policies were rooted in the ideal of marriage, at a time when people had a relatively clear sense of what marriage and nonmarriage meant. Some of these traditional meanings, and the contracting around them, are the subject of the next section.

Domestic Arrangements: Fictional Negotiations,
Traditional Understandings, and the Idea of a
Default Contract

"It takes years to make a friendship: but a marriage may be settled in a week—in an hour."[97] Trollope's line opens not only the issue of friendship and marriage, but also the issues of contract that make it possible for his observations to be accurate.

This section invokes some fictional agreements to illustrate that arrangements, marital and nonmarital, have often been understood as involving an explicit bargain in fact.[98] That bargain may be reached by the softer term *negotiation*,[99] but it is a bargain nonetheless. This section does not treat the issue of enforceability as a "contract" but only argues that a focus on the emotional or sentimental or sexual aspects of personal relationships does not tell the whole story and may even mislead. The idea is that undertakings to live a joint life on a permanent or semi-permanent basis are not made without serious consideration of what that joint life might entail in the actual daily and material base of the relationship. Such undertakings involve bargains and exchanges in fact. Sometimes, as will be argued, that bargain is largely assumed in the idea of marriage (or not). The proposal to marry contains all the terms. As already noted, the marriage contract, as understood by the people proposing and accepting, is more specific regarding mutual obligations than is sometimes suggested.

Although Anthony Trollope was perhaps not thinking about it this way, the point that the standard default contract both exists and is specific underlies his comment that marriage can be settled quickly. This is because the broad outlines of "marriage" and the contract[100] of marriage are generally understood in terms of the obligations assumed in an ongoing relationship. Sometimes, however, the bargain in a marriage contract is rather more explicit on terms in addition to, or different from, the standard default contract.

In dealing with the history of the family in England, historian Lawrence Stone has urged a focus on three modern Western assumptions about domestic life. The first of these assumptions is that "there is a clear dichotomy between marriage for interest, meaning money, status or power, and marriage for affect, meaning love, friendship or sexual attraction; and that the first is morally reprehensible." The second is that "sexual intercourse unaccompanied by an emotional relationship is immoral, and that marriage for interest is therefore a form of prostitution." The third assumption is that personal autonomy "is paramount."[101]

Stone's argument is that the history of marriage and the family is not one uniformly based on these assumptions.[102] Whatever we conclude about the historical issues which Stone addresses, it seems that we must, in discussing our own institutions, understand that older ideas are not dead.[103] Our world is one in which newer ideas are superimposed on older ones, but the older ones survive nonetheless. Society's older ideas included not only ideas suggested by Stone's discussion, but also ideas relating to the permanence and stability of marriage, as well as ideas of strong interests, connections, and affections which are not marital.

Our present cultural assumption is that marriages, to be respectable, must be for love. As Georg Simmel suggested, there is a "disparagement of personal dignity that nowadays arises in every marriage that is not based on personal affection." A "sense of decency," he continued, "requires the concealment of economic motives." This, he noted, is not the case "in simpler cultures."[104]

Whether or not nineteenth-century England was a simpler culture, it seems to have been a culture in which the love and money issues of marriage were much discussed. And while an English sense of decency might have required discussion of "love," English values also allowed Trollope to paint a nonjudgmental picture of a man who proposed to four women in one year, finally marrying the last.[105]

It is reported that Trollope composed hundreds of marriage proposals in his roughly fifty novels. A few of them will be referred to here, including the one that apparently was his own. It seems legitimate to focus on a nineteenth-century English writer here. Even today, discussion of marriage and family typically begins with the traditional views expressed in *Maynard v. Hill* or the definition of *Hyde v. Hyde*.[106] While some variation exists between American and English marriage relationships, the basics are substantially similar; at an any rate, they are similar enough for the purposes of this discussion.[107]

There are, of course, differences between our situation and the social situations Trollope describes. One difference is the role of the father in the marital negotiations of the children. For example, in *Is He Popenjoy?* the father "stipulates" for his engaged daughter a house of her own in London. A married woman, he believes, "should always have some home of her own."[108] Here, both the father's role and the substance of his demand do not accord with middle-class expectations. The role of the father is again strikingly illustrated in a sentence from *Ralph the Heir:* "He engaged hisself to me to marry her."[109]

A second issue is the perception of marital control. In Trollope's era, marital control sometimes meant the direct regulation by the husband of the hourly activity of his often child-wife, including her reading and domestic concerns.[110] Finally, more generally on the question of the status of women, the work of Trollope, which predates women's suffrage in England and largely ridicules women's political rights, contrasts sharply with contemporary views.[111]

While not realistic in the sense of naturalistic fiction or socialist realism, Trollope's work is usually understood to have a profound realism. Nathaniel Hawthorne asked: "Have you ever read the novels of Anthony Trollope? . . . [They are] just as real as if some giant had hewn a great lump out of the earth and put it under a glass case, with all its inhabitants going about their daily business."[112]

Trollope's various marriage proposals represent a set of typical conversations about marriage. One editor has suggested that the classic problem in Trollope is that of marriage for love or money.[113] Trollope's view of marriage—or perhaps ultimately his questions about marriage—intensified over time. In the end, he seems to have had many questions and doubts about the institution. While Trollope thought it necessary that love be stressed in novels, particularly the love of young people, he seemed very clear about the complexity of the motivations of those about to set up joint lives together.[114] This seemed particularly true when his characters were no longer young. Trollope's general view of marriage is found in *Phineas Finn,* in the voice of a woman.

I shall take the first that comes after I have quite made up my mind.
You'll think it very horrible, but that is really what I shall do. After
all, a husband is very much like a house or a horse. You don't take
your house because it's the best house in the world, but because just
then you want a house. You go and see a house, and if its very nasty
you don't take it. But if you think it will suit pretty well, and if you
are tired of looking about for houses, you do take it.[115]

Marriage for Trollope is a solution to problems that vary with the
situation of the individuals involved. Marriage resolves the issue of
leaving the parental nest while simultaneously producing, hopefully, a
situation of which parents can approve. Marriage also solves the problem of who shall be the coparent of desired offspring, or who shall fill
up a life in other ways when offspring are not seen as part of the future.
Marriage provides another producer of income when that is needed or
cook-housekeeper-companion when that is needed. The problem
comes first, the model solution second, and the individual third. Trollope often discusses love in terms of something that one hopes to
achieve after marriage. To learn to love someone is an enterprise for
certain young women after the man has been accepted.

In some of Trollope's work, the explicit individual motivations for
marriage are apparent, and it is clear that the search for a spouse is a
means to particular ends. For example, in one of his later works, *Mr.
Scarborough's Family,* Trollope offered a long negotiation over the marriage contract between a man who wants an heir and a woman who
wants a good establishment with a residence for her friend and companion.[116]

The Proposal and Some Contracts Issues
Trollope's proposal in *Dr. Thorne* (apparently his own proposal to Rose
Hazeltine) suggests that the offer-and-acceptance aspect of the mar-
riage contract may be very elliptical as to details.

> GENTLEMAN: Well miss, the long and short of it is this: here I am.
>   Take me or leave me.
> LADY: Scratching a gutter in the sand with her parasol . . . Of course
>   I know that's all nonsense.
> GENTLEMAN: Nonsense. By Jove, it isn't nonsense at all. Come, Jane,
>   here I am. Come, at any rate you can say something.

LADY: yes, I suppose I can say something.
GENTLEMAN: Well, which is it to be take me or leave me.
LADY: . . . Well, I don't exactly want to leave you. . . . And so it was
settled.[117]

The fact that the parties are "polite lovers," a "gentleman" and a
"lady," assumes something about the context of the transaction. The
indirection of the acceptance says something also. A lady's acceptance
may be hesitant, tremulous, and weak but is nonetheless enough. Even
if there had been a certain amount of pressure put on the lady, duress
would likely not be found.

Bishop notes, "Persons are nowhere compelled to marry."[118] This
is true in the sense that fraud and duress will void a marriage and that
in the modern world direct compulsion is viewed as an evil.[119] But, as a
Trollope novel has it, a girl is "taught to presume that it was her destiny
to be married." A man, by contrast, generally "regards it as his destiny
either to succeed or fail in the world."[120] Marriage is assumed as desirable, for both, but quite differently in Trollope's world.

Capacity to consent is also an issue. An old French argument on
parental consent had it that the consent of elders was necessary because
when a man was under the influence of the most imperious of the passions, he was not exercising free will.[121] So perhaps "love," of itself, dis-
qualifies men and women about to marry from an appropriately contractual state of mind.[122] (The issue of the emotional state undercutting
consent in those ordinarily capable of contracting is familiar in contracts and often quite difficult. It should not be concluded that anything
said here is an attempt to open the issue of lack of capacity generally
because of differential gender socialization.)

The real point, as Llewellyn noted, is that "[a]greement does not
even today carry any necessary connotation of real willingness."[123]
Indeed, "acquiescence in the lesser evil is all that need be understood";
it is essentially a factual question.[124] The problem of 'reality of consent'
is essentially one of determining what types of pressure or other stim-
uli are sufficiently out of line with our general presuppositions of dealing to open the expression of agreement to attack.[125] We assume that
the pressure on women particularly to marry is given, and is no more
of a problem than the pressure to buy food.[126]

The language of Trollope's proposal assumes that a great deal
about the details of the arrangement is known by both parties, as would

be the case in any specific social context (or to the extent not known, as contractual material is not known, not important, until some disaster strikes). The deal itself is standard. The dickered terms, as Llewellyn would have put it, relate largely to the individuals in the deal. At this point, the parties might have wanted to discuss major deviations from the standard arrangement. Projecting the story forward some decades, one can imagine that conventional deviations might have involved the childless marriage; a career (as against a job, or a domestic life) for the wife; the presence of resident in-laws, all quite possibly "dickered" in fact. Beyond this, in the background, the other terms are provided by the situation. Societies indicate the responsibilities of a wife, a doctor's wife, a farmer's wife. The roles are what is being assumed by the agreement to marry. And in one sense the whole matter is, as Trollope says, a "leap in the dark."[127]

In these terms, an arranged marriage is a standardized contract largely mandatory in its terms in which the parties do not select each other.[128] In some cases, nothing much is said by the individual parties because nothing has to be said. The context provides the terms as between the individuals, and the families have done the bargaining that had to be done.[129]

Some marital negotiation may involve ideas contrary to the official ideal of the marriage contract.[130] Consider the following proposal, from Anita Brookner's *Hotel du Lac:*

> "I am proposing a partnership of the most enlightened kind. A partnership based on esteem, if you like. Also out of fashion, by the way. If you wish to take a lover, that is your concern, so long as you arrange it in a civilized manner."
> "And if you . . ."
> "The same applies, of course. For me, now, that would always be a trivial matter. You would not hear of it nor need you care about it. The union between us would be one of shared interests, of truthful discourse. Of companionship. To me, now, these are the important things. And for you they should be important.
> Think, Edith. Have you not, at some time in your well-behaved life, desired vindication? Are you not tired of being polite to rude people?"[131]

This bargain, which does not end at the altar, stresses the social realities of marriage and the importance placed on marriage for women, especially, in terms of respectability and status. The arrangement[132] fails because, in effect, there is too much compromise and not enough love in the deal.[133]

Some contracts, of course, are for nonmarital sex-money arrangements. In Trollope, these are seen as traditional in Europe, and also in fact in England.[134] Far from being expressions of individual bohemianism, they are understood as entirely conventional in nature.[135]

Some nonmarital arrangements[136] can involve fairly explicit contracting. For example, in *Comeback,* by Dick Francis, the following brief encounter is described:

> Into a long smiling silence, lolling back in the armchair, I said casually, "How about a bonk, then?"
> She laughed. "Is that Foreign Office standard phraseology?"
> "Heard all the time in embassies."
> She'd long had the intention and I hadn't misread her.
> "No strings," she said. "Passing ships."
> I nodded.
> "Upstairs," she said economically, taking my glass.[137]

Ross Thomas describes another nonmarital situation: "We had one of those oh so modern arrangements, he lived here and we split expenses. He gave me a check every month for seven hundred and fifty dollars and I paid the bills—food the mortgage utilities things like that. He was sort of a star boarder, I guess."[138] These examples involve language. The language is a clue to transactional patterns that may well be standard and subject to analysis as default contracts.

Some feminist issues involved in the question of marriage and other domestic contracts are obvious. One is status after marriage, summarized in 1700 by the wife-to-be in a play by Congreve, who suggests that even after she had negotiated as fully as possible for what she wanted, it would still be necessary to "dwindle into a wife."[139]

The wife is inferior to the husband in marriage because, for some, the female is inferior to the male in general. Trollope ridiculed the women's rights movement.[140] The link to marriage is made plain in a comment in which one of Trollope's characters defines marriage as the "manner in which the all-wise Creator has thought fit to make the weaker vessel subject to the stronger one."[141] While the statement is rejected by the woman to whom it is addressed, it is rejected on the narrow point that the particular man under discussion is not fit to dominate her.[142]

When Lord Tennyson wrote, in *Locksley Hall*, of the husband to whom the wife was "something better than his dog, a little dearer than his horse," he described a boorish master in a relationship in which there would always be a master.[143] When, in *Mr. Scarborough's Family*, Trollope describes a father urging a daughter to marry a man who will not mistreat her, he is thinking along similar lines, though describing a kinder individual.[144]

Inequality traditionally underlies the idea of husband and wife, even when there is no direct reference to it. In the United States, Justice Bradley's late-nineteenth-century concurrence in *Bradwell v. Illinois*[145] remains a classic statement of the conventional understanding.[146] Justice Bradley wrote: "The paramount destiny and mission of woman are to fulfil the noble and benign offices of wife and mother. This is the law of the Creator."[147] Wife and mother, without economic independence or political rights. The law of the Creator was to be applied universally, despite the fact that women might not marry, since "the rules of civil society must be adapted to the general constitution of things and cannot be based on exceptional cases"[148] The idea of individualized contract is exactly about the possibility of making room for exceptional cases, within or outside of the framework of marriage.

The discussion in this chapter to this point has been intended to illustrate exchanges and bargains-in-fact and to raise certain contracts issues relating largely to issues of entry into domestic contracts. Whether we want to consider these bargain-in-fact "legal contracts" will turn in part on problems of enforcement. These issues require a separate discussion and are the subject of the fourth part of the chapter.

Some Issues of Remedies and Enforcement

We have long indulged in the presumption that no amount of effort or agreement on the part of individuals can result in a contract unless there is a law ready to give that effect to the acts of the parties. Nathan Isaacs writes, "Hence we must argue in a circle: the law will recognize and enforce as contracts such agreements as it chooses to recognize and enforce."[149]

To some degree, the perspective used here assumes a world in which law is ubiquitous, floating over, and capable of creating a context for, all relationships and all behavior. Subject to the self-restraint of constitutions or conventions, everything is, in theory, within the law's reach.

All relationships can also be seen through the law of contracts—some more comfortably than others.[150] By bending and twisting the idea of choice, most relationships can be understood as chosen even if the choice is the refusal of an association. Even the idea that we cannot choose our parents is modified as we see children choosing new parents not only "spiritually," as they used to say, but legally. Within the law of contracts, some bargains are not contracts but are mere agreements, to be left without state intervention in whatever situation may then exist.[151] One issue in determining the answer to the question of which bargains become contracts relates to issues of enforcement.

The contractual view focuses on individual autonomy in a way that denies much reality in the world. It is true in the same sense that stone walls do not a prison make, and that what matters is not the thing but our response to the thing. The contractual emphasis would cut against an observation to the effect that, for example, women do not "choose" their traditional roles.[152] Rather, the argument assumes that one can choose the path of least resistance, and that in fact most people do.[153] In the end, the contractual emphasis is not a truth or a rule of law but a possibility, to be accepted or rejected in particular circumstances.

The problem that some of the Realists saw was that contract law had a single set of rules that applied to all cases. In the context of sales,[154] rather than attempting to define and then impose a perfect model, they developed the Uniform Commercial Code as a framework for different models, different forms, now and in the future. As the statute was a framework for commercial models, the contract was a framework for human behavior. Thus Llewellyn wrote that "the major importance of legal contract is to provide a frame-work for well-nigh every type of group organization and for well-nigh every type of passing or permanent relation between individuals and groups, up to and including states."[155]

The marriage contract was itself such a framework for the individuals, and a variation in that contract—whether or not litigated—would, for those individuals, adjust the framework. Even when a court might say, as in the well-known case of *Balfour v. Balfour*,[156] that a contract between husband and wife could not stand, this was because such a contract was thought to be not intended in fact.[157] It might, then, have been intended on some other facts, including a changed conventional understanding about the legitimacy of such contracts.

Of course any contract may still be "unconscionable" or "unfair," and thus unenforceable.[158] The problem for us is not so much judicial power to police domestic contracts for fairness and the like as our judicial standard. What are the objectives of the state in these contexts? What is fair? How do we know it? Where do we look for state policy on the question? Here the perspective interior to contract law offers certain assistance.

Once we knew, or felt, when a contract was unconscionable or unfair under the assumptions about the nature of marriage, the family, and men and women on which the traditional arrangements were based. Once state policy on marriage referred to an answerable question. We knew that the traditional family was the goal. That family had a certain shape, and people within it had certain roles.[159] Without elaborating the point again here, it is clear enough that the family was not egalitarian either as to adults and children or husband and wife. This point about roles and hierarchy has consequences for the idea of fairness. If a woman is a breeder or entertainer or housekeeper and is generally viewed as replaceable, if not disposable, then a small pension on divorce may be "fair." It may be "fair" that most of the money should remain with the one who had earned it through activity in the market. This would be true, no matter how great the wife's reliance on the idea and even the representation that marriage meant sharing, each bringing what he or she could to the marriage without withholding and without specific valuation. How, after all, could she have "reasonably relied," considering the general cultural stance that insisted that money "really" belonged to those who "earned" it?[160] If charity, goodness, or guilt indicated transfer payments to the ex-wife, then honor to the man who made generous payments. The matter had little to do with her entitlement. And of course her lost opportunity was understood not as lost market-income but as a different spouse. If she, divorced, lacked money or status, the solution was remarriage.

These assumptions are to a considerable degree rejected today as they relate to the marriages and domestic arrangements of young people. Women are formally, and sometimes actually, as free as men to seek opportunities in the market, in the home, in public and private life. This means that domestic arrangements will take many forms, not merely the traditional or conventional one. Here, an explicit agreement-in-fact could be used today as a reference point when the legal system addressed the issues of fairness or unconscionability if the arrangement came into litigation as a contract, or as general background if the issue of fault arises in other ways, since the model of the marriage chosen and a statement of entitlements may well have some relevance to our judicial assessment of equities. Whether or not a legal contract, the agreement-in-fact could be a source of information, establishing the expectations of the parties in a way not relevant only to official enforcement but to issues of fault or good faith that might arise in various contexts.[161]

One way to think about a diversity of marital arrangements is to focus on individual contracts. Another is to think about structured menus, state offered options, to which individuals give their consent. Perhaps the simplest way to think about the issues created by a system of alternative domestic models, including issues of state enforcement of contracts, is to remember the examples we actually have of the different forms of marriage, within the rules of various religious communities. Llewellyn once referred to the "vicious heritage" of viewing the parties to a contract as individuals.[162] The use of religious law helps us recall that point, especially because religious law remains particularly strong with reference to the family. Religious groups are often in the background, behind the individuals who are working through the contractual framework, creating the new family group. Religious law can be used as illustrative of contract terms to suggest the sort of substantive regulation we might be thinking about.

We might think of a contractual menu for domestic arrangements, including marriage and divorce according to different religious rules as well as marital and nonmarital partnerships. This menu might include conventions of Muslim divorce.[163] Another menu option might be a traditional Catholic rule, forbidding birth control and divorce. The menu might include an option for Jewish marriage and divorce, attempting somehow to deal with the "get" issue.[164] The menu would allow a couple to choose an option (then: to modify it? waive provisions? and in fact do all the things that make contract law itself flexible and thus uncertain?). If the couple did not choose, a default option would come into play, which again could possibly be subject to revision and modification.[165]

Discussions of remedies in the context of divorce ordinarily focus on the remedies to be given a spouse (typically assumed to be a wife) disadvantaged by the departure of a partner, often assumed to have the money but be unwilling to give it up. The disadvantage is seen to arise from the fact that the wife either never seriously entered the market or left it early.

The range of choices that the framework[166] might include becomes clear if we think broadly about remedies for breech and recall that the contractual options—following the UCC—might include agreed-upon remedies, as well as statutory remedies.

It is clear that remedies are a cultural institution, and that in this culture, certain remedies are assumed to be inappropriate. We do not hang people for violating the sanctity of contract. Our sense of the appropriate remedy for breach of contracts starts, conventionally, with money damages. When our thinking moves to what the law of con-tracts considers the atypical remedy, some sort of specific performance, we run into serious difficulty in the domestic context. To begin with, it is clear that in many family cases, money is not an adequate remedy, and our thinking does have to turn to other possibilities.[167] Thus, sur-rogacy contracts (in which one wants the child), promises to give a get (a Jewish religious divorce), and promises for the religious upbringing of children all present instances in which money is not really the desired remedy. Yet other more direct remedies may be unavailable because, for example, personal-services contracts are not specifically enforceable and the Constitution guarantees the free exercise of reli-gion or in general because the matter is considered insignificant.[168]

But we should not conclude from this that no legal system can ever attempt specific performance in this context.[169] And, for the sake of per-spective, we might usefully recall the writ for the restitution of conjugal rights. Although the remedy has in fact never been part of American law,[170] restitution of conjugal rights should be remembered as a mea-sure focused on reconciliation and as an example of serious specific performance ideas in the domestic context.[171] (The most that the law could have claimed—and sometimes did—was that enforced proxim-ity would result in increased tolerance and compassion that might ulti-mate translate into something called conjugal affection.)[172] But if we will reject restitution of conjugal rights, perhaps we go too far in the other direction if we say that enforceable contracts must be limited to the economics of the dissolution of the marriage. Possibly we could see a list of enforcement possibilities develop over time as courts consider such theoretical, contractually agreed-upon remedies as waiting peri-ods for divorce itself, or contractual adoption of (for example) penalties for initiating divorce except for fault.

Issues of enforcement focused on particular enforcement measures deal, of course, with an assumption about entitlement. That is, we speak of a remedy for someone who is entitled to that remedy. Often our discussions focus on the reintroduction of categories of fault. To begin with, fault and breach are not identical. But perhaps more fundamentally, while there are such things as guilt and innocence, they are perhaps less easily known than our discussions sometimes assume. The analogue would be to limit discussion of custody problems to conflicts between a fit and a grossly unfit parent where the difficult case—and possibly the typical one—is the conflict between two fit parents.

The following describes a commercial case: "The actual situation is complicated and confused, there are mutual recriminations, each party accuses the other of bad faith, misconduct and faulty performance; until the judicial dice have been rolled, no one has the least idea of which side is in breach and which is not."[173] If this is the truth of a commercial case, it is likely to be even more deeply the truth of many domestic-relations cases. Indeed, it was this problem that provided one of the original arguments for the move to no-fault divorce. It was not that there was no fault, but rather that the system could not usefully expend energy identifying it.[174]

A contracts approach will not eliminate this problem but will allow us to consider the issue by including the understandings of the particular parties.[175] The ideas of breach, or good faith, or fault applied to the controversies of the parties could be individual, subject to some overriding policing ideas. These policing ideas, with such ideas as presumptive contracts and nonvariable terms, permit the articulation of state interests. The contracts approach permits the development of both state and individual interests in a way, it seems, that would be worth our time to explore. An individual agreements/contracts approach does not minimize issues of state interest, to the extent that the ideas of presumptive contracts or nonvariable terms or judicial policing provide ways to accommodate collective interests.

This chapter argues for a stance toward contracting derived from perspectives interior to contract law. It does not argue for any specific contract. Moreover, it concedes in relation to some bargains that the contractual/commercial optic on domestic arrangements would give rise to farce. For example, consider Chekhov's version of the romance of the future in which a broker carries out a marriage negotiation.[176] When the young woman agrees to marry the man the agent asks for a deposit.

The young lady gives the agent ten or twenty rubles. He takes the money, bows obsequiously, and goes to the door.

"The receipt?" She stops him.

"Mille pardons, Madam. I completely forgot! Ha-ha!"

Balalaikin writes the receipt, bows again, and leaves. The young lady covers her face with her hands and falls onto the divan.

"How happy I am!" she exclaims, seized by an emotion she has never before experienced. "How happy I am! I love—and am loved!"[177]

But Chekhov's treatment of the contractual aspects of domestic arrangements is not the only version possible.

The discussion has suggested the utility of an analysis in which all domestic arrangements are (thinly speaking) contractual. The utility derives from an openness to the idea of individual variation, an idea elaborated in realist work on contracts. This approach allows a distinction between negotiated and default aspects of particular relationships, "default" understood as state-defined contractual relationships in the absence of agreement to the contrary. Traditional domestic arrangements were described in terms of these distinctions. For example, conventional marriages would be viewed as resting on a choice of the default position, while less conventional marriages would represent a contract arrangement of a different kind. The "method of silence," or the adhesion aspect of the default position, could work—regardless of whether that default position relates to traditional marriages or to roommate relationships—if the underling social understandings were stable. Problems arise because individuals are attempting to structure and institutionalize new relationships that are not clearly established in the society. Further problems arise because the details of the several default positions are not as clear as they once were. This suggests a role for explicit agreements to clarify the expectations and intentions of the parties and to communicate those expectations to the legal system, should that system ever be invoked. Whether these agreements in fact should be directly enforced will depend, as it has always depended, on a policy judgment itself heavily influenced by underlying social factors, including the behavior, intentions, and reliance of the individuals involved, and the judicial reading of those factors.[178]

Chapter Four

The Family

But his wife's family (the word has a more important application there than here) held a solemn conference.

John Luther Long, "Madame Butterfly"

The family was so important in Japan that marriages were understood as a contract between families rather than between individuals. The House "consisted of all living lineal ascendants and descendants in a particular family, with the oldest male member commonly in the position of Head of the House."[1] Postmortem divorce derives from this idea, since "marriage is a relationship with the family of the deceased which continues after death."[2] The House was formally abolished in the 1948 civil code, although we are told that the idea continued to be significant.[3] In short, the Japanese legal system both before and after the modernization of 1898 took the house as the fundamental unit of society. Thus, Yogo Watenabe writes, "Before World War II, the primary unit in Japanese society was the family rather than the individual."[4]

The family as it appears in Madame Butterfly—*a family that finally expels her, not for her marriage but for her apostasy—is the strong extended family we, in the west, take as the family of the past. As to the past, we often acknowledge both the strength of the family[5] and the complexity of its sanctioning system. This tends to be concealed as to the present, first, by our current emphasis on families as having solely affective functions and, second, by our emphasis on the state regulation of the family. But families may be more complex than we imagine, having their own internal regulatory systems and their own internal divisions.*

The common idea that the family is only regulated by state law is examined through a consideration of Kafka's Letter to His Father. *The letter suggests the existence of a number of interacting legal regimes within the family (state law, religious-social law, father law, individual conscience). These are*

73

*considered through the psychological law ideas of the Russo-Polish theorist
Leon Petrazycki.*

This conception of the strength of family is somewhat strange to the modern audience, as is the idea of family discipline sometimes associated with it. Under the Japanese structure, one could be expelled from the house for marriage without consent. Expulsion from the family is the invocation of the conventional sanction of expulsion or exclusion as applied to a government unit that is not, however, official. The idea of the coercive violence of official law has a parallel, then, in the sanctioning systems of unofficial law.

This idea—that there is a governing unit represented by the family—requires some investigation, if only to raise the question: on what basis does the family govern? What are the laws of family life?

There are different ways to look at the family, assuming for the moment that we agree on a preliminary definition of the unit. For example, one might consider the family as a single authority, a private government comparable to the integrated state or the hierarchical church, ruling the individuals within the family. One might focus on the family as a unit that other larger authorities seek to control.[6] Or one might in effect combine these approaches and discuss the family as a social field, one that is, like society itself, a place of intersecting legal orders, in some sense an entity that other units attempt to control, in some sense a unit attempting to control other units, whether these are individuals or groups. This chapter uses the third approach.

Family Governance

Edmund Wilson, whose assessment of Franz Kafka's work was not particularly enthusiastic, described him this way:

> Franz Kafka was the delicate son of a self-made Jewish merchant in the wholesale-women's-wear business in Prague, a vigorous and practical man, who inspired him with fear and respect, and gave him a life-long inferiority complex. The son was a pure intellectual, who derived from the rabbinical tradition of the mother's side of the family; but he yielded to the insistence of the father and, though at times reduced to thoughts of suicide, he took his place in the dry goods warehouse. His real interest had always been writing, which represented for him not merely an art but also somehow a pursuit of righteousness—he said he regarded it as a form of prayer—and he finally got himself a job in a workers' accident-

insurance office, which left him his afternoons free. He wanted, or thought he ought to want, to get married, but his relationship with his father seems to have deprived him of sexual self-confidence.[7]

Wilson continues his narrative of Kafka's life this way. "He became engaged to a girl whom he described as 'wholesome, merry, natural, robust'; and, after five years of grueling hesitation, developed tuberculosis, on purpose, in his own opinion, to make it impossible for him to marry." Kafka "was by this time, one supposes, too much at home in his isolation to be able to bring himself to the point of taking the risk of trying to get out of it; and he now, at the age of thirty-six, addressed to his father an enormous letter (never yet printed in full),[8] an apologia for his own life, in which he seems to have blamed his failure on him." But then, later, Kafka "did get away to Berlin. He had found an intellectual girl who studied Hebrew with him and whom he seems really to have wanted to marry. Her orthodox Chassidic father was forbidden by the rabbi to allow it when Franz confessed that he was not a practicing Jew; but the girl, in revolt against her family tradition, set up housekeeping with him and took care of him. Though he was eager now to work and to live, his disease had left him little time, and, after less than a year of this life, he was dead at forty-one."[9] Wilson referred to Kafka as "denationalized, discouraged, disaffected, [and] disabled."[10]

Kafka and the Father Letter

Kafka's biography is not merely the story of the artist lacking recognition from his insensitive family, a story that in itself is not unusual. It incorporates father's story (also not unusual), of a businessman who was the son of a butcher. That son, now father, confronts his own son, an artist who seems to neither recognize his parent's struggle nor want to carry the middle-class enterprise forward. In that historical moment, middle-class women have a dependent, but in one sense privileged, role. Max Brod urged that Kafka's parents should do for Kafka what they would have done for a daughter—support him in leisure so that he could write.[11] To review, then, we see that in November 1919, Franz Kafka, who had a troubled relationship with his father for all his life,[12] wrote him a long letter, almost a small book, as Max Brod says.[13] His father seems never to have read the letter, for it was delivered to

Kafka's mother, who did not pass it on.[14] Kafka intended (he says) to send the letter to Milena in July 1920, but as of the end of that month had not done so.[15] Kafka's "Letter to His Father" is read and studied as a constructed text. It is included in a collection of stories called *The Sons*, along with "The Metamorphosis," "The Stoker," and "The Judgment" and in a collection called *The Basic Kafka*. When it was published in English in 1954, the volume including it was titled *Dearest Father*.[16] In our time we can hardly avoid the overtones of the *Mommie Dearest* genre.[17] In Kafka's case, of course, we do not really even know whether the letter is a public or private document. Kafka was notoriously ambivalent about publication. We have the famous problem of Max Brod, the executor who had said he was committed to publication, as the one Kafka instructed to burn his manuscripts. "Letter to His Father" raises the same issue. It was sent to Kafka's father via his mother, who did not pass it on, but returned it—as Kafka may have suspected she would. Was it ever really "intended" for his father? For anyone? For everyone then and to come, except his father? As with Kafka's letters, diaries, and novels, it seems to matter less now than it used to. It is all part of the collected-work genre, a form of narrative in which the child as adult articulates and makes public—presumably in part for the purpose of self-healing—the pains experienced in childhood.

One reading of Kafka today says that out of private pain he built narratives that speak to our general, political situation. Some cite his work politically to say that he anticipated the totalitarian state,[18] others existentially to say that he described the ultimately unintelligible universe. For some, the subject is the text and ideas derived from the text, not the historical family it describes or evokes. Others read Kafka's work more biographically, as Alice Miller does this, seeing the private pain of Kafka as the pain of all children whose parents fail them. She reviews Kafka's history and concludes that he would have been happier and that his writing would have been stronger if he had dealt with his past in analysis. Miller reads the father letter as indicating that the father rejected and even hated the child at times.[19] Kafka "could not possibly know he was portraying what he experienced in childhood in his novels and stories" and suggest that his readers also see the work as products of the imagination.[20] This ignores both Kafka's extreme self-awareness and the alertness of at least those readers who have read more than Kafka's fiction. The movie *Kafka* (Miramax Films, 1992) is built on certain connections between the life and the work.) Kafka's difficulty with his family becomes all but universal.[21] Alice Miller accepts Kafka's facts, and on that basis offers a reading.

But Kafka is a classic problematic narrator. The issue of the lying narrator is familiar: we no longer assume that narrators always tell the truth, that they are not the criminals whose veracity is not to be assumed. Consider one factual question: Did Kafka ever please his father? Did he ever see and feel parental approval, the "[l]ight upon him from his father's eyes" (as Wordsworth put it)?[22] Here is some characteristically ambiguous testimony, analyzed as a pro and con, for and against his father.[23] Kafka writes,

> You have a particularly beautiful, very rare way of quietly, contentedly, approvingly smiling, a way of smiling that can make the person for whom it is meant entirely happy. [You had the power to make me happy. Did you?] I can't recall its ever having expressly been my lot in my childhood [my very doubt suggests con], but I dare say it may have happened, [pro] for why should you have refused it to me [con—you are capable of such withholding] at a time when I still seemed blameless to you and was your great hope? [pro] Yet in the long run even such friendly impressions [pro/con (if any)] brought about nothing but an increased sense of guilt, making the world still more incomprehensible to me [even if pro, con].[24]

Again, a question of fact arises: Was Kafka ever physically disciplined? "It is also true that you hardly ever really gave me a beating."[25] (Hardly ever really? He was abused? He wasn't?) Miller notes as to this point that Kafka's father "presumably did not beat his son regularly," but that this does not mean that Kafka was not mistreated.[26]

> But the shouting, the way your face got red, the hasty undoing of the suspenders and laying them ready over the back of the chair, all that was almost worse for me. It is as if someone is going to be hanged. If he really is hanged, then he is dead and it is all over. But if he has to go through all the preliminaries to being hanged and he learns of his reprieve only when the noose is dangling before his face, he may suffer from it all his life. [Even if he wasn't abused, he was.][27]

The account evokes descriptions of mock executions Dostoyevsky was put through in 1849.[28]

Kafka clearly understood the issues here. He wrote to Milena in July 1920: "Tomorrow I'll send the father-letter to your apartment, please take good care of it, I still might want to give it to my father someday. If possible don't let anyone else read it. And as you read it understand all the lawyer's tricks: it is a lawyer's letter."[29] What Kafka meant by this may be finally unknowable. But it may be suggested that the "tricks" involve his knowledge of [or insistence on] his own "exaggeration." For example: "I'm not going to say, of course, that I have become what I am only as a result of your influence. That would be very much exaggerated (and I am indeed inclined to this exaggeration) [so I do say it],"[30] as well as his general tendency to equivocate, something that Kafka associated with being a lawyer.

Ambiguity and Legal Pluralism

The issue of Kafka as a lawyer has not been entirely neglected. Thus, Robin West writes that Kafka's "training in law and his work in the law-related field of industrial safety for most of his adult life account for part of his deep understanding of the psychological mechanisms of consent and obedience to legal authority."[31]

Posner responds on this point: "From the fact that Kafka studied law and worked most of his adult life for an insurance company, it does not follow that his writing is in any essential sense about law and business."[32] But another view, a monograph on the subject published in 1986, suggests a different analysis, that most critical work on Kafka has "overlooked the fact that Kafka, with or without reluctance, made of the law his primary occupation during a period extending from the time of his enrollment at the university in 1901 to his retirement more than twenty years later from his legal post."[33]

What follows is a preliminary treatment of some very broad issues. Kafka studied law at the German University in Prague and received a doctorate in 1906. At the very least, it is possible that law study was, despite Kafka's well-known comment on "disgusting Roman law,"[34] not uncongenial to his own mental processes. One speculates on the influence on Kafka of at least some aspects of conventional law—not perhaps the rules, but the fictions. One imagines him in the law school classroom, sketching pictures of tortured human beings,[35] listening to a

lecture on the early Roman law idea of coerced consent.[36] It is an idea
that must have interested someone fixated on the issues of the
guilty/innocent, as Milena's obituary of Kafka put it. And one wonders
about the impact on Kafka of the study of the specific fictions that law
employs.[37] (Kirchberger stresses the impact of Ihering and Roman law
on Kafka in her book.[38]) One might play with some examples: the
proposition that a captured soldier is considered dead from the time of
his capture (to ensure that he died a citizen so that a will could be valid)
could operate to reinforce speculation on twin status's (alive from the
point of view of the living captive, dead from the point of view of the
Roman law). This fiction resonates with Kafka's sense that he was not,
for example, as his family saw him and that someone could win in reality but lose in parable.[39] His *Diaries* relate a discussion with Max Brod
to the effect that Kafka would lie contentedly on his deathbed if there
were little pain. "I forgot—and later purposely omitted— . . . that the
best things I have written have their basis in this capacity of mine to
meet death with contentment." His writings about death are "secretly a
game": "It is the same thing as my perpetual lamenting to my mother
over pains that were not nearly so great as my laments would lead one
to believe. With my mother, of course, I did not need to make so great
a display of art as with the reader."[40]

    One can speculate on the impact on Kafka, a failed son, of the rule
of civil and Roman law that a gift can be revoked when there is ingrat-
itude on the part of the beneficiary.[41] Kafka, in the letter to his father,
refers to himself as a disinherited son.[42] What about the gift of life?
Does the idea add something to our reading of "The Judgment"? In
"The Judgment," a father sentences a (bad) son to be executed, and the
son kills himself. Posner seems to suggest that a son who would commit suicide because his father said to him, "I sentence you now to death
by drowning" might be viewed as mentally incompetent. Economic
theory does "not presume that choices made by mentally incompetent
people are value maximizing."[43] One recalls here Kafka's repeated discussions of his father's charge that he was an ungrateful son and his
attempt to offer defenses to the allegation.[44] One notes also Kafka's
diary entry on the importance of remembering the injury that his father
had done him so that the next time he was angry with his father he
would recall his father's behavior.[45] ("In order not to forget," Kafka
wrote, should he denounce me, I write down X, my own denunciation;
but I should not have written it down because now I really hate him,

out of proportion to his offense as I have recorded it, my hatred increasing as he concluded, "I cannot remember what was really wicked in my father's behavior yesterday." [paraphrase], except for quoted material.) One might see the state law as reinforcing Herrmann Kafka's (reported) view that he was entitled to gratitude. Kafka rejects this entitlement in legal-economic terms: "Parents who expect gratitude from their children (there are even some who insist on it) are like usurers who gladly risk their capital if only they receive interest."[46]

Kafka's general view of law can be related to his view of language, which he believes is finally about lies: "Since language only refers to the sensory world, it can never be [an] instrument of truth."[47] Conversation reduces the significance of his ideas; writing letters about certain things involves telling lies.[48] Alone, and without language, there is the possibility of truth—a mist, but truth.[49]

Law in the real world is built on language and is associated, in Kafka's mind, with fraud—as it is in the minds of many others. The negative image of lawyers historically requires no citation and issues of law's problematic relation to an absolute truth have also been commented on.[50] The model of (at least one) of Kafka's approach(es) to law is suggested in a letter concerning his friend's pressure to publish in spite of Kafka's reluctance to do so. "What I say here," he writes, "is naturally just an exaggeration and a bit of spitefulness toward my friends." "The truth," he remarks, "is that I am so corrupted and shameless that I participate myself in getting these things published." Then, to "excuse [his] weakness," he makes "the forces working on [him] out to be stronger than they are." This he knows is a lie, of course. "This is fraud. . . . I am a lawyer, you see—that is why I can't keep away from wrongdoing."[51]

Kafka saw himself as a liar and concealer of truth. He writes to Max Brod, "It is true that I am not writing to you, but not because I have anything to conceal (except that concealment has been my life's vocation)."[52] In his diary, he notes, for example, a "coolness toward [an acquaintance]. He asks me about it. I deny it."[53] He describes a letter to Brod as "lying, vain, theatrical."[54] There is no closure, even on the issue of lies. When the legend of *The Trial* concludes with the idea that lying is universal, K notes that his is a melancholy conclusion, but even this is "not his final judgement."[55] Kafka writes in the letter to his father that "the explanation I gave the director for my resignation was, though not strictly in accordance with the truth, still not entirely a lie."[56] This equivocation goes with his idea of the lawyer. In a letter to Milena, he writes of a question: "I portrayed it just the way I saw it. . . . (It wasn't exactly like that; this is the Jewish lawyer speaking, always quick with his tongue, but still it was partly like that.)"[57] There was, however, no other way as an individual matter. Thus, to Felice he writes, "Subterfuges there have been, lies very few, assuming that it's possible to tell 'very few' lies. I am a mendacious creature; for me it is the only way to maintain an even keel, my boat is fragile."[58]

Kafka's insistence on partialness and qualification relates to pluralist views more than to formal state-centered ideas of law. State-centered theories are typically associated with the idea of a single correct answer. The refusal to define one answer leaves open many answers. The suggestion that Kafka functioned within a framework of multiple legal levels[59] is a way of articulating certain approaches to his fiction, particularly *The Trial*. While some understand that novel as relating to state law (and then the totalitarian state), others have seen the possibility of at least two jurisdictions in that work. While the matter is (of course) not entirely clear, a passage on the policemen representing the state that Kafka deleted would have eliminated the ambiguity.[60] That the law of *The Trial* is not ordinary state law is clear.[61] The argument here is that Kafka's attitude toward language and lying resonates with an approach to law based not on monist but on pluralist ideas and that this approach is evident when applied to the interior life of his own family in the letter to his father.

The idea that there are levels of law in the family is used particularly by the Russo-Polish theorist Leon Petrazycki, who argued that the family was "a legal world with innumerable legal norms, obligations, and rights independent of what is written in the statutes." He stressed that some features might be "common to all systems of the law governing domestic relations," but that one might, of course, find class and variation.

> [These might be] connected with the class structure of a population—the typical domestic law prevailing in the well-to-do and rich strata is distinguished from the same law in the spheres of those who are not well-to-do and of proletarians, while the typical domestic law of the peasants is different from that of the business-

man and the aristocrat. [In fact,] each family is a unique legal world, and each of those taking part in the domestic life including aunts, grandmothers, poor kinsfolk in remote degree, or friends received into the house and into the family, hangers-on, adopted and foster children, and the like) has his own particular position in the legal mentality which prevails in that family—the right to enjoy one's room and certain other objects alone and to take part in enjoying other parts of the dwelling and objects, the right to take part in common meals and pleasures and in family celebrations and the like, the right of a decisive or advisory voice in certain matters of domestic life (economic and personal), the right to certain degrees of civility, love, and gratitude and to appropriate behavior in different cases, and so forth.[62]

The legal world of Franz Kafka's family is divided here into four levels: state, domestic, religious-social, and private.

Legal Levels in Kafka's Family

The material that follows is based on the following categories: state law is the law of the Austro-Hungarian empire of which Prague was a part; domestic law is the law of the household, typically headed by the father; religious-class law (unified here, as Kafka did it) is the religious and social law, the law of the Czech Jewish community; and private higher law is an individual sense of obligation, duty, right and wrong, based on something in addition to the three preceding orders. It can be identified with divine law (in which case it might overlap the religious/social law) and be higher law, or it can be called conscience. It may be that this fourth level mandates obedience to one or all three of the other levels, or it may be that this fourth level involves a different substantive position. The point of all of this is to illustrate that the authority of the family—family government—is exercised through the interaction of several levels of law, of which the state law is only one, in exactly the same way that the state operates as only one component of society as a whole. The family, described as a state in the older literature, is perhaps more like society than it is like the state. The autonomy of the individual is found dominantly at the fourth level, which judges the others and chooses between them when necessary.

Positive Law

Beginning conventionally with a state-centered approach, one notes that the entire family is under the state law.[63] The Familiants law restricted marriage to the eldest son in the family. (Kafka's paternal grandfather [the second oldest son] was not able to marry until 1848, when a 1789 law restricting marriage among Jews to the eldest son was repealed.) The result was unofficial marriages, called in the Jewish community *Bodenchassines*, or "attic weddings," a legal system operating out of an attic.[64]

State law was the law Kafka studied, not because of a special interest in the subject, but because it suited his general indifference to everything except his own internal situation.[65] Lessons interested him only in the sense that "an embezzling bank clerk, still holding his job and trembling at the thought of discovery, is interested in the petty ongoing business of the bank, which he still has to deal with as a clerk."[66] (Again we see the issue of fraud.) That, he indicates, was how trivial everything was in comparison to what really mattered to him.

> [C]ompared to the main thing everything would be exactly as much a matter of indifference to me as all the subjects taught at school, and so it was a matter of finding a profession that would let me indulge this indifference without injuring my vanity too much. Law was the obvious choice. Little contrary attempts on the part of vanity, of senseless hope, such as a fortnight's study of chemistry, or six months' German studies, only reinforced that fundamental conviction. So I studied law. This meant that in the few months before the exams, and in a way that told severely on my nerves, I was positively living, in an intellectual sense, on sawdust, which had moreover already been chewed for me in thousands of other people's mouths.[67]

The main thing was internal—"profound anxieties about asserting [his spiritual and intellectual existence"—and the goal was to find an external situation that would permit his absorption in an internal problem.

Kafka never intended to practice law and in fact became an official. He perhaps did not ever consider himself a conventional member of the legal profession in his time and place. "[A]s an Austrian lawyer, which, speaking seriously, I of course am not, I have no prospects; the best thing I might achieve for myself in this direction I already possess in my present post, and it is of no use to me."[68] His knowledge of state law is, however, to be assumed.

Domestic—Family Law

This law is basically father-law. The four levels in use here are described from the point of view of the son, Kafka. When the son becomes a father, his private higher law might become (from the point of view of his own son) the domestic law of the father. That son could then have his own version of private higher law. The account of a woman, wife or daughter, would contain the many ideas specific to women, particularly, one assumes, in Kafka's culture, with the intensely experienced rules relating to the various appearances—personal and house-hold—of social propriety. The father, Herrmann Kafka, is the governor, the issuer of commands that he himself does not honor. The domestic-family law is in this instance the law of the father-autocrat. It might be a mother-autocrat or even a family council of some shape.

Domestic law should not be understood as trivial. Kafka's vegetarianism, for example, can be seen as food rules but clearly also touched deeper questions, as thus he writes: "I have to not eat as much meat as [my grandfather] butchered."[69] In his general description of his father's law, Kafka writes:

> Since as a child I was with you chiefly during meals, your teaching was to a large extent the teaching of proper behavior at table. What was brought to the table had to be eaten, the quality of the food was not to be discussed—but you yourself often found the food inedible, called it "this swill," said "that cow" (the cook) had ruined it. Because in accordance with your strong appetite and your particular predilection you ate everything fast, hot, and in big mouthfuls, the child had to hurry; there was a somber silence at table, interrupted by admonitions: "Eat first, talk afterward," or "faster, faster, faster," or "there you are, you see, I finished ages ago." Bones mustn't be cracked with the teeth, but you could. Vinegar must not be sipped noisily, but you could. The main thing was that the bread should be cut straight. But it didn't matter that you did it with a knife dripping with gravy. Care had to be taken that no scraps fell on the floor. In the end it was under your chair

that there were the most scraps. At table one wasn't allowed to do anything but eat, but you cleaned and cut your fingernails, sharpened pencils, cleaned your ears with a toothpick.[70]

The difficulty was not with the severity of the laws, but with their application to Kafka only. "Please, Father, understand me correctly: in themselves these would have been utterly insignificant details, they only became depressing for me because you, so tremendously the authoritative man, did not keep the commandments you imposed on me." For this reason, "the world was for me divided into three parts":

> one in which I, the slave, lived under laws that had been invented only for me[71] and which I could, I did not know why, never completely comply with; then a second world, which was infinitely remote from mine, in which you lived, concerned with government, with the issuing of orders and with the annoyance about their not being obeyed; and finally a third world where everybody else lived happily and free from orders and from having to obey. I was continually in disgrace; either I obeyed your orders, and that was a disgrace, for they applied, after all, only to me; or I was defiant, and that was a disgrace too, for how could I presume to defy you; or I could not obey because I did not, for instance, have your strength, your appetite, your skill, although you expected it of me as a matter of course; this was the greatest disgrace of all. This was not the course of the child's reflections, but of his feelings.[72]

Herrmann Kafka is portrayed as the enforcer of the law generally (as to sisters and employees also) and of course as to his son. Kafka describes a punishment, one that is harsh in itself and that involves an expulsion from the family.[73]

> One night I kept on whimpering for water, not, I am certain, because I was thirsty, but probably partly to be annoying, partly to amuse myself. After several vigorous threats had failed to have any effect, you took me out of bed, carried me out onto the pavlatche,[74] and left me there alone for a while in my nightshirt, outside the shut door. I am not going to say that this was wrong—perhaps there was really no other way of getting peace and quiet that night—but I mention it as typical of your methods of bringing

up a child and their effect on me. I dare say I was quite obedient afterward at that period, but it did me inner harm. What was for me a matter of course, that senseless asking for water, and then the extraordinary terror of being carried outside were two things that I, my nature being what it was, could never properly connect with each other. Even years afterward I suffered from the tormenting fancy that the huge man, my father, the ultimate authority,[75] would come almost for no reason at all and take me out of bed in the night and carry me out onto the *pavlatche,* and that consequently I meant absolutely nothing as far as he was concerned.[76]

Father-law is criticized as not universal and not objective. But what is the source of the demand that it should be either?[77] Why should family rules apply to children and not parents? To sons and not daughters? Here, too, one suspects the impact of formal law study, when Kafka, at thirty-six, analyzes the injustice of the domestic order under which he in many ways continued to live.[78]

Jewish (Religious-Class) Law

As to the third level, we see that the father is himself under law, the law of the Jewish community that he in effect obeys, both in relation to his actual religious observance, slight though it is, and in relation to the social codes and standards of child reading. Kafka acknowledges this, saying that "here again you were conforming to the general method of treating sons in the Jewish middle class, which was the standard for you, or at least to the values of that class."[79]

Kafka's indictment of himself for failing his father reflects these aspects of a class and religious code.[80] His attack on himself (in another letter) reflects his father's position.

You who have to fight incessantly for your inner stability, using all your strength and that is not even enough—you now want to found a household of your own, perhaps the most necessary but at any rate the most affirmative and boldest act there can possibly be? You who can barely manage to bear the responsibility for yourself from moment to moment now want to add on the responsibility for a family? What reserve of strength do you expect to draw on? And you also want to have as many children as are given to you, since after all you are marrying in order to become better than you are and the idea of any limitation of children in marriage horrifies you.[81]

This letter was written at about the same time as the letter to his father. The engagement to Julie Wohryzek was broken in 1920. Earlier engagements (to Felice Bauer) had been broken in 1914 and 1917.[82] When he was told that his father had praised him, he said that the report was "hardly convincing," since the reporter "simply takes it for granted that a father can only love and praise his son." Kafka then gives a version of the facts that makes clear that in some moods he accepts his father's view of things, which is influenced by religious and class obligation.

> But in this case what is there to cause a father's eyes to light up? A son incapable of marriage, who could not pass on the family name; pensioned off at thirty-nine; occupied only with his weird kind of writing, the only goal of which is his own salvation or damnation; unloving; *alienated from the Faith, so that a father cannot even expect him to say the prayers for the rest of his soul;* consumptive, and as the father quite properly sees it, having got sick through his own fault, for he was no sooner released from the nursery for the first time when with his total incapacity for independence he sought *out* that unhealthy room. . . . This is the son to rave about.[83]

Kafka considered the issue of his father's Judaism in his letter to him and in other writings. A part of the issue was that the father's connection to the tradition was in ways stronger than his own. The point here is that he understood the normative claims of the tradition and the substantive rules of the middle class.

Private (Higher) Law
Certain ideas seem to involve the fourth, perhaps most private level, which is simultaneously something associated with absolute value or higher law and the attempt to transcend the lies. This level is both above any single category—as higher law—and also a reflection of the deepest part of one of them, sometimes called "conscience" or "self." (Private higher law as an amalgam is familiar in the field of church and state, in which divine law becomes a question of individual belief.)

To begin with, Kafka's father, the governor, is not the only lawgiver. Indeed, Kafka's attack on his father is in part precisely on this point. The father insists on seeing the world as a trial in which he, the father, is the judge. Kafka sees the world, in which he (and his sisters) and his father are all parties, as a trial that is judged elsewhere.

> [T]his terrible trial that is pending between us and you, to examine it in all its details, from all sides, on all occasions, from far and near—a trial in which you keep on claiming to be the judge, whereas, at least in the main (here I leave a margin for all the mistakes I may naturally make) you are a party too, just as weak and deluded as we are.[84]

The "Letter to His Father" invokes the themes of both guilt and innocence, and truth and lying. As to guilt, one can say that while Kafka accuses his father not only of not keeping his own commandments, but also of injustice. The idea has a biblical sound. Shall not the judge of all the earth do justly? (Genesis 18:25). This applies to his son and, for example, the father's employees. The father is finally in a sense judged innocent. Indeed, finally father and son are both innocent, though the [hypothetical] retort from the father suggests that this finding of innocence for the father is only technical, part of a deeper ploy on the part of the son relating to "insincerity, obsequiousness and parasitism." Thus, in the father's eyes—and so then, we might say also in the son's eyes since he absorbs and internalizes the father's values—the son is less innocent, but also in fact *first* in the son's eyes, when the son is the author who creates the father (in the never-to-be-delivered father letter) who urges that the son is less innocent.[85]

One might use, on this point, an actual parental version of Kafka's life, from his mother's letter to Felice, describing a boy who had everything. "Anyone else in his place would be the happiest of mortals, for his parents have never denied him any wish.[86] He studied whatever he felt like, and since he did not want to be a lawyer he chose the career of an official." As Kafka saw it, "All parents want to do is drag one down to them, back to the old days from which one longs to free oneself and escape; they do it out of love, of course, and that's what makes it so horrible."[87]

As to truth, one can say that the (son's version of the) father associates the father with truth and the son with insincerity. This is evident in the first line of the father letter. Kafka writes: "You asked me recently why I maintain that I am afraid of you"—maintain, when it is so clearly untrue. The created father defends his own stance toward his son by saying that he is unable to pretend, being a self-made man, hard up as a child, able through work and energy to have provided the good life for his son. Others, including his son, pretend. He, the father, tells the truth. When the [created] father sees the letter as a strategic move, he judges it—as Kafka himself did by referring to it as a lawyer's letter— on the basis of a higher law.

Kafka was never able to marry. He certainly engaged in sexual relations with women—though sex, like everything else, became ultimately quite secondary to his writing.[88] It probably cannot be known for certain whether he had an illegitimate son who died at seven,[89] or whether his relationship with Milena (a Czech writer) had a physical dimension. Kafka's idea of marriage shows a merger of the several levels. Marriage involves a state directive, a Jewish dimension, a level specific to his father (relating to social standing),[90] and finally a level specific to Kafka. For Kafka, marriage meant much more than companionship or psychological or physical intimacy. It was an institution of ultimate value.

> Marrying, founding a family, accepting all the children that come,[91] supporting them in this insecure world and perhaps even guiding them a little, is, I am convinced, the utmost a human being can succeed in doing at all. That so many seem to succeed in this is no evidence to the contrary; first of all, there are not many who do succeed, and second, these not-many usually don't "do" it, it merely "happens" to them; although this is not that utmost, it is still very great and very honorable (particularly since "doing" and "happening" cannot be kept clearly distinct). And finally, it is not a matter of this Utmost at all, anyway, but only of some distant but decent approximation; it is, after all, not necessary to fly right into the middle of the sun, but it is necessary to crawl to a clean little spot on Earth where the sun sometimes shines and one can warm oneself a little.[92]

Kafka's view of marriage in some ways echoed that of the state that had limited the marriages of his immediate ancestors. The state rules considered marriages not in terms of actual or theoretical intimacy or of domestic comfort, but in terms of the founding of families.

In relation to his father, marriage meant independence. This view of marriage is deemphasized in present feminist writing because of an emphasis—important in context—on problems of spousal relations. But marriage as involving a break from the family of origin is historically and probably still an important aspect of the issue. Tocqueville noted a contrast between Europe and America on the power of the father and the husband over the young woman and then the wife. The unmarried woman was freer in America than in Europe; the wife was more restrained.[93]

Kafka wrote:

> Marriage certainly is the pledge of the most acute form of self-liberation and independence. I would have a family, in my opinion the highest one can achieve, and so too the highest you have achieved; I would be your equal; all old and ever new shame and tyranny would be mere history.[94]

These, then, are the four levels: autocratic law of the father; class and religious law; state law; and individual law. They must of course relate to each other, but how? We can say that religious law and class law influence state law, that state law constrains religious law, that state law and class law and religious law shape the autocratic law of the father, as well as the private individual law of the son, and that they must finally come together—functionally if not substantively—in some way.

Here is one issue as a hypothetical example—birth control in marriage.[95] Prostitution is assumed in Kafka's world, as is sexual involvement (risking venereal disease) with lower-class women whom one does not marry. We might say that the autocratic father favors contraception in relations outside of marriage, that we don't know what he thought about it inside of marriage, that the religion allows it, that the class encourages it, that the state forbids it, and that the private higher law forbids it. Or we might say that the autocratic father opposes it, that the religion opposes it, that the class encourages it, that the state permits it and that the private self insists on it.[96] Combinations might be various. Finally, the individual will do or not do something—the law will be integrated in his head—and the groups will or will not respond.[97] If there is no response, that can be called toleration or even acceptance.

We could add to this the idea called "culture" (class, region, national), which is linked to the question of legal levels and what they mean. That is, "culture" may float above all levels or may be a level attached to each legal regime giving meaning to the norms and structures imposed. As Ruth Benedict argued decades ago, the real point about the family may not be the structure or institutions so much as the culture that gives meaning to those institutions. Marriage for us, she writes, "is a situation which can never be made clear as a mere variant on mating and domesticity." We need "the clue that in our civilization at large man's paramount aim is to amass private possessions and multiply occasions of display," and then we can understand "jealousy" and the "position of the wife." "Our attitudes toward our children are equally evidences of this same cultural goal." For us, "children are not individuals whose rights and tastes are casually respected from infancy, as they are in some primitive societies." Rather, they are "special responsibilities, like our possessions, to which we succumb or in which we glory, as the case may be." Children, for us, are "fundamentally extensions of our own egos and give a special opportunity for the display of authority." The pattern, Benedict insists, "is not inherent in the parent-children situation, as we so glibly assume." Rather, "[i]t is impressed upon the situation by the major drives of our culture, and it is only one of the occasions in which we follow our traditional obsessions."[98]

Understanding this, we are not at the question of how we change law. This, as a mechanical issue, we do understand. Rather, the question is how we can use law to change culture—a question that, it seems, we understand much less. One could say that (illustratively and hypothetically) this cultural value was attached to state law and class law, but not religious law or private law, which see themselves as "countercultural," or that it was attached to all four or that other "understandings" related to the structures.

Finally, as noted earlier, Kafka's complaint against his father relates not to abuse, but to autonomy. But Kafka felt that he could not choose or that he was always in effect forced to choose nothing.

"The simile of the bird in the hand and the two in the bush has only a very remote application here. In my hand I have nothing, in the bush is everything, and yet—so it is decided by the conditions of battle and the exigency of life—I must choose the nothing. I had to make a similar choice when I chose my profession."[99]

The problem was less one of coercion than of incapacity. Lionel

Trilling noted the issues of the depleted interior life in Kafka, comparing his characters to those in Shakespeare.

> Shakespeare's world, quite as much as Kafka's, is that prison cell which Pascal says the world is, from which daily the inmates are led forth to die; Shakespeare no less than Kafka forces upon us the cruel irrationality of the conditions of human life. . . . But in Shakespeare's cell the company is so much better than in Kafka's, the captains and kings and lovers and clowns of Shakespeare are alive and complete before they die. In Kafka, long before the sentence is executed, even long before the malign legal process is ever instituted, something terrible has been done to the accused.[100]

There was, one might say, a problem relating to what Kafka—drafting the sentences several times—referred to as his "upbringing" (*Erziehung*).

> When I think about it, I must say that my education has done me great harm in some respects . . .
>   Often I think it over and then I always have to say that my education has done me great harm in some ways.
>   Often I think it over and give my thoughts free rein, without interfering and always no matter how I turn or twist it, I come to the conclusion that in some respects my education has done me terrible harm.
>   I can prove at any time that my education tried to make another person out of me than the one I became.[101]

The charge is against many individuals and not limited to those involved in formal education. Kafka believed that his freedom to choose lacked substance. The central issue was, then, not so much a problem relating to mistreatment, as Alice Miller saw it, but rather a problem relating to the rights Joel Feinberg referred to as rights in trust.[102]

Kafka's ultimate charge against his father is not that he, as an adult, sees that he as a child suffered pain or lack of support and understanding. It is rather that he as an adult lacks autonomy because of things his father did to him as a child. Perhaps these things were devastating, perhaps not. "Are we once more to play the game of the unhappy children?"[103] So Kafka wrote to Max Brod.

The father participates but is innocent, perhaps because he is the child of a father. The child (says Kafka) also participates but is also innocent.[104] Both are innocent and guilty. Kafka wrote to Milena: "I understand the fall like no one else."[105] It becomes the problem of original sin. The sin is finally the sin of having an heir.[106]

But many, even most of us do have heirs, so that issues of family governance, over time in the life of an individual, shift from the experience of the child as child to the child as parent of his or her own child. Parents may have children to meet the expectation of their own parents, still working out their own lives through the lives of their descendants. Inevitably, they produce children who carry the burden of the parents' lives. This is the subject of the next chapter.

Chapter Five

Children

Let us think first of the child, for his own good.
Kate, Pinkerton's American wife, in Belasco, *Madame Butterfly*

"She named the baby, when it came, Trouble, meaning Joy."[1] The double naming of the child suggests perhaps the ambivalence of the parent. In the Butterfly story we have no sense of the consciousness of the child.

While there is in Long some reference to American and Japanese attitudes toward children,[2] the one real child is the child in Japan. That child, in the opera, is blindfolded so that he cannot see the death of his mother. The blindfolded child, for a Western audience, evokes the image of Cupid and again may draw us to the adults, the couple, and away from the child himself.

Madame Butterfly does not take her child with her into death, though some women have done so.[3] This is, indeed, one context in which the so-called cultural defense has been discussed.[4] Madame Butterfly simply creates a motherless child.[5] But if the death of the child would be the ultimate injury, we might imagine other injuries as part of the cultural setting of childhood. Motherless might be seen less literally, for example, or mothering might be too much, linked to smothering.

Family is related to the state because individuals, socialized in families, grow up to be citizens of states. The idea that one's childhood provides the outlook that one brings to everything, suggests again that we should be interested in the question how in our culture the outlook of childhood is formed.

This chapter examines some problems of law and children through the familiar story of Medea, using an ancient variant in which there is a surviving child, Thessalus. The chapter makes the general point that even as to the Medea story, clearest of all evils, there is considerable uncertainty as to what might have been done to avoid the damage. Beyond that, it may well be that injury to children of some kind and some degree is an almost inevitable concomitant of contemporary American institutions for child rearing.

The Childhood of Thessalus: A Reading of Medea

In the Greek legend of Jason and Medea, Jason abandons Medea for a new wife, and Medea through her powers of sorcery takes her revenge by killing their children, as well as Jason's new wife and her father. Readings of the myth exist in the forms of plays, poems, opera librettos, and paintings. The sorceress appears in law review articles.[6] In one reading, that of the ancient writer Diodorus Siculus, a child named Thessalus survives.

The present chapter uses a mythic "Medea" assembled from various sources.[7] The focus is not on a text or on sources of the myth, but rather on a series of acts, in social context.[8] Here one thinks particularly of an argumentative or philosophical context, for example, in which particular ideas are associated with justifications for violence. The questions it raises, using a myth as a point of entry, relate not to a "text" but to law and social institutions.

Two approaches associated with feminist jurisprudence provide the structure of this chapter. The first involves placing the actor in the context of a richly described social and emotional environment; the second telling the story from another point of view, here that of the child. In the first part of the paper, the context presented relates to arguments that might be made concerning Medea, in her situation, which might explain or even justify her act. When we discuss battered women, this approach results in asking questions relating for example to the socialization of men and women to explore the male biases inherent in certain criminal defenses.[9] The object here is to see Medea, the ultimate bad mother, as something other than as a generalized or stereotypic figure.[10] The second section attempts a retelling of the story of Medea from the point of view of her child as one who observes and experiences adult behavior. Both parts assume that this ancient story can be used as a vehicle for the examination of violence in the family, that it is not simply the story of one demented or demonic figure. This is, however, an issue to be considered. While the first part discusses Medea, the second part treats the marriage of Jason and Medea as an environment for child rearing.

Difficult questions arise immediately in stagings of a Medea play. Thus, we have questions in production: shall Medea be portrayed as someone whose clothing and hairstyle stress her non-Greek aspects, or shall she be portrayed as someone with whom all women in the audience can basically identify? It may be identification with Medea that explains continuing interest in productions of the play, for example the success of Diana Rigg's New York and London performances.[11] But if Medea's responses are emotions to which we can all relate, given sufficient provocation, then Medea's violence represents something about the potential for violence in all women and perhaps all people.[12] And if Medea's attitudes to her children are recognizable even aside from her final act in relation to them, perhaps these attitudes raise questions about the institutions in which we raise children.

The Perpetrator in Context

Medea's crime is not only murder but a more deeply felt violation of the norms of motherhood. Some of the issues it invokes arose in the controversies over the Steinberg-Nussbaum case and the accountability of Hedda Nussbaum, victim and actor, in the story.[13] The discussion continues as problems of spousal domestic violence and child abuse and murder continue to occupy our attention.[14] Is Medea somehow Everywoman?

If the description of women associated with difference feminism is adopted, a description focused on caring, nurturing and the good true and beautiful, how can we explain the existence of so much in that care and nurturing that is not beautiful and not good?

One way is to say that negative images of women as "Mom" are fantasies—like the wicked witch or the female predator—derived from male fears and hostilities. This explanation leaves us (again) with women as innocent victims, largely deprived of what is now called agency. Another way is to assume agency and to directly consider the violence of women.

Even in relation to Medea, we can find accounts that minimize that violence. The stress in Christine de Pizan's fifteenth-century account, for example, is on Medea's strengths, her intellect, her beauty, her power.

Medea . . . was very beautiful, with a noble and upright heart and a pleasant face. In learning, however, she surpassed and exceeded all women; she knew the powers of every herb and all the potions which could be concocted, and she was ignorant of no art which can be known. With her spells she knew how to make the air

become cloudy or dark, how to move winds from the grottoes and
caverns of the earth, and how to provoke other storms in the air, as
well as how to stop the flow of rivers, confect poisons, create fire to
burn up effortlessly whatever object she chose and all such similar
arts. It was thanks to the art of her enchantments that Jason won
the Golden Fleece.[15]

Even here, of course, the story of Medea is a counterweight to the
victim image of women. If we attempt the exercise suggested by feminist writers on the problem of the bad mother, we will place Medea in
context. The following contexts suggest themselves: We can see Medea
as the victim of Jason's betrayal, a member of a social minority—a non-
Greek—abandoned by an opportunistic husband trading up. We can
see Medea as the avenger of that betrayal, one who chooses to take her
vengeance in a way that destroys her children. We can see Medea as a
feminist denouncing the patriarchal culture in which she lived. If she
was a sorceress, we can say that that role was created by a patriarchal
culture and that the strength of even the sorceress or witch comes at a
great price. Finally, we can see Medea as someone on the side of the
gods, the higher law, perhaps something more than human herself.

We might begin here with the discussion by Marie Ashe and
Naomi Kahn. They, like others, use Medea as the ultimate image of the
bad mother, the woman whose "neglectful, abusive, reckless or murderous" behavior injures or threatens her children. They suggest that
one can see the bad mother as a character "in a child's story." Thus, "in
her standard manifestation [the bad mother] appears not in her own
complexity and moral agency, but as 'another' defined from the perspective of a fearful and deprived child."[16]

Ashe and Kahn suggest thinking about women's "embeddedness
within systems that foster violence." But finally, contexts, like inquiries
into gender or racial ties, do not themselves resolve issues of judgment.
Bartlett points out that "feminist methodology will surface and explore
the ties and then consider whether a judgment can stand" in view of
possible distortions and biases.[17] And as Martha Minow has noted, the
contexts of bad mothers include a society unresponsive to domestic
violence that must then have some share in producing violence.[18]

The clearest cases for the context approach are of course those who
are victims themselves, former slaves, battered wives. Even the hardest
case widely discussed to this point, Hedda Nussbaum, involved a

woman whose psychological dependency was so profound that it seemed to outweigh the social and economic advantages that she had. Medea's "love," while great, does not involve this sort of dependency. In its proprietary aspects, indeed, it seems quite male.[19] While one might try to say that Medea was a victim of Jason, it seems also true that if Medea had tired of Jason, she would have left him easily in the exercise of her autonomy.[20]

Context does not initially advance the argument for the defense. Much of the violence in Medea's life is produced by Medea herself.[21] She participated in murder in assisting Jason to obtain the Golden Fleece.[22] She murders again after the episode at Corinth. And Medea is not impoverished and desperate. She is privileged throughout, though not Greek.

While it may be that we believe that the image of the good mother is an aspect of patriarchal society, it is an aspect that is widely internalized, even by Medea. When Jason asks why she is so concerned about the children she answers, "I am their mother."[23] The condemnation of Medea for violation of the norms of that role is to be understood as universal. And, in general, even those who say that patriarchy produces the images of good and bad mothering, see that issues of child abuse (the dark side, as Adrienne Rich saw it) would have to be dealt with. No one defends the abuse itself. The most that it attempted is a plea by way of justification or mitigation.[24]

It is clear that Medea must in some ways stand opposed to the family. In a context in which the primary family duty was to have sons to carry on the line, Medea says: "He will neither see his sons by me alive in the future nor beget a child by his newly wedded wife, since she must altogether die. . . ." As McDermott elaborates, we have in Medea someone who has attacked the family at several different levels. She had earlier attacked the family by her murders in connection with the Golden Fleece. McDermott notes that Medea's "mythic biography can read like a relentless campaign to violate the parent-child bond."[25]

Perhaps we can see Medea as a daughter of Lilith, first wife of Adam in the Jewish tradition, who demands full equality and, not perhaps coincidentally, hates children.[26] Thus, Marina Warner notes that in rejecting maternal love, Medea is linked with "many fantasies of female evil: the inquisition condemned witches for cannibal feasts on children; in Judaic myth, the succubus Lilith was believed to haunt cradles of newborn infants to carry them off."[27]

Here, we have Medea's feminism at its clearest:

Of all things that are alive and have sense, we women are the most miserable breed. First we have to buy a husband with an extravagant dowry, and so take a master over our body—the latter evil more painful than the former. And in this the greatest struggle is whether you take a good one or a bad one, for divorce brings ill repute upon women, nor can a woman spurn her husband. But coming to a new house, with new ways and customs, she must play soothsayer (though she learned no such art at home), to see how best she may handle her bed-mate. And if we work all this out well and our husband lives with us bearing the yoke easily, then our life is enviable. But if not, we might as well die. Now the man, whenever he is tired of the company at home, can go out-of-doors and put an end to his vexation. But as for us, we must look to a single soul alone. They talk about living our lives danger-free at home, while they fight with the spear. But they are wrong. I would much rather stand three times in battle than once give birth.[28]

If we stress Medea's grievances as a feminist, we might see another "context" that would make it possible for her to turn on her children. After all, they, not the males who own the patriarchy, are the direct cause of certain unhappiness. They are the ones crying all night and, we might imagine, clinging to her all day. It is only remotely the man who restrict the mother's autonomy. More immediately it is her children.[29]

Another reason directly involving the children is suggested by the poet Robinson Jeffers: "They have his blood. As long as they live I shall be mixed with him."[30]

In general, we might attribute to Medea some part of the "context" of the twentieth-century mother outlined by Adrienne Rich.

Rape and its aftermath; marriage as economic dependence, as the guarantee to a man of "his" children; the theft of childbirth from women; the concept of the "illegitimacy" of a child born out of wedlock; the laws regulating contraception and abortion; the cavalier marketing of dangerous birth-control devices; the denial that work done by women at home is a part of "production"; the chaining of women in links of love and guilt; the absence of social benefits for mothers; the inadequacy of child-care facilities in most

parts of the world; the unequal pay women receive as wage-earn-
ers, forcing them often into dependence on a man; the solitary confinement of "full-time motherhood"; the token nature of fatherhood, which gives a man rights and privileges over children
toward whom he assumes minimal responsibility; the psychoana-
lytic castigation of the mother; the pediatric assumption that the
mother is inadequate and ignorant; the burden of emotional work
borne by women in the family—all these are connecting fibers of
this invisible institutions, and they determine our relationship to
our children whether we like to think so or not.[31]

A different level of contextual material is suggested by the fact that
Medea is a sorceress, a relative of Circe, whose witchcraft is commonly
referred to. She may not be altogether human; she may be a god.[32] Certainly she is linked to things more than human. "The Gods and I," she
says. At the least, she has the characteristics of a tragic heroine.[33] This
linkage, suggested in the reading offered by John Gardner, stresses the
stubbornness and adherence to one's own orientation that in the case of
Antigone are normally discussed under the rubric "higher law."[34] One
sees that connection again in Gardner's suggestion that a woman
betrayed attains a high level of selflessness, that, "as for Medea, make
no mistake, nothing on earth is more pure—more raised from self to
selfless absolute—than a woman betrayed."[35] The refusal to yield represented by both Antigone and Medea may result in an idea of women
as lawbreaker.[36]

Medea is a woman whose agency is not in question.[37] Mahoney, in
her consideration of agency, quotes bell hooks, who notes that
"oppressed people often cannot afford to feel powerless." Women who
face exploitation daily "cannot afford to relinquish the belief that they
exercise some measure of control, however relative, over their lives."[38]
Mahoney's comment on this is: "this sense of agency often represents
both sound self-knowledge and also denial of the impact on the person
of repression and suffering. It may be both 'true' and 'false' consciousness at once." With this perspective on Medea, we could say both that
she is correct in seeing her own power and agency and also that she is
correct in seeing the impact on her of her status as a woman in a male-
dominated culture.

But contextualizing and explaining the act does not exhaust
Medea's options in dealing with her marriage to Jason. Medea might

also simply excise those events from her account and thereby reinvent her history. In the end, Medea might tell her story rather in the way that it was once offered by Christine de Pizan.

> Medea was one of the most learned women in fortune telling who have ever lived and had the most knowledge, according to what various accounts relate. Nevertheless she allowed her mind to be seduced by self-will in order to fulfill her desire when she let herself be mastered by foolish love and set her heart on Jason, honoring him, giving him her body and bestowing upon him wealth, for which he later so shabbily repaid her.[39]

Christine suggests that Medea was unhappy, that her experiences meant misery. But there is nothing about murder, nothing about the death of children.

Perhaps however, the attempt to contextualize Medea fails. She is in a sense beyond social context, larger than life. This is captured in the dramatis personae in the Robinson Jeffers's play. Each character's name is followed by a description,[40] except the one after whom the play is named, who appears as "Medea."

Of course the list of concerns addressed to this point addressed omits an essential point of view, the perspective of the children, and it is to this we now turn.

The Injury in Context

When we speak of childhood, it is our own childhood that provides the background of our conversation, rather than, for example, the childhood of those to whom we are parents. Perhaps this is inevitable; we are all the heroes of our own lives and the tellers of our own stories. The discomfort that some feminists describe in discussing women's neglect or abuse of children,[41] a discomfort sometimes rooted in awareness of issues of child care, illustrates a more general problem. When we are concerned about parenting, we often focus on its demands. The effects of our own parenting are secondary, for it is our own childhoods that are vivid to us.

Some adults view their shift from childhood to adulthood as a natural developmental processes, analogous to chickens tapping out of shells or larvae emerging from cocoons as butterflies. For some others, the images of adult-formation are somewhat more problematic. The image would be more like the picture of infants potted in vases, breaking free of the ceramic shell, but shaped irrevocably by the experience. We focus more on having been created "vase children"[42] than on our having created them. Thus, the adult can be referred to as the ex-child.[43] Our children's childhoods are an aspect of our adult experience, and, as adults, we see ourselves as doing the best we can. In dealing with Medea, we as parents have the easy out of saying that most parents do not kill their children. But it is simple to see that Thessalus would have been one of the vase children.

In order to consider again the significance of this ancient story, we need a version with a different center and a different narrator.[44] We move, then, to the events at Corinth as Medea's child Thessalus might see them. Instead of seeing the injury as the death of the child, we could put Medea's action on a spectrum of behavior that might include physical child abuse, neglect of children resulting in injury or death in the context of criminal neglect, religious medical decision-making (parents who for religious reasons refuse conventional treatment for their children), and even, for some, abortion and contraception.[45]

Telling the story of Medea through the eyes of named children, one of whom, indeed, survived the killings, we can use the account of Diodorus Siculus: "Jason made his home in Corinth and living with Medea as his wife for ten years he begat children by her, the two oldest, Thessalus and Alcimenes, being twins, and the third Tisandrus, being much younger than the other two."[46] As to the murders, Diodorus writes that "she determined, by the murder of the children of them both, to plunge him into the deepest misfortunes; for, except for the one son who made his escape from her, she slew the other sons and in company with her most faithful maids fled in the dead of night from Corinth and made her way safely to Heracles in Thebes."[47] Thessalus is saved. He is not, however, spared. We need Thessalus as a living child who will grow up and look back. The ghost of a murdered child, Dimitri, for example, in *Boris Godunov*, will not do the work required. He can testify only to his own death.

As a preliminary point, one might comment on constructions of the good mother and the good father. It might be thought that because of the links between aggressive behavior and masculinity, the contrast here for the child is between a nurturing good mother and a judgmental good father. But it is clear that this misses the specifically protective, and even nurturing, aspects of fatherhood that we know under the name "paternal" and "paternalism."[48] The issue, then, may be not so much a distinction between the kinds of nurturing behavior as between those to whom the behavior relates. (The mother nurtures infants and the young, while the father nurtures and protects even adults. It is at this point, indeed, that paternalism gets its bad name because adults are supposed to be in much less need of nurture, and to the extent that we protect them, we invariably, as Dicey pointed out, disable them.)[49] Finally, then, we will reach the idea that the attributes of parents may be less fully gendered than the present discussion assumes. Jason's speeches about his children are in some ways very close to Medea's.[50] Jason speaks of his love for his son in ways that could easily be seen as "maternal." In Seneca's *Medea*, Jason says, "My children are the reason I live on, the thing that makes me able to endure the pain of my ravaged feelings and emotions. I would more quickly sacrifice my soul, my body, life itself."[51]

Medea's violence is a violation of her gendered role (mother) but an expression of her gender (female). Her violent nature is revealed before her act in the uncontrolled emotion that she directs at the children, at Jason, and at the world: "And I know which evils I am about to commit, but [desire is stronger than my deliberations]." Hannah Arendt comments: "The point of the matter is always that reason, knowledge, insight etc. are too weak to withstand the onslaught of desire and it may not be accidental that the conflict breaks out in the soul of women who are less under the influence of reasoning than men."[52]

Certain feminist, rather than misogynist, descriptions of this problem are available. Thus Adrienne Rich: "What woman, in the solitary confinement of a life at home enclosed with young children, or in the struggle to mother them while providing for them single-handedly, or in the conflict of weighing her own personhood against the dogma that says she is a mother, first, last, and always,—what woman has not dreamed of "going over the edge," of simply letting go, relinquishing what is termed her sanity, so that she can be taken care of for once, or can simply find a way to take care of herself?"[53] Rich concludes with a description of emotional violence: "Because we have all had mothers, the institution affects all women, and—though differently—all men. Patriarchal violence and callousness are often visited through women upon children—not only the 'battered' child but the children desperately pushed, cajoled, manipulated, the children dependent on one uncertain, weary woman for their day-in, day-out care and emotional sustenance, the male children who grow up believing that a woman is nothing so much as an emotional whirlwind bent on their destruction."[54]

The idea of maternal power is clear in Jane Smiley's comment that the daily exercise of power over the child, her "actions magnified so enormously by the dependency of another," taught her something about the links between love and power.[55]

While Medea is the prime actor in the story of Jason and Medea, it is not only women who are capable of violent behavior. A child may experience either parent or both as destructive. Corneille has Jason imagining killing his children to get back at Medea.[56] Certainly, the Greek tradition included men who sacrificed their children.[57] Martha Nussbaum reads Seneca's *Medea* as not rooted in gender issues: "Seneca's claim is that this story of murder and violation is our story— the story of every person who loves. Or rather, that no person who loves can safely guarantee that she or he will stop short of this story."[58] Medea has used her children as an instrument. Jason certainly would do the same. Thus, he says, "I want to see you, when you're strong, full grown young men, tread down my enemies."[59] It is the instrumental use of children, the raising of children to achieve parental ambitions, to work out parental grievances or frustrations, that underlies and is the broadest expression of the grievance that the surviving Thessalus might have had.

What we see in both Jason and Medea is a failure to take account of the child as subject. In Euripides' play, the children are identified as the children—they do not even have names.[60] The idea that they might have consciousness, a perspective that might be worth thinking about, is entirely remote from the ideas of the author and indeed most of the commentators.

Thessalus has a life and consciousness of his own. He can be imagined in a variety of ways. As against a child "fearful and deprived" (as Ashe and Kahn suggest we see the child observing the murderous mother), we might see him as a survivor, one of the invulnerable, highly resilient children who sometimes emerge from difficult childhoods.[61] He might be so protective of his victimized mother that one could conceive of Thessalus as a murderer himself, his mother's little soldier.[62] And can speculate on the views of a later, kingly Thessalus, looking back on his part in the murder of Jason's wife, for Medea not only murders her children, she turns them into murderers,[63] in an ancient Greek version of the use of children in parental wars.[64] Or we might imagine Thessalus as a girl, identified strongly with her mother against her abandoning father. But we will likely conclude that Thessalus, whether male or female, has, as Canetti says, one of those minds that "settle in wounds" rather than houses.[65]

But murder, while representing an injury quite different from other injuries, is not the definition of the violence against children in this marriage. Murder is only the logical culmination of something else, in which both parents are implicated. In their discussion of the "bad mother" in psychological theory, Ashe and Kahn include a treatment of the work of Alice Miller.[66] Miller's work makes plain that an emphasis on the physical suffering of children is too limited to reach many dimensions of parent-child difficulty. Until she discovered otherwise, she believed she had had a happy childhood. "I was amazed to discover that I had been an abused child." This abuse is not however, physical; rather, "from the very beginning of my life I had no choice but to comply totally with the needs and feelings of my mother and to ignore my own." She describes herself as "condemned to silence, abused, exploited and turned to stone"—a child who was damaged in the sense that some psychologists call "soul murder."[67] It is about an emotional, rather than a physical context. Moreover—and this is one point one has to stress here—the context is created by good and presumptively loving parents in relation to what may well be an adored child. No adults in the story understand any of their own behavior as bad, or anything to feel bad about.

Miller's account raises serious issues of false consciousness. Certainly Miller's version raises the possibility that the more an adult insists on having had a happy childhood, the more vulnerable he or she is to the argument that this [false] perception only proves the remarkable power of parental manipulation and abuse. At the same time, Miller's account resonates with many others in a way that validates it. Thus, Doris Lessing writes of her life in southern Rhodesia: "The fact was my early childhood made me one of the walking wounded for years. A dramatic remark, and pretty distasteful, really, but used with an exact intention though it makes me easy victim to the kind of the obsessionalist who sees evidence of 'abuse' everywhere. They mean usually sexual abuse. I think that some psychological pressures and even well meant ones are as damaging as physical hurt. . . . Yet my mother was conscientious, hard working always doing the best as she sought she was a good sort of a good sport etc."[68]

With the work of Alice Miller, we reach an attack on parenting so generalized that we cannot view abuse as deviant but must, on the contrary, raise the possibility that it is universal and structural.

Institutional Implications?

It may be true that the more interested we become in context, and in examining serious contextualizations of individuals whose behavior is unacceptable, the more we find that the contextualization makes it difficult to know what is justice in a particular case or what the social structures might be that would minimize some particular problem.

The central point here is that whatever the biological constraints on the organization of human life—and these seem not to be what we once thought—the institutions of family life are largely social and cultural. As to recent and contemporary American structures, while they have been built on an extraordinary level of material satisfaction, they have been in other ways highly problematic.

Using the Medea legend to think about this issue, we might focus on the "causes" of the tragedy. In some Greek versions of the story, the townspeople of Corinth killed the children. But if the townspeople killed the children, then we still have the problem of Medea as the ultimate actor, since Medea has set her children up to be killed by involving them as messengers and carriers in the death of Jason's new wife and her father.[69]

Is Jason's behavior causal? Euripides' Medea sees Jason as the actor, "not your hand, but your insult to me." Perhaps Medea's outrage over Jason's taking a second wife is misplaced because—assuming Jason's vows to be marital[70]—Medea has no claim as first wife. That is, Jason was never married to Medea since she was a barbarian and he could not contract a legitimate Greek marriage with her: "In the strictly legal sense, you have no wife—a northern barbarian, a lady whose barbarous mind has proved its way—forgive me—more than just once, to your sorrow. The law no more allows such marriages into barbarian races than it does between Greeks and horses, say."[71] Of course, even if she is of a lower social status, Jason does not altogether reject Medea. Even if we believe that Jason is unjustified in his abandonment of

Medea,[72] he is not the irresponsible father of the contemporary discussion. Jason is a man who will take care of his children. He will also take care of Medea. He will, however, take a second wife.[73] To this extent the story of Jason and Medea is exactly the story of divorce per se, a question largely ignored in the feminist discussion, where the complete right to divorce is assumed, and the focus is placed on issues of support.[74]

When Medea says in Euripides' telling of the story that Jason is "her whole life," we have some sense of where the difficulty lies. If this is the story of a woman who loves too much, it is also the story of conventional Western marriage in its modern form. In terms of cultural expectation, Jason is the center of Medea's life in a way quite different from the way in which she might be said to have been the center of his life. She—even Medea—was to have been defined by him in a way that he would not have been defined by her.[75] Medea's claim is based in part on past service,[76] and also simply on her present love and desire, with love understood as constituting a claim in the object of love.

The problem in institutional terms is not Medea's love but rather a particular idea of marriage, and the family that includes an understanding of the relation between parents and children. Both the ideas of the relation of the adults and children are of course variable culturally and historically. Comparative material yields the commonplace insight that abuse is defined differently in different cultures. What is problematic in one culture may be normative in another, for example, allowing infants to cry themselves to sleep alone. While "we" speak from within our modern American culture, we are in fact—and perhaps nowhere more than in the family—linked to many cultures, many places, and many times. We can, within our own late-twentieth-century American culture, see echoes of these other places and other times. But the consolidation of values represented in the idea "American child-centered child rearing" results also in a particular structure, one that is "centered" on children within being centered on their autonomy, and one that may subject children to a parental agenda quite remote from one a hypothetical "guardian of the child," for example, might choose.

The standard exposition defines Medea as opposed to an eventually normal maternal love. This normal love, McDermott explains, was to be assumed among the ancient Greeks; Aristotle had said that "parents love their children as themselves."[77] The critical point here is "as themselves." Undifferentiated from themselves. To be sacrificed as they might sacrifice themselves.[78] This, it seems, Medea never sees. Medea does in fact and in conventional ways "love" her children, and it is this sort of love that makes the murder possible. The suicide/murders of mothers and children are a reflection of that love. Jason and Medea are not in their own eyes bad parents until Medea kills her sons. The judgment of their children might well be different.

A part of the story of Thessalus's childhood is that the law has sanctioned the father's behavior and has no particular comment on the mother's behavior until it reaches the point of such damage that we can start talking about serious threats to safety. As noted, there is much damage done short of this point. What is the law's response supposed to be?

One approach leads utopians and philosophers of varying orientations to suggest that children should be protected from the overwhelming emotional impact,[79] often negative, however well intentioned, of their parents. Thus, in *Brave New World*, the description of the Home is that of physical and psychological suffocation.

> Home, home—a few small rooms, stiflingly over-inhabited by a man, by a periodically teeming woman, by a rabble of boys and girls of all ages. No sir, no space; an under sterilized prison; darkness, disease, and smells. (The Controller's evocation was so vivid that one of the boys, more sensitive than the rest, turned pale at the mere description and was on the point of being sick.). . .
> "Yes," said Mustapha Mond, nodding his head, "you may well shudder."[80]

More moderately, we might consider where the awareness of these issues might function in a system that would remain focused on the nuclear family. Here, the issue might arise in our own culture in relation to the home education movement, in which one analysis at least focuses on exactly this issue. Professor Lupu points out that the greatest danger of home education is that the child will be involved only with parents all the time. This raises a problem that he analyzes in terms of an analogy to separation of powers. The critical point for him being that it is essential that children be exposed to the moderating and mitigating impact of other nonparental adults.[81] There is no surprise that the dominant father in Christina Stead's *The Man Who Loved Children* is a father who sees little need for education for his children other than that which he himself provides.

We would *not*, however, use this concern to found a conclusion that single parenting was always inferior or that joint custody was always good. We might in some cases introduce our sense of the child's later adult response into our present calculations. The degree of certainty would vary, as would the weight given the response. The grown-up child's response, "Do you mean I could have been rich?" might get less weight then the response, "Do you mean I could have known my biological parents?"[82]

At this juncture we might say that the answer is not in the specific interventions of family law, but rather in some larger questions of public policy devoted to community building, neighborhood institutions, mediating structures, ways of introducing alternative adult figures into the nuclear family. The central damage to Thessalus is, after all, inherent in the nuclear family, that is, adult behavior in all its variety witnessed intimately and unavoidably by a child. Introduction of other adult figures as mediators or alternatives would break that monopoly on the child's consciousness.[83]

Our interventions might be undertaken in the awareness that families are different, especially, as Tolstoy said, unhappy families. It should be noted that if in some cases this approach results in a victory for biological parents (over some third party, or a state agency), it is not on any theory of parental rights but rather on a temporally expanded view of what is in the interest of the child—who will be an adult.[84]

Certainly it is not enough here to say that the answer is encouragement of extended family structures because extended structures are frequently, though presumably not always, simply extensions of the original nuclear group; that is, the extended family lines up on one side or the other, behind the father or the mother. Extrafamilial intermediate or mediating institutions have a large role here.

There is no conclusion to be drawn but that things are more complicated than any one telling makes them seem.[85]

Still, the standard allusion to Medea is one focused on the murder of her children. The murder is assumed in Marina Warner's comment that "Medea embodies extreme female aberration from the tragedy by Euripides in the 5th century B.C. to the fictional translation of her story in Toni Morrison's masterpiece *Beloved* published in 1987."[86] That kind of reference ignores the question of why, for example, Toni Morrison's figure killed her child—to save the child from a life in slavery. Reasons of one kind or another might distinguish Medea from other murderous parents. Well-known examples have to do with killing children—sacrificing them—in response to a divine command. There exist medieval narratives in which parents kill their children to save them from the ravages of an oncoming army. The closest Medea comes to this sort of argument is in the suggestion that if she does not kill her children, the Corinthians will, but this, of course, ignores the point that the reason the children are in danger from the Corinthians is that Medea has set them up to kill the Corinthian princess. She created the danger in which they find themselves. Medea's reasons have to do with her own, and not her children's, requirements. Hers is the measuring life.

Knox discusses the possibilities open to Euripides in presenting the figure of Medea.

> He might have made Medea a Clytemnestra figure—a magnificent criminal whose violence represents the primitive past the race posed against the civilized rational values of male democracy represented in this case by Jason. He might have created a version of the story in which Medea was punished for her crime and so shown the working of the justice of the Polis represented by Creon or Zeus announced by a god from machine, Hera perhaps would have been appropriate or that old standby Apollo. He might have presented us with a Medea who murdered her children while insane like Ino . . . or who murdered in cold blood but was then consumed by everlasting remorse like Procne.[87]

In fact the story ends, in Euripides, with Medea going off in the supernatural chariot to live out a new, equally violent future. Medea escapes to continue her murderous patterns; myth does not even narrate her death. "I do not remember having read or heard . . . how she died," Boccaccio wrote.[88] John Gardner concludes his *Jason and Medeia* with the image of the snakes and future evil: "Deep in the night old snakes were coupling with murderous intent."[89] In retelling the story of Jason and Medea, John Gardner asked himself what "the characters and events might mean to a modern sensibility . . . how much of the original would still hold, how much we are forced to alter and why, whose reading of experience is more accurate (that of Apollonius or our own) and how much experience has changed."⁹⁰ That is a part of the enterprise here.

One of the features of Euripides' play, as Easterling has noted, is the failure of the chorus to act. Easterling suggests that the Euripides abandons probability in his treatment of the chorus.

> It is highly unlikely that these respectable ladies of Corinth would really have stood ineffectually by when Medea announced her intention to kill their king and princess and then her own children. In real life they would have taken steps to have Medea taken into custody or at the very least would have gone to warn the royal family and Jason.⁹¹

Yet standing by ineffectually is one of the things we often do, as individuals and as officials. Many of our efforts are visible only after the catastrophic fact, partly because we don't know what to do and partly because we fear the consequences of our own interventions. If the family protects against the abuses of the state, the state protects against the abuses of the family, since, of course, groups can oppress members of families as much as members of any other group. Easterling has noted that the story of Medea is roughly this: "The barbarian sorceress with a melodramatic criminal record who could so easily be a monster must become a tragic character, a paradigm, in some sense of humanity."⁹² The chorus says, "Shall we go in? I'm sure we ought to save the children's lives." We should. But how? And at what cost? To the extent that the Medea story is a paradigm of humanity—not of women, not of women in love, but of humanity itself—it yields questions more than answers.

Perhaps we can see the chorus in Medea as something like a child welfare department, well intentioned, overworked, and, at times, tragically ineffective. This would get us to the facts of a recent case before the U.S. Supreme Court involving a four-year-old boy, Joshua DeShaney.⁹³ The Court, in an opinion of Chief Justice Rehnquist, offered the facts as follows:

> Petitioner is a boy who was beaten and permanently injured by his father, with whom he lived. Respondents are social workers and other local officials who received complaints that petitioner was being abused by his father and had reason to believe that this

was the case, but nonetheless did not act to remove petitioner from his father's custody. Petitioner sued respondents claiming that their failure to act deprived him of his liberty in violation of the Due Process Clause of the Fourteenth Amendment to the United States Constitution. We hold that it did not.

The majority wrote that the

harms Joshua suffered occurred not while he was in the State's custody, but while he was in the custody of his natural father, who was in no sense a state actor. While the State may have been aware of the dangers that Joshua faced in the free world, it played no part in their creation, nor did it do anything to render him any more vulnerable to them. That the State once took temporary custody of Joshua does not alter the analysis, for when it returned him to his father's custody, it placed him in no worse position than that in which he would have been had it not acted at all; the State does not become the permanent guarantor of an individual's safety by having once offered him shelter. Under these circumstances, the State had no constitutional duty to protect Joshua.

Judges and lawyers, like other humans, are moved by natural sympathy in a case like this to find a way for Joshua and his mother to receive adequate compensation for the grievous harm inflicted upon them. But before yielding to that impulse, it is well to remember once again that the harm was inflicted not by the State of Wisconsin, but by Joshua's father. The most that can be said of the state functionaries in this case is that they stood by and did nothing when suspicious circumstances dictated a more active role for them. In defense of them it must also be said that had they moved too soon to take custody of the son away from the father, they would likely have been met with charges of improperly intruding into the parent-child relationship, charges based on the Due Process Clause that forms the basis for the present charge of failure to provide adequate protection.

A dissent by Justices Brennan, Marshall, and Blackmun argues, "The Court's baseline is the absence of positive rights in the Constitution and a concomitant suspicion of any claim that seems to depend on such rights." Thus, the majority saw the claim as about "only action." "I would begin from the opposite direction," Justice Brennan said. "I would focus first on the action that Wisconsin has taken with respect to Joshua and children like him, rather than on the actions that the State failed to take."

In a separate dissent, Justice Blackmun wrote that the Court had retreated into "a sterile formalism" in its attempt to draw a "sharp and rigid line between action and inaction." But such formalistic reasoning has no place in the interpretation of the broad and stirring Clauses of the Fourteenth Amendment.

Aviam Soifer summarizes the majority opinion this way: "The DeShaney majority . . . proclaims an abstract, purportedly certain, and general constitutional principle: the state has a limited degree of responsibility." Thus officials must "avoid grossly harmful acts or omissions that grievously harm people" who are in state custody. But in the larger world, "everyone else is fully free and able to take part in the great national free-for-all. Every child, woman, and man, no matter how actually encumbered, is properly relegated exclusively to the political processes and the states for any refuge or redress." According to the majority, in this free world "no one—no matter what that person's condition or age—may look to the federal Constitution for relief, with the possible exception of those rare individuals who are able to prove that invidious discriminatory motivation was the case of their suffering at the hands of government officials."[94]

Another analysis, focused specifically on issues of language and rhetoric, is offered by Martha Minow. In the Court's opinion the categories of public and private, "expressed through words remote from the facts of the case, do the work of judgment." The majority opinion points to these words as the basis for the judgment denying Joshua's recovery. "Such words work as talismans to ward off the facts of the case."

> Justice Brennan's dissent probed beneath these talismans. To do so, he chose different words. . . . Justice Brennan explained that the case was one of governmental inaction only in the sense that the agency failed to take steps to protect Joshua. In another sense, the government actually did act. It acted when it established a system of public social services and directed all other actors—neighbors, school teachers, and medical personnel at hospital emergency

rooms—to direct any suspicions of abuse to the public agency and to rely on the agency to proceed from there. . . .

Although not explored by the dissents, another dimension of state action here was the lower court's decision to award custody of Joshua to his father after his parents' divorce.

Justice Blackmun's comment highlights the complex interconnections between personal and institutional behaviors that maintain a phenomenon like family violence and the cannot be illuminated by simplistic notions like act and omission.[95]

On the point of language, we may also note the remarks of Mary Ann Glendon.

Where the DeShaney opinion is to be faulted primarily is that it failed to take into consideration the increasing influence of legal discourse, especially the Supreme Court's constitutional discourse, on political discussion generally. Words that convey one sense to legally trained individuals may carry a very different meaning to the wider audience that now reads Supreme Court decisions, or, more often, newspaper digests of them.

Her suggestion is that the opinion could have written in a way that would have avoided giving the impression that the American political regime leaves the weakest citizens to fend for themselves. If the opinion writer had taken the time to describe briefly the remedies potentially available under Wisconsin law—such as criminal prosecution of Randy DeShaney, disciplinary action against the social worker, and damages of up to $50,000 from the state—the denial of a *constitutionally* based tort claim would have been contextualized.[96] But these remedies are of course after the fact and essentially too late. Wholesale restructuring might be the result of a focus on these questions. Certainly a part of the issue here is about institutions, and the structuring of institutions touches law.

Chapter Six

Law

"You know, after all, if you have such a fancy for her, I haven't really married her; one can't really consider her my wife." ...
"Not your wife, you say? But, by Jove, though, that's just it; she is your wife."

Pierre Loti, *Madame Chrysanthemum*

The story of Madame Butterfly has as an important part of its background the marriage and divorce law of Japan, under which Yamadori, the princely suitor, has already divorced a varying number of women. "Yamadori who was bred to the law, tells me that our law prevails in such matters, the marrage having taken place here," John Luther Long writes.[1]

What actually was that law? This question might be answered by reference to the professional understanding of the rules of the system, given by an authoritative voice. This authoritative voice differs in the various narratives of Madame Butterfly. Long asserts, "If Pinkerton had told her to go home ... she would have been divorced, without further ado."[2] The lawyer-writer indicates that abandonment by the husband means divorce, even in the absence of judicial or legislative process. In Hwang's M. Butterfly, *abandonment means annulment of the marriage. Pinkerton says, "I split for one month, it's annulled." (The idea of a lease terminable at the end of any month is associated with the rental of the house in the Long story and again with the idea that a Japanese husband would have Cho-Cho-San for a month and then divorce her.)[3] In Belasco there is a reference to divorce by saying (presumably the husband says this) to "walk it back to parent."[4] In one English translation[5] the idea seems to be that abandonment by the husband gives a "right" of divorce.[6] The "law" itself might be any of these or none, since the question of what the law is can be distinguished from the question what the characters seemed to believe the law was.*

Even if we knew what law was and was supposed to do, could law have done it? If the Japanese law had mandated ordinary Western monogamous

marriage, would that have eliminated the system on which the temporary mar-
riages were based?[7] Why are there alternative versions of the Japanese law in
the narratives? Why the failure to distinguish between divorce and annul-
ment, a right to divorce and the fact of a self-executing divorce?

One answer might be that Americans writing about foreign law are
unclear about its details. Questions of translation, for example, are ubiquitous.

Another answer is the considerable slippage between what lawyers think
the law is and what laypersons think.

Yet another is the ambiguity that inheres in law because law exists in lan-
guage, which remains ambiguous despite our best efforts.

Finally, there is some doubt about law *when we attempt to fix its mean-*
ing. Are we talking about statutes? practice? now? then? holdings? Dicta?
Are we talking about instrumental or expressive aspects?

These issues are the subject of this chapter. How is law understood by peo-
ple not primarily concerned with law? Is it precisely or accurately understood?
Can we talk sensibly about law's expressive, as against instrumental, func-
tions? These questions are particularly raised by commentators aware of the
"limits of law." They suggest that if law cannot act instrumentally, it can at
least act expressively, communicating values even where it cannot directly
enforce them. The first part of this chapter considers that proposition, conclud-
ing that the messages of law are highly complex, even contradictory, and per-
haps less well known than lawyers assume. The second part of the chapter
addresses more directly differing ideas of the role of the state as it deals with the
family.

Instrumental and Expressive Functions of Law

The changing role of the family in the law is captured in the headline of
a *New York Times* article published in September 1988: "Family Law:
Battle Ground in Social Revolution." In that article, Linda Greenhouse
writes, "Family law, long a professional backwater, has become a new
constitutional battle ground on which the social revolutions in family
structure, child bearing and personal relationships are being fought."[8]
Family law is an arena in which issues of law and medicine, law and
technology, and law and morals, are being discussed. The field is
understood as being centrally important to our common situation.
Along with this comes a renewed emphasis on the use of law to shape
that situation.

This chapter concerns the suggestion that expressive or symbolic aspects of law should be used in the field of family law to guide people to better behavior. We are reminded of this ancient theme by Mary Ann Glendon's *Abortion and Divorce in Western Law*. Glendon argues that law has both strong educational functions and significant expressive components. Law is a play, a story, a message, shaped by culture and in turn shaping culture. To the extent that law shapes culture, we should use it to send messages. Law, Glendon notes, is "constitutive when legal language begins . . . to influence the manner in which we perceive reality." We must therefore be "attentive, intelligent, reasonable and responsible" in the stories we tell.[9]

Stronger versions of the desirability of a message in family law have also been offered. Jan Gorecki writes,

> Those who are unilaterally guilty of disrupting their marriages . . . should be punished. . . . Their punishment conveys a message to the general society: minimum of responsibility is anyone's family obligation, and so is an effort to avoid inflicting suffering on one's spouse and children, and wrecking their lives. This message, if properly conveyed in the process of instrumental learning, may not but influence general attitudes, and may eventually bring about . . . decline of the total sum of suffering and decrease of the broader social problems generated by widespread family disintegration.[10]

The message that Gorecki envisions is a message to virtue. The message may be enforced if necessary as punishment, as in criminal law. Gorecki argues for retention of recrimination: "In its narrower version, the principle prevents the solely guilty spouse from claiming divorce. In its broader, classical version, it also prevents a spouse from claiming divorce if both he and his counterpart are guilty of matrimonial offenses. . . . The principle of recrimination provides the harmed spouse with an opportunity to receive compensation by use of the threat of vetoing divorce."[11] Glendon sees the messages of law in various ways, sometimes the direct communication of a position—as when she speaks of the present message of no-fault, no-responsibility divorce—and sometimes a message in the form of a compromise or a conversation, in which the law contains (or should contain) the voices of different parts of the cultural discussion. Thus Glendon is concerned not with the absence of a message, but with its content. For example, the law of property settlements in divorce may teach that one can walk away from a spouse (if not children) without assuming financial responsibility.[12]

Commentators may concede the uncertainties of the law-behavior interaction. Glendon says, "No one can chart with confidence the ways in which law, customs, new lines of behavior, ideas about law, and ideas about morality reciprocally influence each other."[13] Her discussion of the law's pedagogic function uses Plato's *Laws* as a text.[14] Plato's treatment assumes, however, an unchanging truth and virtue and the desirability of an unchanging legal structure.

> [An observer of] foreign customs must proceed [to the council] as soon as he gets back. If he has come across people who were able to give him some information about any problems of legislation or teaching or education, or if he actually comes back with some discoveries of his own, he should make his report to a full meeting of the council. If he seems to be not a whit better or worse for his journey, he should be congratulated at any rate for his energy; if he is thought to have become appreciably better, even higher recognition should be given him during his lifetime, and after his death he must be paid appropriate honours by authority of the assembled council. But if it seems that he has returned corrupted, this self-styled "expert" must talk to no one, young or old, and provided he obeys the authorities he may live as a private person; but if not, and he is convicted in court of meddling in some educational or legal question *he must die.*
>
> If none of the authorities takes him to court when that is what he deserves, *it should* count as a black mark against them when distinctions are awarded.[15]

In such a world, no serious problem about the pedagogic preambles or the content of the laws themselves exists.[16] However, this is not our world.[17]

One problem is that "only the most elementary legal information reaches the public, and this almost always in a slightly inaccurate form."[18] Glendon concludes that while there may be problems of communication, "there is no escape from the fact that, willy-nilly, law performs a pedagogical role. It contributes in a modest but not a trivial way to that framework of beliefs and feelings within which even our notions of self-interest are conceived."[19]

Recognition of law as expressive, as a source of symbols and values, has been common in America for some time.[20] This is particularly true in connection with the role of the Supreme Court, where the point is so true that one must work to persuade the public that "constitutional" does not necessarily mean good or wise. This emphasis on expressive functions (linked somehow to instrumental values)[21] has been given new vitality by work in several fields.[22]

Initially, in thinking about this issue we might separate two ideas. First, we look at law because law does in fact express values and thus teaches. We should know as much as we can about what law teaches as a descriptive matter, despite the complex and contradictory substance of the teaching. It is part of knowing the culture in which we live. Second, we look at law because law can and ought to be used to teach specific things. In brief, the expressive functions of law can and should be used instrumentally. Gorecki quotes Brandeis to the effect that "no small part of the law's function is to make men good."[23] Atiyah, describing this aspect of law, refers to the "hortatory" function.[24]

The first position can accommodate, though it does not require, ideas of uncertainty, indeterminacy, and even chaos in law. The second idea works best when we assume that in talking about law we deal with a thing that can be known accurately, at least in theory. Clear messages can be sent and received, even when they are complex. The complexity of legal messages is not necessarily a problem for those interested in the expressive function. Indeed, on some versions, a tension in the message, or a contradictory message, is viewed as a compromise between conflicting positions, or as a way of incorporating aspects of the public debate. Thus, Glendon writes: "The 1976 West German divorce law . . . added to the Civil Code section on the effects of marriage the following sentence: 'Marriage is concluded for a lifetime.'" She indicates that, from one point of view,

> this insertion, part of a last-minute compromise between the coalition government and the Christian Democrats, is strikingly out of place in a divorce statute, just another sop to the losers. Yet . . . it acknowledges an important ideal of a large segment of the popu-

lation, while accommodating to some extent in practice those who do not share or cannot live up to the ideal.[25]

On the same basis, Max Rheinstein views the fault system as a compromise.[26]

Attempts to make abortion illegal remind us of Prohibition, both because the prospect of large-scale refusal to comply is so real, and because the symbolic victory (independent of enforcement) may be sufficiently important for those opposed to abortion that they will risk substantial noncompliance.[27] Glendon illustrates a compromise with the French abortion law that requires some (undefined) distress on the part of the woman.[28]

Messages Sent

We might compare this idea of a clear legal message with some other ideas about law in general. As Robert Gordon points out, "History helps to teach us that the rule of law 'system' is fundamentally misdescribed, that inspected at close range, it's not really a system at all, but a complex mess of competing and contradictory systems."[29] Grant Gilmore comments, "When we think of our own or of any other legal system, the beginning of wisdom lies in the recognition that the body of the law, at any time or place, is an unstable mass in precarious equilibrium."[30] Gilmore's remarks are particularly striking, coming from a scholar who spent his professional life working in fields—contracts and commercial law—in which formalism and theory were dominant ideas and certainty a prime legal value. If these legal contexts could produce and illustrate Gilmore's view, we would expect that this sense of instability and uncertainty to pervade family law, where the need for individualization is taken for granted. Indeed, these descriptions of law in general have their analogues in work on family law. Thus, Carl Schneider describes the complexity of the sources of family law, the nontheoretical nature of family law scholarship, and the "rarity of attempts" in this field to "go beyond the specific."[31] He writes: "It is hard to produce a systematic view of an unsystematic subject, and perhaps family law must always be ad hoc, responsive to local conditions, sensitive to the day's sensibilities, and willing to compromise irreconcilable differences."[32] Judith Areen describes the relatively "undeveloped state of secular thinking about family life," with particular application to surrogacy questions.[33] Martha Minow discusses the Supreme Court decisions in relation to group conflict, suggesting that the Court has used debates about family, state, and individual to mediate larger social struggles, and that "it should not be surprising that constitutional rhetoric about the family is confused and inconsistent."[34]

When we look at what law is—things we might legitimately look at in determining a message—we see constitutions, legislation, judicial opinions, official behavior of all sorts. All contribute to the "symbolism" of law or the message that law sends. This message or symbolism will necessarily not be uniform or consistent, since law carries many values. This is true in all areas of law, but particularly in family law, inevitably focused on individuals and using open standards. It is not merely, as Tennyson had it, that law is a "wilderness of single instances."[35] It is that each single instance can be said to stand for different things—which is what the techniques (as against the principle) of precedent are finally about. The point is familiar in general. The leading example is probably *Everson v. Board of Education*,[36] in which the holding and rhetoric were so far apart that dissenting Justice Jackson invoked the precedent of Byron's Julia, who "whispering 'I will ne'er consent,'—consented."[37]

In the area of family law, we might consider the messages sent by a single text, *Marvin v. Marvin*.[38] First, the opinion recites the facts of cohabitation as if they matter to the legal system, thus reinforcing the idea that law's function is principally to be responsive to social facts. "During the past 15 years, there has been a substantial increase in the number of couples living together without marrying."[39] Then the court opts for a kind of responsibility, by generally recognizing the enforceability of cohabitation contracts, as long as the explicit consideration is something other than meretricious sexual services. The last point is a signal in the direction of traditional moral values and the existing case law.[40] Finally, the court, having gone a long way toward recognizing quasi or alternate[41] marriage, speaks eloquently about marriage.

> The mores of the society have indeed changed so radically in regard to cohabitation that we cannot impose a standard based on alleged moral considerations that have apparently been so widely abandoned by so many. Lest we be misunderstood, however, we take this occasion to point out that the structure of society itself largely depends on the institution of marriage, and nothing we have said in this opinion should be taken to derogate from that

institution. The joining of the man and woman in marriage is at once the most socially productive and individually fulfilling relationship that one can enjoy in the course of a lifetime.[42]

In Leonard Bernstein's *Candide,* we have the following response by Pangloss to the question, If marriage is so wonderful, why is there so much divorce? "Why marriage, boy, is such a joy, so lovely a condition, that many ask no better than, to wed as often as they can, in happy repetition."[43]

Considered as a teaching tool, the *Marvin* opinion can be used for many lessons or it can be used for one: expansion of rights of cohabitants. The *Marvin* case, or any case, can be reduced to a proposition or a statement of law, or a holding, or a finite point of view on a problem. However, this approach (which the formal system, integrating its various structural parts and its majority and dissenting opinions, makes possible) is not the approach that those interested in expressive or symbolic functions would take. Even if one did this, the central question of message would remain. Is "expansion of the rights of cohabitants" a symbolic move away from the values of responsibility and cohesion associated with marriage, or a symbolic move toward those values now associated with nonmarital arrangements?[44]

The problem of "what is the law" is behind one of the criticisms of a well-known 1958 study comparing law and community moral standards on a number of family law issues.[45] This book attempted to compare the public's moral sense of a problem's correct answer with a projected legal answer.[46] On some problems, the study did not distinguish between general principles and details. Thus, on issues relating to the legal age of marriage and the problem of parental consent, it was noted that on "neither of these issues did the disagreement found relate to the principle involved. It related, instead, only to the *ages* at which marriage should be legally possible, and consent unnecessary."[47]

"Law" was used in the study to mean "the choices that the courts in the jurisdiction probably would have made—by virtue of existing statutes, precedents or analogies—if the specific situations were presented to them in litigious form." They are not, the authors say, the "law-in-action," rather "law ready to be applied if and when the occasion calls."[48] A definition of *law* published in an earlier account of the project was "Choices that have been made by the courts (in opinions) and the legislature (in statutes) when actually confronted with such or similar situations."[49] When were the choices made? How similar is similar? The study was not focused on knowledge of law, but rather on the discrepancy between the law and the moral sense of the community. It indirectly relates, however, to knowledge of law problems to the extent that we are, in effect, talking both about the authors' knowledge of law, and the respondents' knowledge of law to the extent that they were ignorant of the legal consequences of their answers. "[I]t is apparent that the respondents had not the slightest awareness of the practical implications of their answers."[50] The "Big Brother" approach involved in implementation, the review suggests, might, if surfaced, have revealed different attitudes. Another reviewer, concerned with the same sort of problem, suggests that "there is a risk that [as to the problem of parents denying college or a career choice to their children] most respondents did not have a clear image of what legal intervention would entail."[51]

In 1975, the Cohen-Robson-Bates study was described as the "most extensive and sophisticated study on the congruence of public sentiments and family law then available.[52] As a number of reviewers suggested, the treatment of law was static. The law, said one review, was taken to mean "law ready to be applied," "an application of statutes and judicial precedent without insight or imagination."[53]

The complexity of legal messages suggested here goes beyond what might be viewed as an ordered dialogue or a deliberate attempt to incorporate many voices. The pluralism of law is something less planned, less obviously representative of the opinions of identifiable groups. The pluralism of law may not even reject judgments that are surely universal, easy cases. The law of contracts continues to suggest, for example, that a man's feeling for his bull is more important than his feeling for his son.[54]

Assuming there is a law, or rule of law that can be known accurately in principle, we confront the problem of whether it is known in fact. It is suggested that law is known, though somewhat inaccurately, by the public. Even Stanley Kowalski knows that Louisiana is under the Napoleonic Code. His description of the Code in *A Streetcar Named Desire* emphasizes community property, without a focus on possibilities of separate property. He says, "There is such a thing in the state of Louisiana as the Napoleonic Code, according to which whatever belongs to my wife is also mine—and vice versa."[55] The point is made that the message sent is received, but imperfectly.

Messages Received

What do we know about how law is understood?

One approach turns to empirical studies. That material itself is not voluminous.[56] However, a general feeling exists that people do not know much about the law or the legal system.[57] One problem relates to the sources of information about law. Newspapers and broadcast media are listed as prime sources, with informal networks of friends and family following.[58] Lawrence Friedman, reviewing Michael Kammen's book on the Constitution, suggested that people learned what they know from the six o'clock news.[59] Information may be filtered through individuals and groups in a way that is independently worth our attention.[60]

Another response is impressionistic. Thus Thurman Arnold tells us, "The trader takes heart by learning that the law ignores the more profitable forms of dishonesty in deference to the principle of individual freedom from governmental restraint. The preacher, however, is glad to learn that all forms of dishonesty which can be curbed without interfering with freedom or with economic law are being curbed."[61]

Still impressionistically, another answer might go to other sources, other understandings, and use those sources as material speaking to this question. At the level of popular material,[62] journalism or detective fiction, one finds understandings of the law that are not necessarily those of Austinian jurisprudence. This chapter is not, of course, an examination of even detective fiction as a source of information about knowledge of law in the culture. At most, it suggests that some material gives the impression that some ideas (multiple legal systems, limits of law) are known. Any serious study that attempted to use fiction in this way would have to take account of the point that one cannot take an inaccuracy (for example) as an indication of the author's actual knowledge, for it might be intentional.[63] One would have to deal with the question of why deliberate inaccuracy might exist.[64] There is a relation between detective fiction and popular culture as a whole. J. I. M. Stewart suggests that, for example, "Holmes has even entered the mythology of the folk, so that if in a pub a man is called 'a ruddy Sherlock Holmes' the expression is . . . generally understood. . . . Understood, as are references to Shylock and Romeo, although "nobody has ever been called 'a peeping Poirot.' "[65]

Some law resonates. Do we know which?

In mystery stories, one sometimes finds that multiple legal systems are understood as operating in the world. Ed McBain's *Blood Relatives* tells of a woman wondering whether sexual relations and marriage between cousins are forbidden by the state or only by the church.[66] A reference to "real" (official) as against "religious" law can be read as meaning that the speaker knows something in addition to "real" law. It can also be read as impacting on what "real" law is taken to mean. Arthur Upfield sees two systems, aboriginal and Western, tracking the same criminal.[67] Sometimes the issue of the limits of state enforcement in relation to multiple systems of authority is clear. Thus, Philip Mason's *Call the Next Witness* contains a move and counter-move description of a murder trial (based on a case in India in 1931) that centrally involves the relative power of family groups and the Indian legal system.[68] When it deals with the official system, detective fiction may be far from sanguine about its operation. Austin Freeman writes that "unspeakably dreary and depressing were the brief proceedings that followed, and dreadfully suggestive of the helplessness of even an innocent man on whom the law has laid its hand and in whose behalf its inexorable machinery has been set in motion."[69]

Some detective stories are filled with legal technicalities, for example, those of Cyril Hare (Alfred Alexander Gordon Clarke), who was a barrister and then a county court judge.[70] Those may initially reflect a professional and not popular understanding of law. These points suggest the possibility of a general knowledge not of legal rules or doctrines but of legal pluralism and the limits of law in the culture.

One also suspects the possibility of vast ignorance of the role of law, going far beyond ignorance of specific rights or rules in the legal system. Most obviously this may be true of children. Stephen Wizner offered an anecdote relating to a nine-year-old child in a burglary trial.

"Did we win or lose?"
"We won."
"Yeah? What did we win?"[71]

The child was told that "what he had 'won' was a decision that he 'didn't do it.'" The child answered—" 'but I *didn't* do it.'"[72] However, ignorance and misunderstanding may also characterize the thinking of adults. Questions might be asked, not about knowledge of rules in the state legal system, but about legal ideas more broadly. A study of knowledge of law might well start with questions devoted to the problem of marriage as a state-created relationship. For example, do people know that two people must participate in an officially structured procedure? *Hewitt v. Hewitt* involved two people who lived together from 1960 until 1975.[73] In that case, the defendant "told her that they were husband and wife and would live as such, no formal ceremony being necessary."[74] States of knowledge in this case may be suggested as ranging from knowledge of canon law marriage via language in the present tense, to knowledge failing to include the idea that both people have to do something to get married.[75] Do people know that they do not have to "ask" for a divorce? Did this, in any case, mean, ask a spouse to be a plaintiff in a divorce action, that is, to participate in a particular kind of charade, on the one hand, and economic bargaining, on the other? That "grounds" are generally no longer necessary? Will it turn out that the law that people "know" is the law of their childhood? How do people answer or think they should answer the question "were you ever married" when their marriages have been annulled? Any relation here to people's answers and the void/voidable distinction? Do you have to return wedding gifts? Will the answers here turn on ideas not of validity but of vesting? Or equitable compensation?[76]

Some of these questions raise issues of the internal law of each family, (or each individual) in the sense suggested by Leon Petrazycki.[77] ("[E]ach family is a unique legal world.") On this view, each family might, for example, have its own law of divorce, existing inside the state law, and interacting with it, influenced by it, but also perhaps shaping it.[78]

Some journalistic discussions of the family in America contain comments about family law that initially seem to fall in the "ignorance" category. Thus, Barbara Ehrenreich, in *The Hearts of Men*, writes: "Men cannot be forced to marry; once married, they cannot be forced to bring home their paychecks, to be reliable jobholders, or of course to remain married."[79] What is meant by the idea that people cannot be forced to do something? Is this about a theory of sanctions, or the limits on physical compulsion? Does she mean that American law does not command men to marry? What is meant by the idea that men do not have to—cannot be forced to—bring home their paychecks? Is there some underlying problem about the idea of the support obligation? Finally, while at the time Ehrenreich wrote people could not be forced to remain married, she presumably knew that the history of the law of divorce is about the problem of forcing reluctant couples to remain married. Or even to cohabit.[80] Yet perhaps these comments by Ehrenreich can be best understood not as a description of actual or possible legal rules, but as a description of effective law or legal results in fact. As to support, for example, Ehrenreich apparently does not think that the existing laws really do create a support obligation, since they do not, as she says, compel the purchase of life insurance policies.[81] It may be that people know something about the practical limits of law,[82] as much as about the power and efficacy of law.

Family law is a particularly important point at which to examine problems of the expressive function of law. It already contains many examples of messages, though there has been a change in the kind of message being sent over time.[83]

Truman said of Eisenhower in 1952: "He'll sit here, and he'll say, 'Do this! Do that!' *And nothing will happen.* Poor Ike—it won't be a bit like the Army."[84] The point about law is not that nothing happens, but that things happen that we did not expect and that the simple cause and effect relationship in which law shapes behavior is far from proven.[85] This does not make law trivial or insignificant. It does limit what we can realistically expect law to do alone. Note in this connection Schneider's comment that enforcement problems in family law are ubiquitous, even where the law purports to act.[86] The difficulties in child custody, for example, require no citation. Proposals are heard to the effect that law should contain more, despite the acknowledgment that the effectiveness of law is limited. For example, Max Rheinstein concludes that law is not a prime determinant of behavior in relation to marital stability. "Experienced observers have long known what we have laboriously tried in this book to prove, namely, that a strict statute law of divorce is not an effective means to prevent or even to reduce the incidence of marriage breakdown."[87] Abel suggests that this observation might have been a "foundation for the study, not an afterthought."[88] Mary Ann Glendon notes that the relation between law and behavior are uncertain, and that other factors are critical.[89] Scholars whose concern is law/society issues suggest that law may not be very important in causing particular behavior.[90]

Even if we assume some effectiveness, the problem remains "what message?" One possibility is a message of facilitation of private choice, which may finally lead to the proposition that marriage is not a useful legal idea. Thus E. M. Clive raises the question of the future of the legal concept of marriage.[91] In the context of article 12 of the European Convention on Human Rights, which treats the right to marry, he asks: "What are the underlying assumptions of that provision? Would it be breached if a country abolished marriage as a legal concept but gave its inhabitants complete freedom to participate in such religious or social marriage ceremonies as they thought fit?"[92] Another message would try to invoke the now-gone consensus of the Christian nation.

We agree that the consensus is gone. However, that agreement creates a problem, since we want our law of the family to be not merely not evil, but affirmatively good.[93] As Lee Teitelbaum suggests,

> It does not seem enough . . . to content ourselves with saying only that some rule cannot be shown to produce evil. While that may suffice for a commercial contract or the occasional tort, there is some feeling that family relationships should be founded on rules and practices we can call good.[94]

But what we can call good, and how to justify the description, remains unclear. Clifford Geertz tells us, "Like just about every other long-standing institution—religion, art, science, the state, the family— law is in the process of learning to survive without the certitudes that launched it."[95] The process is associated in law with the realists, and so we return to Grant Gilmore. He wrote in 1951,

> At twenty years distance we may with the prescience of hindsight pass judgment. Llewellyn and his co-conspirators were right in everything they said about the law. They skillfully led us into the swamp. Their mistake was in being sure that they knew the way out of the swamp: they did not, at least we are still there.[96]

Gilmore himself thought that in general law followed society, so that a just society resulted in a just law. But, he wrote, "Law never creates society; society creates Law. Law never makes society better; a better society will improve the law."[97] Decades later, it is as true in family law as in much else. Just before his death Gilmore said,

> We stand at the end of a half century during which the body of the law has been at fives and threes—not to say, sixes and sevens. The imposing structure of our nineteenth century law—and a magnificent creation it was—lies in ruins. It has not been rebuilt—nor will

it be, although there are a good many would-be master builders eager to offer their services. If any of your instructors was rash enough to tell you what the law is, you would not believe him; if you did, you would be poorly equipped to operate in the real world.[98]

But there is something in family law that makes the matter peculiarly difficult. The problem is centrally that we care so much, and that law, finally, can do so little. As to this, it may be that the public is more sensitive to reality than some lawyers. Here is Trollope, particularly acute on the failure of the law to provide an adequate remedy. *Kept in the Dark* involves a wife's concealing her previous engagement; rejected by her husband, she considers the law's relevance to her situation. The limits of law could not be more clearly set out.

> She could not force him to be her companion. The law would give her only those things which she did not care to claim. He already offered more than the law would exact, and she despised his generosity. As long as he supported her the law could not bring him back and force him to give her to eat of his own loaf, and to drink of his own cup. . . . He had said that he had gone, and would not return, and the law could not bring him back again.[99]

The strength of inquiries into the expressive functions of law is that they focus not only on the formal content of the decision, but also on its effect and tone. They direct attention away from the decision maker, powerful and authoritative, and toward the audiences that the decision both addresses and reflects. While emphasis on rule and decision making gets us to clarification and thus simplification, emphasis on rhetoric gets us to complexity and contradiction. Given the circumstances, while we must somehow still decide things, we might do well to announce our decisions in a less certain voice.

Family and State
What is it that we expect of the state with reference to children? We can begin with Bentham's account.

"The feebleness of infancy," Bentham wrote, "demands a continual protection." The development of the human being, physical and intellectual, takes many years, and while at a certain age, the child will gain strength and passion, it is without "experience enough to regulate them." The human child is "[t]oo sensitive to present impulses, too negligent of the future," and the result is that "such a being must be kept under an authority more immediate than that of the laws."[100] That "more immediate authority" to which Bentham referred is typically the authority of natural or adoptive parents. As Goldstein, Freud, and Solnit write, parents "offer children protection and nurture, and introduce them to the demands and prohibitions as well as to the promises and opportunities of society."[101] It is this combination of parents and children that provides a core meaning for the term *family*.

> Immemorially, the family has been an important element of our civil society, one of the supports upon which our civilization has developed. Save as modified by the Legislature, in domestic affairs the family has remained in law a self-governing entity, under the discipline and direction of the father as its head.[102]

The nineteenth-century American account of the family often associated family life with ideas of governance, that is, with rules, authority, and discipline. Thus, Horace Bushnell of Connecticut wrote of family government: "Of course it is to be *government*." It was not to be a "mere nursing" and/or "an exhorting, advising, consulting relationship." Family governance was not a matter of the "lavishing of devotion" or of "parental self-sacrifice." Rather, the basic point of family government was "that it governs, uses authority, maintains law and rules, by a binding and loosing power, over the moral nature of the child."[103] A classical discussion of this is Locke's *Essay Concerning Certain False Principles,* rejecting Filmer's approach to the justification of monarchy through analogy to biblically based paternal authority.[104]

Noting that with the rise of the modern state many of the functions of the family passed to the state, Roscoe Pound wrote in 1916: "Along with the development of individual interests at the expense of the interests of the head of the household," there had been "a weakening of the household as an entity ruled from within and as an agency of social control."[105] He saw that in

> the law today, not only duties of care for the health, morals and education of children, but even truancy and incorrigibility are

coming under the supervision of juvenile courts and courts of domestic relations, where in the past there was little of no occasion for the law to think of them.[106]

Note also that social interests—both an interest in "protection of dependent persons" and an interest in "securing to all individuals of moral and social life," and in the "rearing and training of sound and well-bred citizens"—have greatly limited a parental claim to custody and control[107] and have tended to de-emphasize the governmental aspects of family and to stress instead affective characteristics.

It is not necessary to see this as a contemporary development. Some, indeed, have placed it much earlier. Thus, it has been said, "By the middle of the eighteenth century family relations had been fundamentally reconsidered in both England and America."

> An older patriarchal family authority was giving way to a new parental ideal characterized by a more affectionate and equalitarian relationship with children. This important development paralleled the emergence of a humane form of childrearing that accommodated the stages of a child's growth and recognized the distinctive character of childhood. Parents who embraced the new childrearing felt a deep moral commitment to prepare their children for a life of rational independence and moral self-sufficiency.[108]

At the moment, however, attention is once again being given to the connections between the family and the state and particularly to issues of the internal regulation of family life. This chapter, as part of this inquiry, focuses not on the idea of judicial intervention in crisis situations, but on the issues raised by the overriding state presence. The inquiry seems to result partly from the work of feminists concerned with a variety of problems located in the domestic order[109] and partly from the discussion of some of those concerned with the apparent failure of at least some families to train for citizenship. Whatever its sources and motivation, however, the inquiry unquestionably touches issues of major importance for the quality of individual life.

The proposition that micro legal systems have as much to do with individual happiness as macro systems is a familiar one.[110] The family is fundamentally one such micro system, existing with others, which can be analyzed along the spectrum of such systems. Michael Reisman has noted,

> It is a matter of common experience that the family unit is a primary social and socializing unit and that the general community allocates a broad measure of discretion to parents in choice of purposes and modalities of disciplining, intervening, perhaps too rarely, only when gross deprivations of intensely demanded community standards occur.[111]

The problem of family governance relates then, first, to the issue of something called "the family" in its relation to "the state" and, second, to the issue of the internal functioning of the family.

We can begin by recalling that families were once described as forms of public order. Heman Humphrey, a Congregational minister and president of Amherst College, wrote in 1849, "Every family is a little state, or empire within itself." "Nations may change their forms of government at pleasure, and may enjoy a high degree of prosperity under different constitutions," but it was clear that "in the family organization there is but one model, for all times and all places." That model was patriarchal: "Every father is the constituted head and ruler of his household." This was an aspect of the divine plan, and the father, "supreme earthly legislator over his children," was accountable to God "for the manner in which he executes his trust; but amenable to no other power, except in the most extreme cases of neglect or abuse." Thus, "The will of the parent is the law to which the child is bound in all cases to submit, unless it plainly contravenes the law of God." It followed that, from one point of view, the role of the state was extremely limited: "Nor has civil *government* any right to interfere with the head of a family, unless it be where he is guilty of extreme neglect, or abuse." Even here, the issue of accountability relates the state role to a higher authority.

> But in all ordinary cases, even of great delinquency, the guilty parent must be left to answer for "his abuse of power, or neglect of duty," to him who "ruleth over all." It would be impossible for any government in the world, to take upon itself parental authority and discharge parental duties; and if it were possible, such an

innovation would soon derange and destroy the whole social system.[112]

Humphrey is used to represent the authoritarian, as contrasted with
the sentimental, approach to child rearing.

At the same time, it was conventional to cite connections between
family and state. Tocqueville wrote that order at home resulted in order
in the state: "Where the European tries to escape his sorrows at home
by troubling society, the American derives from his home that love of
order which he carries over into affairs of State."[113] The United States
Supreme Court, in an exemplary American discussion on the relation
between marriage, family and the state, insisted that society was built
on marriage.

> Marriage, while from its very nature a sacred obligation, is never-
> theless, in most civilized nations, a civil contract, and usually reg-
> ulated by law. Upon it society may be said to be built, and out of its
> fruits spring social relations and social obligations and duties, with
> which government is necessarily required to deal.[114]

Marriage was of course the basis of the legitimate family. The family continues to be seen as having a relation to the civil order,[115] in part
because portions of society, at least, have found that schools cannot do
the whole job of training for citizenship. Since the family is a source of
the health of the state, while the state regulates the family, a British ana-
lyst asks: "Who is to say that the crisis in authority in British society
today is not to be partly attributed to changing domestic relations?"[116]
He argues that although the human being is a "rational animal" he or
she might be "also termed the 'irresponsible animal'" since a person
"lightly launches into the atmosphere of society substances [legal models, in this case] which may have a similarly destructive tendency."[117]
Americans raise the same question. Does breakdown of the family lead
to breakdown in the social order?

This question assumes that the family, however significant its
emotional roles, is more than a place for the satisfaction of the needs of
the two individuals of the marital couple. Arguing that "the family
plays a central role in modern society" and has not been preempted by
governmental institution, Lee Teitelbaum has urged that "[i]ntermedi-
ate administrative and regulatory organizations, such as the educa-

tional system and the juvenile court, have not entirely occupied the fields once primarily committed to family authority." And even where such agencies have time to play major roles, "their activities, to a considerable extent, are still dependent on familial decisions."[118] Teitelbaum notes, "Families have much to do with social control as well," despite the fact that "they no longer provide the principal mechanism for that purpose." Families participate directly in the creation and definition of criminal behavior.[119] "A blow by one spouse to another is an act, but the actor will only be treated as a spouse abuser if the victim defined the conduct as intolerable and communicates that view to an official agency." Similarly, "A blow by a parent to a child is an act." This means that "whether it is child abuse rather than reasonable parental discipline depends largely on whether the family (or some other person) so identifies it." Teitelbaum concludes on this point: "What counts as deviance by children within the home is, as well, largely defined within the home. The kinds of conduct that a family may define as disobedient are virtually infinite because the particular commands that parents may give, and that children may disobey, are virtually infinite."[120] Thus, Teitelbaum indicates, there is continuing power in the family (often negative) over individual psyches.[121]

Certain facts in the world support and even expand Teitelbaum's assessment of family power. To take an extreme example, fundamentalist Muslim parents recently killed their westernized daughter apparently as an exercise of family authority.[122] Groups referred to as cults have disciplined their children in a way that has been attacked by state authorities as child abuse. Recall the Island Pond community in Vermont, in which a large number of children were for a time thought to be victims of child abuse.[123] Parents have refused to pay for college for children who fail to conform to their expectations. Divorced fathers have failed to support their children in the manner to which they would have been accustomed but for the divorce.

In some of these cases, we feel that the state should intervene, although the conceptual significance of intervention is doubtful.[124] We note that the family is an independent source of power that on the one hand operates as a check on the state as another mediating institution, parallel to churches, trade unions, and corporations, but on the other hand abuses its authority and thus requires coercive supervision by the state.[125]

If we consider the history of the family not as an affective unit—a haven from the heartless world[126]—but as a kind of unit of government, our images are clear and rooted in ancient legal systems. We recall the wealth *patria potestes*—the right of the father at Roman law to kill his children.

> It was a maxim of Roman jurisprudence that the Patria Potestas did not extend to the Jus Publicum. Father and son voted together in the city, and fought side by side in the field; indeed, the son, as general, might happen to command the father, or, as magistrate, decide on his contracts and punish his delinquencies. But in all the relations created by Private Law, the son lived under a domestic despotism which, considering the severity it retained to the last, and the number of centuries through which it endured, constitutes one of the strangest problems in legal history.[127]

Another link between family and state authority took the form of rules in colonial New England to the effect that everyone had to live in family units so that they would be under family governance,[128] a power altered but visible (though derived from a different source) in the rules of colonial Connecticut and Massachusetts[129]—apparently never enforced—authorizing the death penalty for disobedience to parents. The modern story might begin with the power of the family before the French Revolution to imprison misbehaving relatives through a writ issued by the royal authority at the request of the family.

> [T]he family had demanded the support of the state in order to reinforce its authority over its recalcitrant members ever since the end of the *ancien régime*. The Napoleonic Code had maintained part of the old power of the family, formerly based on the procedure of the *lettres de cachet de famille*. Article 375 of the Civil Code stipulated that every father whose child afforded "compelling grounds for dissatisfaction" . . . [could] cause him to be imprisoned for a period of one month if he is less than sixteen years of age, and for a period of six months if he is older.[130]

The connection between this writ and the continuing role of the family in relation to civil commitment seems obvious and may be connected to the power of the Anglo-American family to disinherit.[131] As Massachusetts has it,

If a testator omits to provide in his will for any of his children, whether born before or after the testator's death, or for the issue of a deceased child, whether born before or after the testator's death, they shall take the same share of his estate which they would have taken if he had died intestate, unless they have been provided for by the testator in his lifetime or *unless it appears that the omission was intentional and not occasioned by accident or mistake.*[132]

The central meaning of family governance from the point of view of the state was expressed in one court's comment,

Anything that brings the child into conflict with the father or diminishes the father's authority or hampers him in its exercise is repugnant to the family establishment, and is not to be countenanced save upon positive provisions of the statute law. . . . Any proceeding tending to bring discord into the family and disorganize its government may well be regarded as contrary to the common law.[133]

It is worth noting here that the state is not simply the direct mechanism of involvement with any particular family, but also with the ideology of the family in general. The adoption of state conceptions of justice—in fairness and process—would have as much impact on the family as would state officials moving in to regulate. Thus, state intervention may take the form of educational campaigns[134] directed to such problems as appropriate family behavior or appropriate family governance.

But what is family governance? Surely it is something about which we can say more than that it is patriarchy, the rule of the fathers. On what basis do these fathers rule? What are rights within the family?

To begin with a minimal right, we can speak of a right not to be mistreated within the family,[135] As with public education, the "right" may not be constitutional but political.[136] However, the more difficult problems in theory are not about mistreatment or abuse, but about autonomy. Feinberg describes a category of "rights-in-trust"—rights that "look like adult autonomy rights except that the child cannot very well exercise his free choice until later when he is more fully formed and capable." These rights are "*saved* for the child until he is an adult" but "can be violated 'in advance,' so to speak, before the child is even in a position to exercise them." Certain adult behavior "guarantees *now* that when the child is an autonomous adult, certain key options will already be closed to him."[137] It was this right, as will be discussed, that Franz Kafka believed had been denied to him by his father-autocrat-patriarch.[138] A central question for the outside official legal system is how and whether to protect that right, since it is on that psychological capacity, created in the family, that all other capacity would seem to depend.

It may be that homes are universally appalling and oppressive. It is not necessary to use Freud to get to the idea that parents should not educate or raise their own children.[139] As Alice Miller notes, the doting parents of Wordsworth's *Intimations* ode are also inevitably the sources of psychic if not physical pain.[140]

It may be that there can be no end to the grievances that children have against parents. R. D. Laing noted that he spent much of his life attempting to understand the relations between the people in the adult world into which he had been born: "From as far back as I can remember, I tried to figure out what was going on between these people. If I believed one, I couldn't believe anyone else."[141] Max Brod (whose childhood was on some scales much worse than Kafka's) and Edmund Wilson both felt that Kafka was excessive in his denunciation of his father. But we are not, I think, as certain as Alice Miller that the child is always innocent.[142] We often think that parents are in some respects children themselves, doing damage, as it were, to the new generation before fully dealing with the damage done to them: "Man hands on misery to man."[143] The only certainty is that the grandchildren will have grievances against the children, whose parents were once children themselves.[144] The point here is that the present American emphasis on incest and abuse—in short, deviance and pathology in the family—distracts us from the more general point that even the "normal" family has problems. Whether we define this issue politically (in terms of families encouraging particularism)[145] or psychologically (with children as the carriers of the unlived lives of the parents)[146] or economically (with parents as the monitors of future economic status),[147] these problems are systemic and have little to do with, for example, the absence of what is termed parental love.

The question remains: Where are the remedies for problems as large as these? The home and the family remain primary institutions in our culture, and with them comes the problem of legal definitions of appropriate parental authority and of the relations between the family and the state.

A passage deleted from *The Trial* suggests that the state might intervene on Joseph K's side. "The state is offering to come to my assistance," whispered K into the ear of one of the men. "What if I transferred the trial into the domain where the writ of the state law runs? The outcome might very well be that I would have to defend you two gentlemen against the state!"[148] The deletion suggests a point about the father letter. State law, of course, existed, but outside intervention was not sought. Kafka's injuries had in fact no state-provided remedy. Max Brod discusses the question: What difference would the approval of his father have made to Kafka?[149] The question opens the difficult possibility that normalization works against genius. It is, at the personal level, the analogue of the issue of art and oppression at the political level. Indeed, as against the state, the authority of the father might have to be defended.

The question for the present discussion is what an analysis focused on levels of law in the family can add to the almost ubiquitous discussion of state-family relations. Family life in its dailiness can look very different under different social conditions. Thus, for example, marriage looks different when women are not educated for dependency and are not in fact dependent on men for economic and social status. Because of changes in the status of women, the state ceased to enforce a specific, male-dominated model of marital happiness. As nineteenth-century feminists noted, the old law was all too similar to the law of slavery or indentured servitude.

> He has made her, morally, an irresponsible being, as she can commit many crimes with impunity, provided they be done in the presence of her husband. In the covenant of marriage, she is compelled to promise obedience to her husband, he becoming, to all intents and purposes, her master—the law giving him power to deprive her of her liberty, and to administer chastisement.[150]

In the same way, we can say that parenting will look different when the drive upward for social and economic security no longer dominates intergenerational relationships. But does this process end with egalitarian relations between parents and children as the goal? Even the apparently self-evident words *parents* and *children* require work, and this is true even if we ignore the ambiguities created by the new birth technologies. Do we mean children as infants, in fact, dependent, requiring nurture and discipline? Do we mean children in law, below some age of minority (note various ages of minority for different purposes) for some person in some context? Do we mean children who are dependent in fact, regardless of age, either because of some individual difficulty or some societal pattern that requires them to be financially dependent long past legal majority? When we reverse parents and children (and this may happen long before anything as official as a guardianship proceeding acknowledges the shift in roles), and cause children to become the caretakers of their own parents, what then of issues of family authority and governance? At this point, it no longer makes sense to speak of parental authority as lying in the biological parents, though we may well think in terms of family privacy authority or autonomy in urging the state to enforce the decisions of children with reference to their aged parents. Even egalitarian child-rearing, it would seem, opens quite different issues concerning the creation of autonomy and "intergenerational justice."

Two broad approaches to these issues may be distinguished. One approach—which may also be consistent with certain readings of liberalism—would attempt a universal norm imposed on, or encouraged in, all families. Lawrence Friedman has written of the modern desire for total justice. This, he notes, extends to the family. "Justice is, or ought to be, available in all settings: in hospitals and prisons, in schools, on the job, in apartment buildings, on the streets, within the family. It is a pervasive expectation of fairness. And it is substantive as well as procedural.[151] This emphasis on the just family might be a goal of state efforts through education, for example.

A different but equally universal goal would in effect associate the family with approaches that are not centrally about justice. This family might be benign, although by certain standards unjust. If the contrast suggested by some discussions seems to be of justice and fairness versus unfairness (particularly in the context of gender and social and economic roles),[152] another contrast sees justice as opposed to mercy. The last thing we want from the family, Llewellyn suggested, is what we actually deserve.

No man will ever understand the age-old problem of "justice" as a going concern who does not keep in mind that one of the vital desires of human beings—which social institutions must provide for—is not even-handedness, but understanding treatment of individual idiocy or weakness. The boss is great because he helps out those in trouble. He helps you out first, and helps without regard to whether you have been at fault. If you have, he bawls you out—as is his function. It *does not stop this help.* You have no use for what reformers keep calling "justice," even-handed, and the law. You need the undeserved aid reformers will denounce as favoritism, influence, corruption. And this you get from marriage, as from the boss. . . . The family you are born into serves this need—it sprang from marriage; a marriage is its major part. And if or when that family ceases to perform the functions, a further marriage may provide escape and cure.[153]

Other views of the injustice of family life are less comforting. The family, Walzer tells us, is the home of favoritism.[154] What of grievances, for example, of older and younger children?

When does the next generation have some entitlement to knowledge of the secrets of the earlier generation? Such secrets may be based on events or decisions taken before children were born or when they were very young, when, in short, they were not players. The classic example in family law is the "you are an adopted child" secret. We do not enforce the telling of this secret. Once it is told, there is sometimes a basis for revealing the correlate secret (that you are the child whom X, a now identified person, gave up for adoption). This is often justified by medical necessity in the child. Other possible secrets relate to earlier marriages, lovers, and pregnancies. Is this sort of thing also to be analyzed as an issue of justice within the family? Is it likely that one approach (e.g., "full disclosure") will work for all families and all secrets?

Lionel Trilling suggest that the family is where we learn injustice, often before we learn justice. "In all of us," he writes, "the sense of injustice precedes the sense of justice by many years. It haunts our infancy, and even the most dearly loved of children may conceive themselves to be oppressed."[155] Dickens and Blake, he writes, saw the image of injustice in the unhappy child, and Dickens, like Burckhardt, "connects the fate of nations with the treatment of children." So too,

Benjamin Franklin (whose autobiography Kafka apparently gave to his father) saw powerful feelings for justice as an adult as rooted in childhood experience of injustice.[156]

A universal substantive standard encouraged or even imposed by the state is not, however, the only possibility. Another approach is pluralist in emphasis and assumes that there is a form of family authority that the state recognizes and to which it often defers, even when it does not approve. The family decision might be one in which the parents act against an official sense of what is in the best interest of the child, perhaps because the parents have put their own or some other interest ahead of the interests of the child. Parents might, for example, disinherit some children and favor others or favor men over women (adults or children), all in tension with public norm. The recognition of the family as a governing unit (which may be patriarchal rather than democratic, traditional rather than enlightened) implicates issues of multiculturalism and religious freedom. It is centrally about problems of self-definition since the issue will become an exploration of the limits on this tolerance of different family structures.

At the extremes, we know some answers. We do not allow parents to murder their children as an exercise of family authority. We do not allow parents to refuse life-saving medical treatment for minor children. Other issues are still coming into litigation.[157] A common line of analysis, consistent with traditional liberalism, would focus on the general limits of authority, whether state or family, over individuals.

Even the distinction between universal standards and a stress on pluralism does not end the matter. All pluralist orientations are not, of course, the same. Thus, the view of the family taken in the present chapter—that the family is less a hierarchical state than a varied and complex society—can be compared to that put forward some time ago by Erik Erikson in *Childhood and Society*. "The American family," Erikson wrote, "tends to guard the right of the individual member—parents included—not to be dominated." Each member of the family "reflects a variety of outside groups and their changing interests and needs." These needs are, for example, "the father's occupational group, the mother's club, the adolescent's clique, and the children's first friends." These groups are "interest groups" that "determine the individual's privileges in his family" and also "judge the family." Erikson continues in the role of the mother:

The sensitive receptor of changing styles in the community and the sensitive arbiter of their clash within the home is, of course, the mother; this necessity to function as arbiter is one more reason why the American mother instinctively hesitates to lavish on her children the kind of naive animal love which, in all its naiveté, can be so very selective and unjust; . . . . The mother remains, in a sense, above the parties and interests; it is as if she had to see to it that each party and interest develops as vigorously as possible—up to the point where she must put in a veto in the interest of another individual or of the family as a whole. . . .[158]

Issues, according to Erikson, are finally settled by majority. "The family is successful if the matter is settled to the point of 'majority concurrence,' even if this is reluctantly given; it is gradually undermined by frequent decisions in favor of one interest group, be it the parents or the babies." The contrast here is to families based on hierarchies. This "give-and-take cuts down to an extraordinary degree the division of the family into unequal partners who can claim privileges on the basis of age, strength, weakness, or goodness. Instead, the family becomes a training ground in the tolerance of different *interests*—not of different *beings.*"[159]

A presentation analogizing family interests to interest groups in the larger state tends to assume autonomy, rather than thinking about the conditions of its creation, which is a prime concern of Kafka's letter to his father. Erikson's analysis and the present inquiry relate the internal political processes of the family to the political processes of the outside culture. (The points made by way of comments on Erikson's approach generally track the criticisms made of interest group pluralism.) Erikson's assumptions are optimistic about the family and about the political culture. Domination of the group or individual by the whole is successfully vetoed. Consensus is in fact achieved. Conflict is in fact minimized. Preferences exist and are not formed, or if they are formed, we do not worry much about how. Autonomy for functional purposes is assumed. The system, as Erikson sees is, involves an "automatic prevention of autocracy and inequality," breeding people ready to compromise.

A different pluralist inquiry, illustrated by the earlier discussion of Kafka, begins with the typical pluralist method—disaggregation—but after that looks for the codes as experienced by individuals rather than interests advanced by them. This multiple-levels method may be less cheerful than an interest group approach. Some of this may reach deeper questions relating to individual views of human nature. For a particularly dark assessment, see Freud's *Civilization and its Discontents.*

> The bit of truth behind all this—one so eagerly denied—is that men are not gentle, friendly creatures wishing for love, who simply defend themselves if they are attacked, but that a powerful measure of desire for aggression has to be reckoned as part of their instinctual endowment. The result is that their neighbor is to them not only a possible helper or sexual object, but also a temptation to them to gratify their aggressiveness on him, to exploit his capacity for work without recompense, to use him sexually without his consent, to seize his possessions, to humiliate him, to cause him pain, to torture and to kill him.[160]

A pluralist approach might stress that certain interests in the family, as in the society, are seen but rejected; others are strategically managed and even created for some purpose or other. Pluralist theory can note that it is appropriate under the private code of the son to manipulate the mother or appropriate under the religious/social code of the mother to manipulate her children. It also suggests that state policies, whatever they turn out to be, should be undertaken with a view toward the complexity of the social field being regulated.

Certain approaches to issues of children suggest a very active role for the state. Thus, a court noted in 1840,

> There is no parental authority independent of the supreme power of the state. . . . The moment a child is born, it owes allegiance to the government of the country of its birth, and is entitled to the protection of that government. And such government is obligated by its duty of protection, to consult the welfare, comfort and interests of such child in regulating its custody during the period of its minority.[161]

Similarly, another court said in 1908,

> A child is primarily a ward of the state. The sovereign has the inherent power to legislate for its welfare, and to place it with

either parent at will, or take it from both parents and to place it elsewhere. . . . The rights of the parent in his child are just such rights as the law gives him; no more, no less. His duties toward his child are just such as the law places upon him.[162]

Such readings of the relation of government to the child are, of course, controversial, but the idea that the state has an important role in relation to the family is assumed. We are likely to agree initially that "abuse and injury are intolerable even when practiced behind family walls," though when we consider the matter against particular cases, we will of course see difficulties.[163]

But to what have we committed ourselves in terms of state behavior when we say this? We are not certain how to define abuse, whether it is measured by consequence or intent or whether the consequences must be physical or emotional, real or anticipated. Thus Elshtain notes, "We are in the midst of a socially constructed crisis concerning this society's treatment of its children. The way this issue, or any highly charged matter, gains public attention is a complex going together of political, economic, and cultural forces." But the point is that these questions invoke issues of social construction.[164]

Teitelbaum notes, in the context of legal discussion,

The line between permissible corporal punishment and child abuse is sometimes said to depend on whether the force used is "designed or known to create" a substantial risk of death, serious harm, or disfigurement. . . . There are, of course, relatively clear instances of abuse, but many instances are ambiguous in the sense that they could be considered either as appropriate or as inappropriate discipline.[165]

And, of course, there is a large debate over the limits on state intrusions generally. Ira Ellman outlines the issues this way:

The dilemma of child protective services lies in fashioning programs that actually help abused or neglected children, while not causing harm by unnecessary intrusions into a parent-child relationship. On one hand, there is a natural tendency to intervene not only when necessary to protect a child from danger or physical abuse, but at any time when it seems clear to the observer that the child's treatment is wrong. On the other hand, many fear that the intervention will turn out to be mistaken, as in the principal case, or unhelpful, because of limitations in agency resources or skills, even where the home environment is inadequate. Both commentators and practitioners naturally divide into two camps, the interventionists and the noninterventionists. Interventionists have greater faith than noninterventionists in the skills of the behavioral sciences to recognize and repair the damage caused by inadequate homes. Noninterventionists place more emphasis on the harm caused children, even neglected children, by taking them from their home or even by less drastic interventions which nonetheless weaken the autonomy and authority of their parents.[166]

One might stress education as a primary solution for children when abuse and neglect are not involved.[167]

With the growth of the modern state, we look to the state to solve problems of the family, as we look to the state to solve many others. State authority is assumed to be large. The state is joined by the professionals whose activity may or may not be viewed as "private." Stressing the role of the state, we associate issues in the family with family pathology or dysfunction rather than with the problem of the power of intermediate groups, and thus even where the role of the family as an authority is accepted, its role may be limited to training for citizenship.[168] This approach, much as one that sees the family only as an affective group, assumes and may intensify state power. It is true that this intensification of state power is associated with an emphasis on the rights of individuals, but this protection of the individual may be at the cost of the family as a whole.

Chapter Seven

Breaking the Butterfly

I have had a visit today from Mme. Ohyama, wife of the Japanese ambas-
sador. . . . I sketched the story of the libretto for her, and she liked it, espe-
cially as just such a story as Butterfly's is known to her as having happened
in real life.

Giacomo Puccini to Giulio Ricordi

Mme. Ohyama admires the libretto to Puccini's opera because it is parallel to
a true story. So, too, we are told that the Long account is "possibly based on a
real event."¹ Without reaching the question, "What allows us to decide that a
particular version of reality is true?" we might ask the apparently simpler
question, "Exactly what is Butterfly's story?"

The aria "Un Bel Di," probably the best-known melody in Puccini's
Madame Butterfly, *can be used to focus the issues. Three years after Pinker-*
ton's departure, Cho-Cho-San is waiting for him to return. Responding to
Suzuki's suggestion that Pinkerton is gone forever, Butterfly insists that he
will return: One fine day, they will notice a ship. She will wait. She sees a man
coming. Chi sara? *who is it?* che dira? *What will he say? Pinkerton will be*
the man, and he will say things that recall their life together. He will call her
by the names he once used. Cho-Cho-San sees his return as the beginning of a
happy future that will continue her account of their past. She waits specifically
for a return, and not, for example, a conversation that might complete unfin-
ished business, providing an opportunity for her to tell something or to learn
something. She indicates no doubt about the fact of the return or concern over
the nature of their encounter.

Butterfly is presented in the opera as tragic, but also as essentially quite
simple, even naive. She is unchanged, a girl-woman throughout, so that
Pinkerton's callousness becomes a kind of child abuse. Although Pinkerton has
married and Cho-Cho-San has had a child, time itself has little impact. This is
not the reunion after eight years of Anne Elliot with Captain Wentworth in
Persuasion. *It is even less the possible meeting between Ellen Olenska and*

Newland Archer after a thirty-year separation with which Edith Wharton teases us in The Age of Innocence.[2] *Pinkerton says that he will come back with the roses and the robins nesting. He speaks in the tradition of folk songs in which a man assures a woman that he will return within a year, in a period measured by the agricultural cycle. He offers himself as a "faithful Johnnie," who will return again "when the corn is gathered and the leaves are withered."*

But he does not return, and Butterfly waits.

Three years later, Pinkerton suggests in a letter to Sharpless that Butterfly may not remember him. To those who start with Butterfly's position in mind this is incomprehensible. We might declare it disingenuous, or a projection onto Pinkerton's onetime love of his present disinterest. But perhaps the idea that Butterfly might have forgotten him and moved on is consistent with Pinkerton's sense of who Butterfly actually is, perhaps a version of the wife of the samurai in Rashomon—*"angel outside, whore inside."[3] His whole story might be quite different from hers. Perhaps he did really love her once, under whatever definition of love we choose to invoke. Long's version includes the speculation that Pinkerton "might have intended to return to her." And if so, might he not again intend to return?[4] The Pinkerton of David Belasco says: "If Little Butterfly still remembers me, perhaps you can help her out and make her understand. Let her down gently. You don't believe it, but for two weeks after I sailed, I was dotty in love with her."[5]*

Or perhaps he did not think too much at all. We could see again the narrator of Madame Chrysanthemum, *stressing the consensual or even commercial aspects of the arrangement. Or something lighter, in the tradition of the casual seducer, the sailors of Purcell's* Dido and Aeneas *who visited the nymphs of Carthage and simply lied about the future. (They "silenced their mourning with vows of returning, never intending to visit them more.")*

Or, perhaps, he might say that he was simply trying not to give offense, trying to do what the other person expected, as was conventional in Japan.[6]

Finally, the details of the future as seen in "Un Bel Di" can tell us little about the truth of an actual meeting, if one were ever to take place. Because the narrative is about the future, we might say this is not, and could not be, a narrative based on truth. It could at most speak to the truth of Butterfly's subjective belief in a future in this form.

But if a narrative of the future has a problematic relation to truth, narratives of the past, we say, are different. But this may be a mistake, for various reasons. All narratives—whether cast as fiction or nonfiction, fantasies of the future, or accurate accounts of the past—have an uncertain relation to truth and may leave us unclear in all cases about what follows from the account. It

is in part for this reason that some have resisted the idea that individual nar-
rative could be useful for law, which must, it is urged, base its conclusions on
some sort of demonstrable or generalized truth.

Thus, finally, we reach the issue often described as the problem of
Rashomon, *a story about another young Japanese bride.*[7] *As lawyers view the*
problem, Rashomon *is about present conflicting accounts of past events. Of*
these, we tend to say, the law must choose one.[8] *One might say that the image*
of the butterfly as all chaotic life is fine for an observer. But when we deal with
Butterfly the human being, who may or may not be reliable as a witness to real-
ity, the law must pass on the question in the role of judge and participant.
Often the mandate for law seems to contain this corollary: If the accounts con-
flict, someone is lying and the law must decide who it is. Sometimes, however,
the Rashomon *problem is understood as a difference of perspective or inter-*
pretation. No one is lying, but everyone is self-interested and involved in offer-
ing a worthy presentation of self. This approach makes the law job, to use
Llewellyn's language, much harder.

This concluding chapter reviews the Rashomon *problem and discusses*
some issues current in scholarship on law and narrative. It reopens the general
issues of narrative and law reform treated in chapter 1.

While part of the debate over narrative in law has to do with the status of
narrative as scholarship, another part focuses directly on narrative and legal
processes. In this context the call for narrative is often associated with a call for
more or less thoroughgoing law reform. In both contexts, a subargument con-
cerns a question that looks something like this: Does narrative introduce a dis-
tortion into a legal and political process that is going along reasonably well?
Or is narrative a necessary corrective in a process that is to begin with prob-
lematic, because biased in favor of certain groups, ideals, and assumptions,
often in the name of the generally accepted wisdom?[9] *This chapter urges that*
law based on a dominant narrative is inevitably partial, distorted, and that
many narratives are necessary for law. Consideration of "law" and legal
behavior in this context should go beyond the conventional emphasis on judg-
ing in adversarial proceedings.

Legal Conversations

Because, as a general matter, we do not have direct access to the minds
of others,[10] we are forced to judge their motivations, their aspirations,
and their understandings of the world by their behavior and their
accounts of themselves. But the understanding that we will gain is

imperfect. Our own observation is limited. For a variety of reasons, others may not reveal themselves in a clear way. Even if they do, we must confront the conflict among the various stories "others" tell.

Some of the most contested aspects of the storytelling movement in law have related to the privileging of certain voices, particularly the claim that the minority or outsider voice[11] has a different and, because historically silenced, more important sound. This is not the claim here. Rather, this chapter considers competing narratives on the assumption that initially all narratives have a claim to be heard. This does not mean that they will all be accorded equal weight. It does mean that all voices should be acknowledged.[12]

Rashomon

The *Rashomon* problem raises the question of which of several conflicting accounts is true, or at least more true.

The term *"Rashomon* problem" or *"Rashomon* effect" has entered the legal literature, as it has entered the general vocabulary.[13] It refers to the 1950 film by the Japanese master Kurosawa, a drama in which we have three central characters and several minor ones. The central characters are the husband, the wife, and the bandit, the minor ones the woodcutter (who is also a witness), a priest, and an onlooker to the proceedings who seems to serve the function of commentator, in the fashion of a Greek chorus. The narratives of the encounter between the three principals are framed by a scene of a heavy rain from which several people have taken shelter in an ancient ruin, the Rashomon gate.[14] Within this frame, they describe the different narratives that have been presented apparently in a legal setting, the prison inquiry.

The film starts the narrative exposition with the bandit's story. He describes going through the woods, seeing a beautiful woman, desiring her, and deciding to rape her without deciding to kill the husband. When he does kill the husband, he does so because the woman, in the course of the rape, has become resigned at least and possibly even willing, to the point that the sexual act might be viewed as consensual. In the bandit's account, the woman has asked him to kill her husband.

The wife says that after the rape—she begins her story after the event in which the bandit indicates her change of mind—she was so completely distraught (in part because of her husband's coldness toward to her) that she simply fainted. Her narrative reports nothing about the murder itself, but the conclusion that she killed her husband is suggested by the visual images of the position of the parties, she above her husband, dagger pointed down. (In the short story she says that she killed him.)

The husband, who is dead, speaks through a medium. His version of the story is that he was so completely destroyed by the sight of the rape of his wife that he could only weep and, in the end, kill himself.

The woodcutter has two versions of his story. The first is about finding things: a woman's hat, some rope, and finally the body. Later he says that he, indeed, did see the whole episode and that the bandit killed the husband. His version has a furious wife attacking both of the men for their weakness. He testifies both to the fight and the murder. The woodcutter is shown to be not simply a witness but also a participant in the suggestion that he has stolen the critical weapon that is either a dagger or a sword.

Rashomon is frequently described as a film about four different points of view.[15] This description suggests that what we are seeing is the actual subjective point of view of each person speaking, unmediated by any technique or construction. This is not, however, what the film actually suggests. The commentator, who regularly uses the word "story," makes plain throughout his many lines that the presentation of self that is involved makes the narrative much more than an expression of an actual psychological point of view. It is closer to a presentation for the sake of persuasion of a viewer than an exposition for the expression of a viewpoint held to be subjectively true.

The questions raised by *Rashomon* are, of course, not new. Different people will relate the questions to the work of different authors. Sometimes these works claim to be true. Thus, De Laclos is "editor" of a collection of letters presented as a real correspondence in *Dangerous Liaisons*. It is the pretense of reality, a tradition that is reflected still, for example, in the movie *Fargo*, which Ethan Coen describes as "a story which pretends to be true."[16] *Rashomon* does not, in this sense, pretend to be true.

In addition to multiple perspectives, *Rashomon* raises the issue of misunderstanding. We do not understand the communications of others even when they believe that they are communicating clearly. In its opening speeches, we hear of the bandit falling off his horse. Someone says, "Well, you fell off your horse," and the bandit replies by saying in effect, "Look at what you know. I was sick and I had to lie down, and so I got off my horse." At the end, when a baby has been found and the woodcutter, who has already been revealed to be a thief, grabs it, the priest says, "What would you steal from this child absolutely everything he has?" The thief replies, in effect, you have misunderstood me. I have six children of my own. I was prepared to take him home and raise him because we won't notice the addition of one other.

In addition to these issues, we have issues relating to issues of social construction. Even if we describe a reality we believe to be true, is it? Is the wife in *Rashomon* a "true" picture of any Japanese woman at any time? Did Puccini draw his Asian "little girls" because Asian women were like that? Because he had a personal interest in certain types? Because he adhered to a cultural stereotype of Asian women held by Westerners? Do we avoid this problem if we go to an authentic Japanese voice in the filmmaker, Kurosawa? Will we find there a true description of Japanese women? Or will we find ourselves in the world of Japanese stereotypes of women? And what shall we do with the issues of cross-cultural influence suggested by the fact that the novelist, Akutagawa, was influenced by Western writers?[17] Or that the music in *Rashomon* is an easily recognizable reworking of Ravel's *Bolero*?[18]

We never do find out what "really" happened in the grove.

What does this mean for our approach to law's understanding's of social facts?[19]

Let us look briefly at the family. This book has used a sense of family focused on the couple, and the children of the couple. It is this family, what is called the natural family, that underlies the Court's opinion in a recent case on a presumption of legitimacy.[20] A broader view of history, Aviam Soifer suggests, would yield the point that there are many kinds of family in America. A still broader view might suggest that it is not merely that there are many kinds of family but also that the immediate relations between parents and children—the natural biological family—are not as quite as solid and unconstructed as the discussion of the biological family typically suggests. It is not necessary to go to science fiction or the inquiries of anthropologists—looking perhaps for tribes with two sexes but five genders, or groups that locate themselves in families in time (ancestor connections, descendent connections) rather than in space—to find the suggestion that the nuclear family itself is not to be taken as given. If you don't have a good father, Nietzsche wrote, acquire another one.[21] Sterne offered a legal debate over the relationship, if any, between mother and child.[22] "It has not only been a question, Captain Shandy, amongst the best lawyers and civilians in this land . . . '[w]hether the mother be of kin to her child,'— but after much dispassionate enquiry and activation of the arguments on all sides—it has been adjudged for the negative—namely, 'That the mother is not of kin to her child.'"[23] And fifteenth- and sixteenth-century paintings show the family of Jesus as a matriarchal line from the grandmother to her daughters as mothers and their children.[24]

The naturalness, the givenness of the grouping, then, may always be in question. And there is nothing necessarily immutable about it. Lawrence Friedman has argued that in this culture more and more appears to be voluntary.[25] Where the situation is not voluntarily chosen initially, we understand the parent-child relation as something that we can avoid or escape. In the same way that husbands and wives can divorce, children can be emancipated, and can be adopted, even as adults.

Certainly some affiliations are involuntary from the point of view of some particular group. And perhaps not merely involuntary to begin with, but irrevocable. But from another point of view—that, quite possibly, of the state—even these affiliations are understood as voluntary to a degree. We see religious affiliation in terms of volition. Gender identification is subject to change.[26] Even the natural biological fact— for example, skin color—has a constructed social meaning. All the red-haired, left-handed, green-eyed people of the world could be natural groups, stigmatized or worse, yet in this culture are not. In a sense, groups are always constructed. Out of the countless relations into which a human being is born, these particular relations are identified by some culture, larger or smaller, as important.

If everything is constructed, courts, like the rest of us, cannot look "at" society.[27] Courts, like the rest of us, are always in effect looking through society and culture at something (or nothing). And the problem judges have in dealing with the real truth of the world and the image of that world in law is rather similar to the problem judges have in dealing with the idea of law in general. It is really quite like the question whether judges discover or make law. Judges may be more or less sympathetic to litigants, more or less appreciative of historical materials. They also may be more or less engaged in prudential calculations involved in the recent emphasis on the socially conventional as natural rather than as constructed. Another way to say this is that when we start using the language of social construction, we might recall that the role of the judge is also a social construction, one that at times may impose its own conditions.[28]

Consideration of the outer reaches of social construction takes us past reformist and even utopian thinking into science fiction and meta-physics, speculative writing that considers whether reality involves eternal recurrence, or whether our memories have been implanted by a robotics engineer, or whether time in fact runs in a direction opposite to that of our ordinary understanding.[29] But these have nothing much to do with law, except in the sense that they begin to touch the issues that, under ideas of religious liberty, are generally thought to be beyond law's reach.[30]

The largest issues raised here concerning the ultimate nature of reality are not questions unique to law. But there is something worth noting in law's approach to these questions. We can frame the question by the comment quoted in a casebook on evidence: "The most conspic-uous difference between the law's problems in determining historical facts and those of other disciplines lies in the procedure of decision." The Hart and McNaughton extract notes that other disciplines rely pri-marily on the method of inquiry, reflection, and report by trained investigators. In other disciplines the final conclusions as to key facts are drawn by experts, and the conclusions may be changed if they are found later—after further inquiry and reflection—to be wrong." By contrast, "law depends in most formal proceedings upon presentation by the disputants in public hearing before an impartial tribunal, in modern times a tribunal previously uninformed about the matters in dispute. And findings of fact by the tribunal are usually final so far as the law is concerned."[31]

But the finality of "the law" here refers, it seems, to the law of a case, the particular dispute. Quite evidently, the legal description of the world does change.

Law and Narrative

Sarat and Kearns explain that in Robert Cover's work on law and vio-lence all "legal interpretive acts signal and occasion the imposition of violence upon others: A judge articulates her understanding of a text, and as a result, somebody loses his freedom, his property, his children, even his life."[32] The Sarat-Kearns analysis notes that there are two senses in which Cover thinks of judges as people of violence. The first involves the force that is used by judges as officials: "Judges are people of violence because they are able to bring physical force to bear in making their interpretive acts work in the world."[33] But in a second sense judges become people of violence "when they repress and reduce the rich normativity of the social world."[34] This was the sense in which Cover thinks that law is jurispathic. "Confronting the luxuriant growth of a hundred legal traditions, they assert that this one is law and destroy or try to destroy all the rest."[35] Cover believed that "too often, too routinely" judges defer to that violence; too often, too routinely, judges aggressively assert the supremacy of state law. In either posture, Cover believed that jurispathic state law is needlessly destructive of the nomos it must regulate.[36]

Law's violence may involve the selection of a single narrative support from the many narratives available. Consider the levels of narrative available with reference to the history of the Plymouth Brethren, a group that came into litigation in a child custody dispute. The autobiography of the English literary figure Edmund Gosse can be used to illustrate the point that the rigidity of sectarian religious practice can damage children.[37] We also have Garrison Keillor's account of his childhood within the Brethren and Paul Boyer's historical discussion of the Brethren in the context of other apocalyptic sects.[38] Keillor suggests that he was eager to be rid of the restrictions of the Brethren. His family's dinner conversation was not much about the distant future, he writes, because of the imminence of the Second Coming.[39] When we put the narratives in a spectrum, won't we become less certain about the damage done by the affiliation with the religious group? Gosse's book includes an account of the development of a "dual" nature and descriptions of the response of the child to the overwhelming demands of the father; such a response could arise in many contexts besides Christian fundamentalism. A good part of Keillor's indictment, for example bad food and learned shame about one's body, marks the upbringing of many children.[40]

"Law," however, tends to choose one of narrative and suppress the others. Law will speak as though there is a single thing meant by *fundamentalism, family, marriage*. In the end, law will break the butterfly on a wheel, imposing a conventional understanding. The force may be as the line from Pope suggests, excessive.[41] But the creation of order in society presumably requires a certain amount of force. The butterfly must be described and given form. And every part of this is a limitation.

A discussion of this problem with reference to the Amish in *Wisconsin v Yoder* suggests a similar point. In *Yoder*, the Supreme Court granted the Amish an exemption from the compulsory education law to the extent of two years of high school. The exemption was required, the Court said, by the free exercise clause of the First Amendment. The majority opinion, one scholar concluded, was based on the idea that "The Amish could do no wrong and the state could do no right." It was rooted in judicial assumptions about reality, here the reality of the lifestyle of the Amish.[42] The descriptions of reality that are the necessary foundation of speech, thought, and of the legal enterprise is the breaking of a butterfly on a wheel, a version here of the law's violence. *Yoder* found the Amish lifestyle sympathetic. Less favorable descriptions were available, which might have reinforced arguments for the state.

It is this issue that seems often to be at stake in the debate over narrative. Order is required. But how much? And at what price? One strategy used to reduce the intensity of this question rests on ideas of universal reason. A community shares a vision of the good life, generalizable values and experiences. The law, it is said, must rest on the general state. The use of this idea in *Bradwell v Illinois* shows both the strength of the point and its tendency to reflect a particular view of the general. That view, as the concurrence in *Bradwell* illustrates, can change. It changes under the impact of new stories. A single narrative will not provide the base of understanding and information that the legal enterprise in its various forms requires. The only way to provide that base is to provide more narratives.

Finally, the problem of generalizability that has concerned commentators[43] omits the way in which the argument on the importance of narrative is close to the argument on transformative power of art. The point is not that the narrative represents a general claim, representative of the claim of an existing group. Rather, the point is that a narrative can make visible a previously unrecognized claim. "Things are because we see them," Oscar Wilde wrote. "What we see and how we see it depends on the Arts that have influenced us." In fact, "life imitates art far more than art imitates life."[44] Art is not, on this view, apolitical or decorative; it is not "merely art" (see chap. 1). As Jane Smiley argues, narrative changes our sense of what is true.[45] Others seem to say something similar by thinking in terms of a total and radical transformation of the reader.[46]

A related set of ideas would invoke an enhanced vision or experience. It is not necessarily about blindness to sight, or nothing to everything, and not necessarily the entry into a new world. Rather, it is the kind of radical enhancement that we can hear, for example, when we first hear entirely familiar music through a very good sound system or when a well-known orchestral work is heard for the first time in a performance with a vocal line and is thus connected to literature of the song cycle. The objects of the experience were familiar to begin with, and they are both the same and changed.

The Conventional Wisdom: A Long Conversation

Just as speculations about ultimate reality are not the basis of most utopian writing—utopian blueprints are in a sense practical—they are also not, finally, the basis of legal writing. The law behaves on the basis of common sense, as though we sit on a solid chair, as if time runs forward, and as if the past is to a significant degree knowable, whether or not usable. Law is about the daily understanding of things. It operates at the level at which people do or do not sleep under bridges and steal bread. Simmel, comparing law and fashion, said that in effect they were both based on the externals of life, those parts turned to society.[47] Fashion was a framework, he said, within which we seek our inner lives. So too is law.

Much of the conversation between law and literature enters the relationship between law and storytelling in the same way that Karl Llewellyn dealt with the problem of truth in the conventional judicial statement of facts, with a reference to the constraints imposed by the rules of evidence. But it is clear in Llewellyn's account that evidentiary rules are not entirely founded on the search for truth.

It is also clear that when a case offers an account of facts, a reader must sit loosely with that account. Llewellyn's statement of the problem remains exemplary: "What is the relation of this statement of 'the facts' to the brute raw events which happened long before?' he asked. "What is left in men's minds as to those raw events has been canvassed, more or less thoroughly, more or less skillfully, by two lawyers."

But canvassed through the screen of what they considered legally relevant, and of what each considered legally relevant to win his case. It has then been screened again in the trial court through the rules about what evidence can be admitted. The jury has then reached its conclusion, which—for purposes of the dispute—determines contested matters for one side. The two lawyers have again sifted—this time solely from the record of the trial—what seemed to bear on points upon appeal. Finally, with a decision already made, the judge has sifted through these "facts" again, and picked a few which he puts forward as essential—and whose legal bearing he then proceeds to expound. It should be obvious that we may now be miles away from life. Again, we may not. By some miracle it may be there is no distortion. Or by some other each successive distortion may have nearly canceled out the last. But it is current doctrine that the age of miracles is past.[48]

It has been suggested that the idea that a judicial or adversarial proceeding is useful in all contexts "overestimates the power and efficacy of the adversary process as a means of finding a truth—even current, provisional, working, technical truth—that the 'loser' will concede to be the truth."[49]

It remains the case that the general American academic approach to legal questions concentrates on litigation as the essence of what state law is about. The search for truth is thought to be centrally important because the adversarial model, the criminal trial (based on an allegation of criminal activity) or the civil trial (based on an allegation of a less significant wrongful act) both locate their source in behavior in the past, which is assumed to be fixed, if not in fact perfectly knowable.[50]

But law means more than trials and judging. If we focus on those parts of law directed to the future, toward the making of policy through legislation and the official shaping of collective and institutional life, we see a different relationship between law and narrative. To begin with, we deal here not with contested facts in litigation but with what are sometimes called legislative constitutional facts.[51] They are simply a part of the judge's understanding of reality. Whether the narrative is offered to a legislative committee or a wider public audience, we operate free of evidentiary rules. Narrative is understood in this context as based on an attempt to persuade rather than an attempt to report objective truth. The "truth" here would involve both the truth of the narrative offered and the "truth" meaning probability of the projection into the future, the impact of the policy or the legislative change. By contrast, for example, to the ideas that the Supreme Court uses in deciding or not to take a case, in the legislative context, the individual speaker may or may not be "representative" of anything beyond himself or herself—and may or may not claim to be.

The narrative involved in the legislative process or the policy process seems not so concerned with the issue of filtering out those accounts that are not true as it is with accommodating accounts that are both irreconcilable and deeply held. If the question is how we can incorporate the various accounts of *Rashomon*, the answer might be, through *Rashomon*, which holds them all. *Rashomon, the Mystery*, would have to attempt a different kind of resolution, closer to the resolution of a trial,[52] perhaps declaring some accounts true, some false, some to be passed over in silence. As to trials, we have fairly elaborate processes to deal with issues of competing narratives, although contested areas remain. The discussion over whether victims' impact statements distort the criminal process is one example. Perhaps the approach to multiplicity available to a legal academic or a legislator is less available to a judge or a policeman. But it is hard to think that what Piaget saw as the objections of others, internalized in reflection, would not be useful for all of these.

As to lawmaking more generally, and particularly whether an individual narrative should carry weight in determining our understanding of the facts, we have been in doubt. The idea that narrative gives voice to the voiceless is consistent with ideas of participatory democracy and therefore is seen as good. But when what may be an idiosyncratic view is translated into a "majority" opinion, the process is problematic, as is the idea that "victim" narratives have more value than other narratives. (If this is true, we will tend to compete for victim status.) This is particularly true if the individual or minority voice is seen to be unconcerned with truth altogether.[53] Although it is common to say that law is concerned with many values, truth just one among them, there may remain a level at which law is fundamentally concerned with truth. Thus, William Twining has noted that our deepest sense of the injustice of certain legal results rests in the idea that, for example, the convicted criminal was innocent in fact.[54]

To the extent that the use of narrative is understood as an attack on some idea of universal reason—since the particularity of the narrative is subversive of the universal generalized statement—it is parallel to an attack emanating from a quite different quarter, which attacked universal reason in the name of faith or higher law. In both instances, there is the claim that something significant has been omitted from the generalized account, and in fact in both cases these might be described as the experience of the individual of reality itself.

But do we have to say that law is based on universal reason? Isn't it as likely, and more manageable, to say that law is based on the conventional wisdom? The great advantage of doing this is that conventional wisdom changes, sometimes quite rapidly. In American life, for example, an approach that sees law as the guardian of morality in family life and that judges questions in terms of the moral categories "good" and "bad" yields in a relatively brief period of time to a view of law that sees the legal system as facilitative of individual choices.[55] It is the conventional wisdom that changes the word *bastard* to *natural child* to *love child* and finally to *child of a single parent,* just as the conventional wisdom that shifts (or will shift) the meaning of *single parent* from "immoral woman living on state benefits" to "economically independent person, male or female, choosing to raise a child alone." Law will also influence the conventional wisdom, but as noted in the earlier chapters, the degree to which this is true not known and probably overstated by lawyers.

The insistence on reason as an argument against narrative is an argument for finality and closure in an area in which results must be provisional at many levels.[56] It is the demand for coherence in a context in which finally coherence cannot obtain and may not even be relevant.

In the end, of course, law will reach a kind of closure. At least provisionally it will decide if something seems more likely to be true than not. (In another sense the discussion will go on long after that closure so that one always will be reopening the decisions of law in particular cases as to particular policies.) The point of this inquiry has been to present, as to ideas and motivations conventionally treated as quite simple, understandable, and agreed upon, the underlying complexities revealed through literatures that are not legal. These can be social scientific or humanistic. They are, in many cases, literatures focused on particularity. Richard Rorty has noted that our society "recognizes that moral progress has, in recent centuries, owed more to the specialists in particularity—historians, novelists, ethnographers, and muckraking journalists, for example—than to such specialists in universality as theologians and philosophers."[57] Since law is both particular and general because lawyers are both specialists and generalists,[58] lawyers can see themselves on both sides of this dichotomy. But the emphasis on narrative falls on the side of particularity.

In a recent treatment of this issue, Martha Minow quotes Lon Fuller: "The trouble with the law does not lie in its use of concepts, not even in its use of 'lump concepts.' The difficulty lies in part in the fact that we have sometimes put the 'lumps' in the wrong places, and in part in the fact that we have often forgotten that the 'lumps' are the creations of our minds." She comments, "Rather than relying on old 'lump concepts,' without thinking about them, those who use legal arguments should explore the relationships between concepts and think up analogies that break out of ill-fitting conceptual schemes. By seeing something in a new light, seeing its similarity to something else once thought quite different, we are able to attribute different meanings and consequences to what we see."[59]

The problem is, exactly, the relationship between the "generalization" and the "imperative."[60] Generalization is finally necessary for daily life. Generalization and even stereotyping allow us to function.[61] But when the generalization, detached from the constant sense of its approximate nature, becomes normative, we have taken a step in the direction of an unnecessary suppression of possibility. Perhaps certain words should be used only in quotation marks, to remind us that these are words and not realities.[62] In our context, we could say "families," or "marriage" as a way of communicating the varieties of experience captured in these names.

Like the standard acknowledgment that law is effective at the margin, the admission that generalizations are imperfect is made and then immediately forgotten, in a discussion built typically on professionally based assumptions of law's central and overriding importance (a point made in chapter 6). A nonprofessional position might be quite different. Flaubert, for example, wrote that a conventional understanding of law is "nobody knows what [the law] is."[63] Even the major categories of law, public and private, should not be taken as a two-part division of the world. Public and private together do not constitute everything. As Simmel understood, there is also an "inner."

This final chapter has reviewed some relationships between law and literature, concluding with a discussion of the uses of narrative for law. The most difficult approach to the law/literature question is the one ordinarily described as "storytelling," and it is here that this book makes its primary argument to the effect that first, all stories must be told, all voices heard and acknowledged. Official law will, inevitably, use its violence in relation to some of those voices, in the interest of a stable social order. The issue is not whether this will happen, but whether we can keep it from happening too much and with inadequate justification.

Conclusion

Outlining various possible relationships between law and literature, we make a mistake if we treat the two prime categories as clear and only the connectives as problematic. When we speak of law as literature, law in literature, literature as a subject of law and legal regulation, and so on, we should remember that these formulations assume a certainty in the basic terms that is far from obvious. Law is not merely an autonomous system of state-sponsored rules. On certain views, "private" groups can be considered among the sources of law. So, too literature, understood at the moment as referring largely to high culture, poetry, fiction, and drama, was once defined differently and much more broadly. Moreover, the connection between law and literature, as has recently been demonstrated, was once much closer.[1]

Law and *literature*—the more general term *narrative* has often been used in this book—have been used here both to explore certain contemporary issues in family law and to raise more general issues about law and society. The presentation has sought to avoid a central danger, the adoption of a partial truth,[2] that which is "conventional" or "dominant," as the whole. An idea of truth has been discussed that is not the precisely defined factual truth so often used in law. We can see that other sense of truth in a maxim of Goethe's—"It is not always needful for truth to take a definite shape; it is enough if it hovers about us like a spirit and produces harmony; if it is wafted through the air like the sound of a bell, grave and kindly."[3] This approach to truth, however, may not facilitate the resolution of disputes, which it is precisely one of the law's jobs to conclude. Legal officials cannot rest at listening to bells or observing, from an Olympian distance, dialectical social or legal behavior. At the same time, legal officials, even operating within role constraints, can choose to see more or less, and to hear more or less. They should, I think, choose to hear more, to be more open to analogy and to descriptive and narrative material, particularly in the many legal contexts in which the resolution of disputes does not occur in the course of adversarial proceedings. "Hearing" a story might not involve believing it or accepting its truth. It would typically involve an acknowledgment of it, a recognition of its existence, as a precondition of political dialogue.

Law, at its most functional, can be seen as akin to plumbing. But law is its own endeavor, a technical field, perhaps a discipline, which has often been seen to require a particularly wide vision. Thus, Learned Hand, among others, argued for a humanistic understanding of law and law training, as human beings search for what we see as acceptable compromises and solutions. "An education which includes the 'humanities' is essential to political wisdom," Hand wrote, adding, "[by] 'humanities' I especially mean history; but close beside history and of almost, if not quite, equal importance are letters, poetry, philosophy, the plastic arts, and music."[4]

I do not know why Hand included music, but I would suggest the possible relevance of Cioran's comment: "When we have no further desire to show ourselves, we take refuge in music, that Providence of the abulic."[5] *Abulia*, a loss of willpower, is not a word we necessarily associate with those directly concerned with the applications of power. But perhaps the idea has some relevance to law, at least to the extent that a kind of deliberate abulia, based on self-restraint, intellectual modesty, and prudence[6] would reduce law's violence.

In the end, the argument offered here rests on a view first of the limits of law and second of the relation between law and other humanistic undertakings. It adopts Learned Hand's explanation of the need for the humanities in law. This explanation is focused not on a problem with rules of law, but on what is ordinarily seen as the human condition. "Most of the issues that mankind sets out to settle, it never does settle," Hand remarks. "They are not solved, because, as I have just tried to say, they are incapable of solution properly speaking, being concerned with incommensurables." Even if that was not always true, he continues, the opposing parties seldom agreed on a solution; in fact the dispute may be fought again. When the dispute disappears, "it is replaced by some compromise that, although not wholly acceptable to either side, offers a tolerable substitute for victory."[7] The one who would find the substitute, Hand concludes, "needs an endowment as rich as possible in experience," experience that creates generosity in the heart and insight in the mind.

Hand's argument can be supplemented by the words of an ancient text: "Ben Zoma said, 'Who is Wise? The one who learns from everyone, as it is said "From all who would teach me, have I gained understanding."'"[8]

Notes

Introduction

1. See James Hall, *Dictionary of Subjects and Symbols in Art*, rev. ed. (New York: Harper and Row, 1979), 54.

2. Primo Levi, *Other People's Trades*, trans. Raymond Rosenthal (New York: Summit, 1989), 18. Woody Allen and Marshall Brickman in *Sleeper* conceived the transformation in the other direction, when the poet of the future, Luna, sees the butterfly turning into a caterpillar by and by.

3. Juan Eduardo Cirlot, *A Dictionary of Symbols*, 2d ed. (New York: Barnes and Noble, 1995), 35.

4. J. C. Cooper, *An Illustrated Encyclopedia of Traditional Symbols* (London: Thames and Hudson, 1978), 27.

5. The association of law and violence in current discussion—law's violence against both individuals and competing normative orders—results in part from Robert Cover's work. See "Nomos and Narrative," *Harvard Law Review* 97 (1983): 4. See also Austin Sarat and Thomas R. Kearns, eds., *Law's Violence* (Ann Arbor: University of Michigan Press, 1993).

6. Cicero, *De Republica*, trans. Clinton Walker Keyes (Cambridge: Harvard University Press, 1928), 317 (I.18).

7. Alexander Pope, *Imitations of Horace*, in *Complete Poetical Works*, ed. Herbert Davis (New York: Oxford University Press, 1966), 336.

8. Dickens's Mr. Skimpole speaks "gaily, innocently, and confidingly": "Here you see me utterly incapable of helping myself, and entirely in your hands! I only ask to be free. The butterflies are free. Mankind will surely not deny to Harold Skimpole what it concedes to the butterflies!" Charles Dickens, *Bleak House*, ed. Stephen Gill (Oxford: Oxford University Press, 1996), 90. On butterflies among the Japanese (and the naming of dancing girls for butterflies), ("Cho" in Japanese), see Lafcadio Hearn, *Kwaidan: Stories and Studies of Strange Things* (Boston: Houghton Mifflin, 1904).

9. Such as James Fitzjames Stephen's terrible image of an eyelash being pulled out with tongs, conveying the harm done when laws or public opinion try to regulate, for example, the internal affairs of the family or relations of love or friendship. See *Liberty, Equality, Fraternity* (London: Cambridge University Press, 1967), 162.

10. The emphasis is on the libretto. See Paul Robinson, "A Deconstructive

Postscript: Reading Libretti and Misreading Opera," in *Reading Opera*, ed. Arthur Groos and Roger Parker (Princeton: Princeton University Press, 1988), 328, noting that "an opera cannot be read from its libretto." Since the "meaning of opera is at bottom musical" and opera's "essential argument is posed in musical language," an interpretation "derived exclusively, or even primarily, from the libretto is likely to result in a misreading." There is of course no attempt here to discuss the music of Puccini or anyone else.

11. John Luther Long, "Madame Butterfly," *Century Magazine*, January 1898, 374–92.

12. Belasco's *Madame Butterfly* is described as "founded on John Luther Long's Story." David Belasco, *Six Plays* (Boston: Little, Brown, 1928). There is no suggestion of coauthorship in that text. The 1907 edition of Puccini's *Madame Butterfly* (Dover rpt., 1990) says that it has a "Libretto by Luigi Illice and Giuseppe Giacosa based on the story by John Luther Long and the play by David Belasco." This is the Library of Congress cataloging data. There is also a reference to a libretto based on the story by Long and "the play by Long and David Belasco" on the page containing the list of characters. This attribution seems not to have been generally accepted. It is not used here. Puccini was also aware of *The Mikado* (George Marek, *Puccini: A Biography* [New York: Simon and Schuster, 1951], 213).

13. David Hwang, *M. Butterfly* (New York: Penguin, 1989). On issues of representation, see Martha Minow, "From Class Actions to 'Miss Saigon,': The Concept of Representative Law," in *Representing Women: Law, Literature, and Feminism*, ed. Susan Sage Heinzelman and Zipporah Batshaw Wiseman (Durham: Duke University Press, 1994), 8.

14. Pierre Loti, *Madame Chrysanthemum*, trans. Laura Ensor (London: KPI, 1985).

15. Carl Dawson sees the Long story and its heirs as a challenge to and "tacit criticism" of the Loti version. See *Lafcadio Hearn and the Vision of Japan* (Baltimore: John Hopkins University Press, 1992), 40. Henry James's introduction makes plain that Loti's own impressions may not be accurate in the ordinary sense. "I have been assured," James writes, "that *Madame Chrysanthemum* is as preposterous, as benighted a picture of Japan as if a stranger, disembarking at Liverpool, had confined his acquaintance with England to a few weeks spent in disreputable female society in a vulgar suburb of that city." Pierre Loti, *Impressions*, with an introduction by Henry James (Westminster: Archibald Constable, 1898), 16.

16. J. R. R. Tolkien, *Poems and Stories* (Boston: Houghton Mifflin, 1994), 29.

17. Mary Russell Mitford, quoting her mother, who was describing Jane Austen (*Life and Letters of Mary Russell Mitford*, vol. 1, ed. A. G. K. L'Estrange [New York: Harper and Bros., 1870], 235). Austen's nephew, J. E. Austen-Leigh, disputed this account on several grounds, among them that Austen would have been a child at the time she was purported to have displayed the described behavior. See Austen-Leigh's memoir, appended to Jane Austen, *Persuasion* (New York: Penguin, 1985), 390–91.

18. Chris Baldick, *Concise Oxford Dictionary of Literary Terms* (New York: Oxford University Press, 1990), 145.

19. See Robert Birmingham, "Remarks," *Connecticut Law Review* (1997), 827, 837ff.

20. Cover, "Nomos and Narrative," 53.

21. George Steiner, *Real Presences* (Chicago: University of Chicago Press, 1989), 137.

22. Eugen Ehrlich, *Fundamental Principles of the Sociology of Law*, trans. Walter L. Moll (Cambridge: Harvard University Press), 1936.

Chapter One

1. Long never visited Japan and apparently received most of his information about it from his sister, the widow of a missionary. See his obituary, *New York Times*, November 1, 1927, p. 27, col. 3.

For consideration of another Puccini work, see J. M. Balkan, "Turandot's Victory," *Yale Journal of Law and the Humanities* (summer 1990), 299.

2. Law, of course, has many objectives, only one of which is truth. For an overview of law's truth, see William R. Bishin and Christopher D. Stone, *Law, Language, and Ethics: An Introduction to Law and Legal Method* (Mineola, N.Y.: Foundation Press, 1972), chap. 6.

3. Robert Wilson, *Ripley Bogle* (London: Deutsch, 1989), 120. Legal versions of "telling one's story" are often thin and linear, for example, telling where one was on the night of the tenth.

4. Stanley Appelbaum, *Puccini's Madame Butterfly: Libretto* (New York: Dover, 1983), vii.

5. Jewish Publication Society, *The Writings*, new translation of the Book of Esther (Tel Aviv: Maariv Book Guild and American-Israel Publishing, 1974), 405–6.

6. Lewis B. Paton comments, "There is no noble character in the book" (*A Critical and Exegetical Commentary on the Book of Esther* [Edinburgh: T. and T. Clark, 1908], 96). Emil Fackenheim refers to a "curious Midrash" that says that the only festival to be celebrated in the world to come will be Purim, which has at its center the Book of Esther (*What Is Judaism?* [New York: Summit Books, 1987], 274).

7. Paton, *Critical and Exegetical Commentary*, 150.

8. Elias J. Bickerman, tracing the Candaulus theme, comments, "According to the rabbis, Vashti told the king '[I]f I come before the lords of the kingdom they will kill you and marry me.'" *Four Strange Books of the Bible: Jonah, Daniel, Koheleth, Esther* (New York: Schocken, 1967), 185.

9. Paton, *Critical and Exegetical Commentary*, 150.

10. Ibid. A later commentator suggests that only courtesans attended the banquets when the men were drinking: "By coming to the King's party, Vashti would lose face, she would degrade herself to the position of a concubine" (Bickerman, *Four Strange Books*, 186). It is an explanation based on feminist dignity, but it does not reinforce ideas of female solidarity.

11. Elizabeth Cady Stanton, *The Original Feminist Attack on the Bible (The Woman's Bible)* (New York: Arno Press, 1874). Hereinafter cited as *Woman's*

Bible. On Stanton and the Bible, especially Exodus, see Carolyn C. Jones, "Feminist Views of Exodus: Narrative of Liberation or Oppression?" *Utah Law Review* 297 (Spring 1986).

12. *Elizabeth Cady Stanton, Susan B. Anthony, Correspondence, Writings, Speeches,* ed. Ellen Carol DuBois (New York: Schocken, 1981), 233.

13. In the Jewish tradition, drunkenness is associated with Purim in the sense that one is supposed to be intoxicated. See Fackenheim, *What Is Judaism?*

14. *Woman's Bible,* 85. See also the address by Anna Shaw to the Woman's National Council, February 25, 1891, *Woman's Journal,* March 7, 1891, 1–2.

15. *Woman's Bible,* 86, slightly misquoting Tennyson's *The Princess* (probably best remembered today through Gilbert and Sullivan's parody, *Princess Ida*).

16. *Woman's Bible.* The stress on dignity and modesty can result in a reading in which Vashti's disobedience exemplifies the *true* duties of a Christian wife: "A wife need not and may not obey her husband in what opposes God's laws and the laws of feminine honor and decency. All praise to the heroic Vashti for her decent disobedience" (Herbert Lockyer, *All the Women of the Bible: The Life and Times of All the Women of the Bible* [Grand Rapids: Zondervan Publishing House, 1977], 166). For a similar position, see Abraham Kuyper, *Women of the Old Testament,* trans. Henry Zylstra (Grand Rapids: Zondervan Publishing House, 1961). Note also the suggestion that Vashti's arrogance had something to do with her royal lineage, in that she is a granddaughter of Nebuchadnezzar, "who scoffed at kings and unto whom princes were a derision" (Louis Ginzberg, *The Legends of the Jews* [Philadelphia: Jewish Publication Society of America, 1947], 375).

It is clear that the Vashti story is, as the *Interpreter's Bible* indicates, a requirement of the plot of the Book of Esther. The story requires that Vashti make room for Esther, cousin and adopted daughter of Mordecai. Esther, concealing the fact that she is a Jew, is chosen by Ahasuerus as his queen. Esther is later able to defeat the courtier Haman, who proposes to exterminate the Jews (George Arthur Buttrick, ed., *The Interpreter's Bible: the Holy Scriptures in the King James and Revised Standard Versions with General Articles and Introduction, Exegesis, Exposition for Each Book of the Bible,* 12 vols., vol. 3, [New York: Abingdon-Cokesbury Press, 1951–57]).

17. *Woman's Bible,* 86.

18. Vashti Cromwell McCollum, mother of the plaintiff Terry McCollum in the 1948 case on released time. *McCollum v. Board of Education,* 333 U.S. 203 (1948).

19. Vashti Cromwell McCollum, *One Woman's Fight* (Garden City, N.Y.: Doubleday, 1951), 11–12. She writes that "in any case, I have always been eager to set people right when they assumed that I was named after the once-popular novel of purple passion, *Vashti; or, 'Until Death Us Do Part'"* (12).

20. Stanton referred to a divorce in *Woman's Bible,* 85 n. 17. See also *Smith's Bible Dictionary* (New York: Jove, 1977), 25.

21. Ginzberg, *Legends of the Jews,* 378.

22. *Woman's Bible,* 87. The text records that the king later remembered

Vashti, but not how he remembered her, or what he did later on. On gaps in the biblical texts, see Meir Sternberg, *The Poetics of Biblical Narrative: Ideological Literature and the Drama of Reading* (Bloomington: Indiana University Press, 1987).

23. Ernest R. Mowrer, *Family Disorganization: An Introduction to a Sociological Analysis* (Chicago: University of Chicago Press, 1927), 260 (discussing the diary of Miriam Donaven). In the case of Mrs. Chapman we have some indication of what the husband and the Shakers thought. See Eunice Chapman, "The Memorial of James Chapman," in *The Other Side of the Question* (Cincinnati: Looker, Reynolds and Co., Printers, 1819), 22, and "The Remonstrance of the Shakers to the Legislature of the State of New York," *The Other Side of the Question*, 30.

24. Mowrer, *Family Disorganization*, 261.

25. "We live our lives by telling ourselves stories. There is *the* story, of course: the story of what happens, which in real life has no teller, at least none that we can hear." Rebecca Goldstein, *The Late Summer Passion of a Woman of Mind* (New York: Farrar, Straus and Giroux, 1989), 55.

26. The narrators would, of course, have quite different perspectives. For a consideration of the story with an emphasis on Ahasuerus, see Maurice Samuel, *Certain People of the Book* (New York: Knopf, 1955).

27. Feminist scholarship makes a major claim to build on reinterpretation of experience through the process called consciousness-raising. Katharine T. Bartlett writes, "Consciousness-raising is an interactive and collaborative process of articulating one's experiences and making meaning of them with others who also articulate their experiences" ("Feminist Legal Methods," *Harvard Law Review* 103 [1990]: 863–64).

James Elkins suggests that, in the context of marriage counseling, the point is to move from stories involving self-deception or dishonesty to stories that are (more) truthful. "The truth of narrative is fundamental to the healing process" ("The Stories We Tell Ourselves in Law," *Journal of Legal Education* 40 [1990]: 62). In some processes, however, the truth to be reached is a given—e.g., the facts of patriarchy or women's subordination—and not yet-to-be-found. Further, the truth of how we feel or felt—which is often what our therapeutic narrative is about—is only part of the relevant truth. The surfacing of the truth is the beginning, and not the end, of an analytic or evaluative or transforming project.

On multiple selves, and particularly issues arising when early selves try to bind later selves—the Ulysses and the Sirens problem—see Jon Elster, *Ulysses and the Sirens: Studies in Rationality and Irrationality*, rev. ed. (Cambridge: Cambridge University Press, 1984); and Elizabeth S. Scott, "Rational Decision-Making about Marriage and Divorce," *Virginia Law Review* 76 (1990): 58–62.

28. Judith, the imagined sister of Shakespeare, as described by Virginia Woolf in *A Room of One's Own* (London: Hogarth Press, 1929); though a child prodigy, Maria Anna, the sister of Mozart, "never developed into anything more" (*Grove's Dictionary of Music and Musicians* [London: Macmillan, 1941], 3:570). See also Linda Nochlin, "Why There Are No Great Women Artists," in

Women, Art, and Power and Other Essays (New York: Harper and Row, 1988) (on the issue of talent and training).

29. The idea that narratives, even autobiographical narratives, are constructed is standard in certain fields. In other contexts, the idea seems to be that the narrative is to be taken as true. In certain narrative approaches, the issue of literal truth does not arise. It does not matter if certain tribes exist. For such tribes, see Arthur Alan Leff, "Law and," *Yale Law Journal* 87 (1978); Alf Ross, "TûTû," *Harvard Law Review* 70 (1957): 812.

30. Patricia Williams, "On Being an Object of Property," *Signs* 14 (1988): 5.

31. John Stuart Mill suggested that "the knowledge which men can acquire of women, even as they have been and are, without reference to what they might be, is wretchedly imperfect and superficial, and always will be so, until women themselves have told all that they have to tell." *The Subjection of Women* (Cambridge: MIT Press, 1970), 26.

32. "The verisimilitude of the story, along with its assessable literary structure, will allow us to ascertain whether we can trust it as a vehicle of insight or whether we are being misled." Stanley Hauerwas and David Burrel, "From System to Story: An Alternative Pattern for Rationality in Ethics," in *Why Narrative? Readings in Narrative Theology,* ed. Stanley Hauerwas and Gregory Jones (Grand Rapids: Eerdmans, 1989), 187.

33. Have we enough information about Vashti to reconstruct such a calculation? Did she have children, for example? Or did she know what she was risking? Kuyper thought she did (*Women of Old Testament,* 172).

34. Hwang, *M. Butterfly*, 95.

35. See Roscoe Pound, *Jurisprudence* (St. Paul: West Publishing, 1959), 4:124–27 (reviewing the law of persons).

36. See Leonard Shengold, *Soul Murder: The Effects of Childhood Abuse and Deprivation* (New Haven: Yale University Press, 1989).

37. See Aileen Kraditor, *Ideas of the Women's Suffrage Movement,* 2d ed. (Garden City, N.Y.: Doubleday, 1981); and Carol Weisbrod, "Images of the Woman Juror," *Harvard Women's Law Journal* 9 (1986): 59.
This discussion draws on Carol Weisbrod, "Practical Polyphony, Theories of the State, and Feminist Jurisprudence," *Georgia Law Review* 24 (1990): 985.

38. Frances E. Olsen, "Feminist Theory in Grand Style," *Columbia Law Review* 89 (1989): 1147.

39. Catherine MacKinnon, *Feminism Unmodified: Discourses on Life and Law* (Cambridge: Harvard University Press, 1987), 115.

40. Leslie J. Harris, "New Perspectives on the Law of Rape," *Texas Law Review* 66 (1988): 915 (book review of Susan Estrich, *Real Rape* [Cambridge: Harvard University Press, 1987]).

41. Carole Pateman, "Women and Consent," *Political Theory* 8 (1980): 162. See also Gary Peller, "The Metaphysics of American Law," *California Law Review* 73 (1985): 1151.

42. Jean Bethke Elshtain, *Public Man, Private Woman* (Princeton: Princeton University Press, 1981), 250.

43. See Erving Goffman, *The Presentation of Self in Everyday Life* (London: Penguin, 1959), 13, 14, 18 (citing Harry Stack Sullivan, *American Journal of Psychiatry* 10 [1954]: 987–88, on the same issue with reference to the insane pretending to be sane).

44. Lucinda M. Finley, "Choice and Freedom: Elusive Issues in the Search for Gender Justice," *Yale Law Journal* 96 (1987): 935 n. 99, (reviewing David L. Kirp, *Gender Justice* [Chicago: University of Chicago Press, 1985]).

45. Goffman, *Presentation of Self,* 57.

46. Of course, as Katherine O'Donovan notes, Catherine MacKinnon must face the problem of accounting for the authenticity of her own view. "Engendering Justice: Women's Perspectives and the Rule of Law," *University of Toronto Law Journal* 39 (1989): 139 n. 61.

47. See, e.g., Estrich, *Real Rape.*

48. Mary Joe Frug, "Securing Job Equality for Women," *Boston University Law Review* 59 (1979): 55; Frances E. Olsen, "The Family and the Market: A Study of Ideology and Legal Reform," *Harvard Law Review* 96 (1983): 1497. More broadly, the problem is women's inability to value or to make choices at all.

49. Jessie L. Embry, *Mormon Polygamous Families: Life in the Principle* (Salt Lake City: University of Utah Press, 1987), 12. See also Cass R. Sunstein, "Feminism and Legal Theory," *Harvard Law Review* 101 (1988): 826, (reviewing MacKinnon, *Feminism Unmodified*).

50. John Stuart Mill, *The Subjection of Woman,* 23.

51. Keith Thomas, *Man and the Natural World: Changing Attitudes in England* (New York: Pantheon, 1983), 43. See also Matilda Jocelyn Gage, *Woman, Church, and State* (Salem, N.H.: Ayer, [1900] 1985), at 56; Herbert Thurston, "Has a Council Denied That Women Have Souls?" *Month,* January 1911, 559.

52. See Francis Lieber, "On Penal Law," in *Contributions to Political Science* (Philadelphia: J. B. Lippincott, 1881), 491.

53. Dorothy Sayers, *Are Women Human?* (Grand Rapids: Eerdmans, 1971).

54. Llewellyn said long ago, "Society moulds and makes the individual; but individuals are and mould society. Law is a going whole we are born into; but law is a changing something we help remodel. Law decides cases; but cases make law. Law deflects society; but society is reflected in the law." Karl N. Llewellyn, "Behind the Law of Divorce," pt. 1, *Columbia Law Review* 32 (1932): 1283. This essay, described as "bizarre" in William L. Twining, *Karl Llewellyn and the Realist Movement* (London: Weidenfeld and Nicolson, 1973), 194, makes plain the connection with the law of divorce and marriage itself. Moreover, the piece stresses the importance of description. Llewellyn himself was concerned with bourgeois marriage, while noting regional, religious, and class variations. See also chapter 3.

55. See Joseph William Singer, "Persuasion," *Michigan Law Review* 87 (1989): 2442.

56. This is a major theme in Austen's novel, *Persuasion.*

57. On narrative generally, see the symposium, "Legal Story Telling," *Michigan Law Review* 87 (1989). See also Julius G. Getman, "Voices: Human Voice in Legal Discourse," *Texas Law Review* 66 (1988): 577; and Mark G. Yud-

off, "Tea at the Palaz of Hoon: The Human Voice in Legal Rules," *Texas Law Review* 66 (1988): 589.

58. Whose "silly sensual leer" is she really talking about, the psychohistorian wonders.

59. Aviam Soifer, "Listening and the Voiceless," *Mississippi College Law Review* 4 (1984): 320 (describing literature, but the point is valid as to narrative generally). The present defenders of narrative, whether as writers or as persons analyzing narrative for legal purposes, are not the first people to make this argument, of course. See, e.g., John T. Noonan Jr., *Persons and Masks of the Law: Cardozo, Holmes, Jefferson, and Wythe as Makers of the Masks* (New York: Farrar, Straus and Giroux, 1976).

60. Milner Ball, "The Legal Academy and Minority Scholars," *Harvard Law Review* 103 (1990): 1855.

61. "Since then, at an uncertain hour, / That agony returns, / And til my ghastly tale is told / This heart within me burns" (Coleridge, *The Rime of the Ancient Mariner*), used as the epigraph in Primo Levi, *The Drowned and the Saved*, trans. Raymond Rosenthal (New York: Summit Books, 1989).

62. For example, the stories of women divorced in *Bucholz v. Bucholz*, 197 Neb. 180, 248 N.W.2d 21 (1976) (regarding claim that marriage involved a property right) or *Sharma v. Sharma*, 8 Kan. App. 2d 726, 667 P.2d 395 (1983) (attempt to seek free-exercise exemption from divorce law for high-caste Hindu), who argued that they should not be divorced and suffered substantially.

63. This relates to points made in Martha Minow, "Beyond Universality," *University of Chicago Legal Forum* 1989:115; and Randall L. Kennedy, "Radical Critiques of Legal Academia," *Harvard Law Review* 102 (1989): 1745. For a presentation that both records questions about narratives and offers an argument against asking such questions, see Patricia Williams, *The Alchemy of Race and Rights* (Cambridge: Harvard University Press, 1991), 50–51, 242.

64. For a nineteenth-century evaluation of biblical texts along these lines, see Simon Greenleaf, *The Testimony of the Evangelists Examined by the Rules of Evidence Administered in Courts of Justice* (Grand Rapids: Baker Book House, 1965).

65. Tomalin, "Book Review," *Observer Review*, March 14, 1971.

66. Historical scholarship is supposed to be about truth, though there can be a question about how that truth is established and by what sort of thing it can be evidenced. See Ian Hacking, *The Emergence of Probability: A Philosophical Study of Early Ideas about Probability, Induction, and Statistical Inference* (Cambridge: Cambridge University Press, 1975), 33 (on the fifteenth-century attack on the Donation of Constantine. As Hacking sees it, it was proved to be a forgery by an argument that the Donation was not the sort of thing that would have happened, rather than by using "evidence").

67. Even if it has been a trivial subject by some standards, one can adapt Gershom Scholem's comment that "nonsense is always nonsense but the history of nonsense is scholarship" (of debated origin, quoted in Jaroslav Pelikan, *The Medley of Theology: A Philosophical Dictionary* [Cambridge: Harvard University Press, 1988], 224).

68. See Ball, "Legal Academy."

69. And may also reject the idea that language has meaning. For a discussion of this issue, see Richard S. Kay, "Adherence to the Original Intentions in Constitutional Adjudication: Three Objections and Responses," *Northwestern University Law Review* 82 (1988): 226 (in context of constitutional interpretation).

70. "To disclaim objective standards of truth is not to disclaim all value judgments. We need not become positivists to believe that some accounts of experience are more consistent, coherent, inclusive, self-critical, and so forth." Deborah Rhode, "Feminist Critical Theories," *Stanford Law Review* 42 (1990): 626.

71. The convention is to automatically attribute authenticity or truth to the later reading—not necessarily an analytic reading of one's life—but it is only a convention. See also James Averill, "The Acquisition of Emotions during Adulthood," in *The Social Construction of Emotions,* ed. Rom Harre (Oxford: Blackwell, 1986), 114 (discussing getting in touch with one's feelings as being "not so much a process of discovery as it is an act of creation").

72. Perhaps the victim is an expert about that part of oppression that he/she experienced. Thus a recent writer on the Holocaust spoke of it as series of family tragedies (Paul Webster, *Pétain's Crime: The Full Story of French Collaboration in the Holocaust* [London: Macmillan, 1990]). But the victim is not necessarily an expert as to the whole.

73. Often they are not explicit. See Kathryn Abrams, "Hearing the Call of Stories," *California Law Review* 79 (1991): 971.

74. See Kennedy, "Radical Critiques."

75. For example, if she really believed them, she would have divorced her husband—unless excused from her "duty" to divorce. Since she did not divorce him, she didn't believe in her own ideas and [therefore?] they are less likely to be true? See William O'Neill's discussion of Havelock Ellis in *Divorce in the Progressive Era* (New Haven: Yale University Press, 1967), 124–26 (challenging the credentials of Ellis as a man unable to make a success of so universal an institution as marriage). This overlooks that while the term *marriage* is universal, the institution is not; that unhappy experiences may qualify people to offer critiques. Is female dependence to be celebrated as an aspect of the different voice (so that the desire for independence becomes something to be rejected as a part of the male ego trip)? For a hard view on the necessity of independence, see Joan Smith, *Misogynies: Reflections on Myth and Malice* (London: Faber & Faber, 1989).

76. Judith Resnik and Carolyn C. Heilbrun, "Convergences: Law, Literature, and Feminism," *Yale Law Journal* 99 (1990): 1920 (discussing the problem of revising the canon).

77. Ronald D. Laing, *The Facts of Life: An Essay in Feeling, Fact, and Fantasy* (New York: Pantheon, 1976) (what others call me is their map of me; what I call myself is my map: where is the territory?). Is there a core "I" under the many ways to say "I" in Japanese? Note also that values highly specific to individual families, e.g., family pride, may be as important as any other social identifica-

tion. See David Daiches, *Two Worlds: An Edinburgh Jewish Childhood* (Tuscaloosa: University of Alabama Press, 1989), 10.

78. Martha Fineman makes the same point—that what is centrally relevant is the argument, not the speaker—and urges that this is so in part because a contrary emphasis gives a false idea of the significance of the individual in relation to social or political problems. "Challenging Law, Establishing Differences: The Future of Feminist Legal Scholarship," *Florida Law Review* 42 (1990): 41.

79. There seems no point in trying to enumerate the various ways in which one's work, product, or expression might be "about" oneself.

80. This would be the strong version of the outsider claim. See Robert Merton, "Insiders and Outsiders," *American Journal of Sociology* 78 (1972): 13. Merton notes that Simmel is the source of aphorism: We don't have to *be* Caesar to understand him; but note that Simmel was a man who could discuss the moral problems of people with "psychologically fine ears," those who suddenly and involuntarily received insights into other people that those others would prefer to keep private. Georg Simmel, "Discretion," in *The Sociology of Georg Simmel*, ed. and trans. Kurt Wolff (Glencoe, Ill.: Free Press, 1950), 323. It is one thing for such a person to claim value in the outside perspective, quite another for that perspective to be used as a sole source by those whose empathic capacity is either not known, or known to be fairly limited.

81. Thus Voltaire comments on Montesquieu's defense of the sale of offices in monarchies (though not despotisms): "[W]e can forgive him: his uncle purchased [an office], and left it to him. After all we find the man. No one of us is without his weak points." Montesquieu, *The Spirit of the Laws*, trans. T. Nugent (New York: Hafner, [1949] 1975), 69 n. v.

82. We work in a field in which "wrong but interesting" is a legitimate category. This is not true in all fields.

83. There must be those, in both victim or oppressor categories, by race or class, who are unable to identify their own individual stories with the conventional stories of their group. On the fluctuating aspects of (ascribed) identifications, see Einstein: "If my theory of relativity is proven successful, Germany will claim me as a German and France will declare that I am a citizen of the world. Should my theory prove untrue, France will say that I am a German and Germany will declare that I am a Jew" (quoted in Merton, "Insiders and Outsiders," 28). On problems of inclusion/exclusion generally, see Martha Minow, *Making All the Difference: Inclusion, Exclusion, and American Law* (Ithaca: Cornell University Press, 1990).

84. For discussion of the interaction of the American legal system and religious legal system in American family law, see Carol Weisbrod, "Family, Church, and State: An Essay on Constitutionalism and Religious Authority," *Journal of Family Law* 26 (1987–88): 741.

85. *New York Times*, January 16, 1905, p. 5, col. 2. See generally Aranson, "Divorces on Condition," *Green Bag* 3 (1891): 381. Conditional divorce might solve the current "get" problem. L. Epstein remarks that conditional divorce at the time of the marriage is "halakacally sound, but very impractical" ("Adjustment of the Jewish Marriage Laws to Present Day Conditions," in *Proceedings of*

the Rabbinical Assembly 35 [1935]: 231). For a review of objections based on religious law, see Moshe Meiselman, *Jewish Woman in Jewish Law* (New York: Ktav Publishing House, 1978), 106–15. For a discussion of the "get" issue, see Leo Pfeffer and Alan Pfeffer, "The Agunah in American Secular Law," *Journal of Church and State* 31 (1989): 487. On groups generally, see Aviam Soifer, *Law and the Company We Keep* (Cambridge: Harvard University Press, 1995). See Kate Simon, *Bronx Primitive: Portraits in a Childhood* (New York: Harper and Row, 1983), 47, for a narrative of a culture in which despite the availability of divorce, "the Jewish women were as firmly imbedded in their marriages as the Catholic."

86. See Deut. 25:5–6. On polygamy in Jewish law see Moses Mielziner, *Jewish Law of Marriage and Divorce* (1884; rpt., Littleton, Colo.: F. B. Rothman, 1987), 28–32 (describing rabbinic ban on polygamy in the West).

87. For another approach to religious divorce, see Edwin B. Firmage, *Zion in the Courts: A Legal History of the Church of Jesus Christ of Latter-Day Saints, 1830–1900* (Urbana: University of Illinois Press, 1988), 322–31 (discussing Mormon divorce). Note that it is also possible to conceive marriage as neither for life nor for an indefinite period, but terminable by divorce, permitting divorce, but as temporary for a specified period of time. See Shahla Haeri, *The Law of Desire: Temporary Marriage in Iran* (London: Tauris Publishing, 1989). See also David Pearl, *A Textbook on Muslim Law*, 2d ed. (London: Croom Helm, 1979), 75–76.

88. Margaret Lee, "Final Words on Divorce," *North American Review* 50 (1890): 263–64.

89. Jan Gorecki, "Moral Premises of Contemporary Divorce Laws: Western and Eastern Europe and the United States," in *Marriage and Cohabitation in Contemporary Societies: Areas of Legal, Social, and Ethical Change: An Introductory and Interdisciplinary Study*, ed. John Eekelaar and Sanford Katz (Toronto: Butterworth, 1980).

90. The most liberal divorce regime does not require parties to divorce. On family law as an overarching scheme within which people seek their individual good life, see Inga Markovitz, "Family Traits," *Michigan Law Review* 88 (1990): 1740–41, reviewing Mary Ann Glendon, *Transformation of Family Law: State Law and Family in the United States and Western Europe* (Chicago: University of Chicago Press, 1989).

91. We could, for example, return to the issue of Vashti's narrative and compare it to the narratives of the others in her world (the king, the ministers) and ultimately to the official legal system and our own legal systems.

92. These rules may include rules about what may or may not be done, or discussed or acknowledged. They may be rules about controlling fictions. As Simmel noted, there is utility in the reserves and discretion of marriage (*Sociology of Georg Simmel*, 326–29 n. 183). We pretend to others and perhaps to ourselves that we are living according to the norm, which itself rejects pretense.

93. William Graham Sumner, *Folkways: A Study of the Sociological Importance of Usages, Manners, Customs, Mores, and Morals* (1906; rpt., Dover, 1959), sec. 364 (noting that the family—not marriage—is the real institution).

94. Ellen Key, *Love and Marriage* (New York: G. P. Putnam's Sons, 1911), 321–22. See Karl N. Llewellyn, "Behind the Law of Divorce," pt. 2, *Columbia Law Review* 33 (1933): 251 n. 4 (regarding his mother—conservatively acting, but radically thinking—and Ellen Key). Ellen Key is called "conservative" in that she stressed love and motherhood; "radical" in that she believed in free divorce and motherhood for single women. On Ellen Key generally, see Nancy F. Cott, *The Grounding of Modern Feminism* (New Haven: Yale University Press, 1987), 46–49.

95. Leon Petrazycki, *Law and Morality*, trans. Hugh Babb (Cambridge: Harvard University Press, 1955).

96. This might be restricted by contract. Thus Scott, "Rational Decision-Making," notes,

> A variety of binding precommitment options would, of course, theoretically be possible. The most extreme would be a legal prohibition against divorce. Like Ulysses, the married individual would be irrevocably bound to the original choice. In terms of precommitment analysis, a no-exit rule would make the inconsistent short-term preference unavailable (theoretically), forcing the individual to abide by the commitment. Less extreme precommitment mechanisms could impose costs on the decision to divorce and directly or indirectly support the choice to continue in the marriage. A couple could agree before marriage to impose economic penalties, benefiting the spouse or children, on the partner seeking divorce. Some precommitment mechanisms would impose costs on the decision to divorce, while at the same time discouraging impulsiveness. An agreement or a legal rule requiring mandatory delay before divorce (a two- or three-year waiting period, for example) would discourage impulsive divorce and provide sufficient opportunity for a reconciliation. A similar effect would result from an agreement to submit to counseling, mediation, or arbitration, or a requirement of psychological evaluation of the children to assess the probable effect of divorce. (43–44)

97. Erving Goffman, *Relations in Public: Microstudies of the Public Order* (Harmondsworth, Middlesex: Penguin, 1971), 185.

98. Ibid.

99. Martha Minow, "Identities," *Yale Journal of Law and the Humanities* 3 (1991): 326–29. Note particularly Minow's discussion of finding room for a private self within the social identity.

100. It is the public and official aspect of marriage that creates the contrast to friendship. We are not asked to register our friendships unless we are trying to set them up as marriages (though, as Aviam Soifer reminds me, we may choose sometimes to publicly record them). Our friendships exist and change according to their own rules and sanctions. Note also the distinction between consort and companion. Though identified as a single role, this role may in fact be varied—i.e., is emphasis placed on consort or companion aspects?—along a public/private line.

101. As Lawrence Friedman suggests, this is in part due to the effect of marriage on property ownership. See Carol Weisbrod, "Comment on Friedman

Paper, 'Rights of Passage,'" *Oregon Law Review* 63 (1984): 633. We want to identify ownership and inheritance rights. It is still true, as Friedman once noted, that family law is adjunct to the law of succession (*American Law* [New York: Norton, 1984], 150). At the same time, however, we might note that the state adjudication of property is not the only adjudication possible.

102. Denis de Rougemont, *Love in the Western World,* trans. Montgomery Belgion (New York: Schocken, 1983), 293.

103. See Scott, "Rational Decision-Making"; Bartlett, "Feminist Legal Methods."

104. De Rougemont, *Love in Western World,* 293.

105. We would not be the first culture to have defined an institution in such a way as to make it difficult, if not possible, to meet all of its requirements. See Ruth Benedict, *The Chrysanthemum and the Sword: Patterns of Japanese Culture* (Boston: Houghton Mifflin, 1946).

Chapter Two

1. Pierre Loti had himself married a temporary wife. He wrote to a friend: "Last week I was married . . . to a young girl of seventeen. She is called Okanesan. We celebrated with a lantern procession and a tea party. The validity of this marriage is entirely at the whim of the two parties" (quoted in introduction, *Madame Chrysanthemum*), viii. See Benedict, *Chrysanthemum and Sword,* 184, on the differences between the wife and the mistress.

2. See Rebecca Bailey-Harris, "Madame Butterfly and the Conflict of Laws," *American Journal of Comparative Law* 39 (1991): 157.

3. Temporary marriage was available to Japanese and foreigners.

4. See Bailey-Harris, "Conflict of Laws." On contemporary marriage in Japan, see *New York Times,* February 11, 1996: low-expectation marriages result in high stability.

5. On the derivation of "pidgin," see Jonathan Spence, *God's Chinese Son* (New York: Norton, 1996), 8.

6. Other narratives that reflect values that are not parallel to those of the culture or the law, and that would represent minority or individual positions, could also have been chosen. That is, in a period that focused generally on low-expectation marriages, stories might exist that described high-expectation marriages, and in a period that viewed marriage in terms of personal satisfaction, narratives might exist that focused on duty and social meanings and/or that stressed that personal satisfaction was not an independently achievable goal but a by-product of other behavior. At this point, one might wonder whether our sense of the central and marginal stories was correct.

7. Llewellyn had said as much ("Behind Law of Divorce," pt. 1, 1281).

8. M. I. Finley, *The World of Odysseus,* 2d ed. (Harmondsworth: Penguin, 1954), 137.

9. See, e.g., Ruth Benedict, *Patterns of Culture* (Boston: New American Library, 1959), 210, who describes an Eskimo marriage in which the murderer of a husband, under principles of restitution, takes the place of the husband.

10. Lawrence Stone, *The Family, Sex, and Marriage, 1500–1800* (New York: Harper and Row, 1977).

11. See O'Neill, *Divorce in the Progressive Era.* Carl Degler, *At Odds: Women and the Family in America from the Revolution to the Present* (New York: Oxford University Press, 1980), 168, notes that O'Neill's view relates to families: "Yet from what we know about divorces in the late 19th century, most of them dissolved marriages, not families. About 60% of all divorces between 1847 and 1906, for example, did not involve children."

12. Joel P. Bishop, *Commentaries on the Law of Marriage and Divorce* (Boston: Little, Brown, 1881), vol. 1, sec. 2.

13. *Marvin v. Marvin*, 18 Cal. 3d 660, 684, 557 P.2d 106, 122, 134 Cal. Rptr. 815, 831 (1976) ("The joining of the man and woman in marriage is at once the most socially productive and individually fulfilling relationship that one can enjoy in the course of a life time.").

14. Elaine May, *Great Expectations: Marriage and Divorce in Post-Victorian America* (Chicago: University of Chicago Press, 1980), 47.

15. Ibid., 90.

16. Ibid.

17. See Ben Lindsay and Wainwright Evans, *The Companionate Marriage* (New York: Boni & Liveright, 1927).

18. Peter Berger and Brigitte Berger, *The War over the Family: Capturing the Middle Ground* (Garden City: Anchor Press/Doubleday, 1983), 166–67.

19. Ibid.

20. Ibid.

21. Ibid., 167. See also Catherine K. Riessman, *Divorce Talk: Women and Men Make Sense of Personal Relationships* (New Brunswick, N.J.: Rutgers University Press, 1990), 21–74.

22. Brigitte Bodenheimer, "Reflections on the Future of Grounds for Divorce," *Journal of Family Law* 8 (1968): 189–90.

23. Nancy F. Cott, *The Grounding of Modern Feminism* (New Haven: Yale University Press, 1987), 156.

24. Ibid.

25. At least in some parts of the culture. Mirra Komarovsky, *Blue Collar Marriage* (New York: Vintage, 1967), 125, refers to "the meagerness of verbal communication that characterizes [blue collar] marriages" and also "the absence of certain norms," particularly the spouse as confidante/best-friend norm: "In interpreting specific cases, such norms were judged very weak or non-existent, not only because they were not voiced, but because emotionally significant experiences were regularly shared with others in preference to one's mate without any perceptible feeling that this reflected upon the quality of the marriage. Moreover, some persons acknowledged their ignorance of the thoughts and feelings of the mate without the apology or defensiveness usually accompanying violations of norms."

26. Berger and Kellner discuss marriage as a reality-creating institution that tends to eliminate competitive orderings and accounts in part through the "dominance of the marital discourse" ("Marriage and the Construction of Real-

ity," *Diogenes* 46 [1964]: 12). See also Riessman, *Divorce Talk*, 51, on the intimacy requirements of marriage.

27. O'Neill, *Divorce in Progressive Era*, 220.

28. But not, of course, entirely. See Lee E. Teitelbaum, "Placing the Family in Context," *U.C. Davis Law Review* 22 (1989): 801.

29. O'Neill, 220.

30. For a recent examination of modern divorce stories, see Riessman, *Divorce Talk.*

31. Susan B. Anthony, "The Status of Woman, Past, Present, and Future," *Arena Boston* 17 (1897): 902–4.

32. Cott, *Grounding of Modern Feminism,* 158. See also Densmore, "On Celibacy," *Journal of Female Liberation* 1 (1965): 22 (noting the enormous emphasis being placed on sexuality as a roadblock on the way to liberation), quoted in Jessie Bernard, *The Future of Marriage* (New Haven: Yale University Press, 1982), 222–23: The "supposed need" for sex had therefore to be "refuted, coped with, demythified, or the cause of female liberation is doomed." Usually "what passes for sexual need is actually desire to be stroked; desire for recognition or love; desire to conquer, humiliate, or wield power; or desire to communicate." See also O'Neill's reference to the classic feminist demand "for more work and less sex" (*Divorce in Progressive Era,* 127). Ethel Persons has pointed out that it is far from clear what role genital sexuality has in the formation of female identity—perhaps much less than in the formation of male identity. "Sexuality as a Mainstay of Identity," *Signs* 5 (1980): 618–21.

33. Presumably the goal of men as well as women. Edward Sapir referred to the "useful tyranny of the normal." *Selected Writings of Edward Sapir in Language, Culture and Personality,* ed. David Mandelbaum (Berkeley: University of California Press, 1949), 514.

34. Susan Sontag, "The Third World of Women," *Partisan Review* 1973: 189. Sontag omits from this list some other possibilities. See Densmore, "On Celibacy."

35. Roderick Phillips, *Putting Asunder: A History of Divorce in Western Society* (New York: Cambridge University Press, 1988).

36. See Gerhard Mueller, "Inquiry into the State of a Divorceless Society," *University of Pittsburgh Law Review* 18 (1957): 545: "The title of this paper is misleading, for England was not entirely divorceless during the period of inquiry. [Divorce by act of the legislature had become available for the cause of adultery.] After a parliamentary divorce the innocent party was at liberty to remarry. Very rarely a parliamentary divorce was granted for cruelty."

37. Pound, *Jurisprudence* (St. Paul: West, 1959), 2:392, sec. 77m.

38. *Maynard v. Hill,* 125 U.S. 190 (1888), often quoted for its general language on the importance of marriage.

39. Roscoe Pound, "Law in Books and Law in Action," *American Law Review* 44 (1910): 21.

40. See Lynn Wardle, "No-Fault Divorce and the Divorce Conundrum," *B.Y.U. Law Review* 1991:79.

41. Lawrence Friedman and Robert Percival, "Who Sues for Divorce? From Fault through Fiction to Freedom," *Journal of Legal Studies* 5 (1976): 76.

42. Ibid., 78.

43. Ibid.

44. See Nancy F. Cott, "Divorce and Changing Status of Women in 18th Century Massachusetts," *William and Mary Quarterly* 33 (1976): 586.

45. Ibid.

46. Lawrence Friedman, "Rights of Passage," *Oregon Law Review* 63 (1984): 652.

47. 1839 Laws Va., chap. 262 (cited in Friedman, "Rights of Passage," 652 n. 10).

48. Friedman, "Rights of Passage," 652 n.10.

49. See Nelson Blake, *The Road to Reno: A History of Divorce in the United States* (New York: Macmillan, 1962) (discussing the Chapman case); Blake, "Eunice against the Shakers," *New York History* 61 (1960): 359.

50. These are of course narratives for public consumption, raising even more clearly than private diaries the issue of construction of a story for a particular purpose. If we want to say that the story is in fact a lie, we must consider the possibilities that the lie is thought to be functional, perhaps because it will be believed, or perhaps because it will be disbelieved (X transparently lies to protect Y; so that everyone will believe that Y really is so awful that his character needs protection, while X is established as good).

Regarding the divorce novel as narrative see James Barnett, *Divorce and the American Divorce Novel, 1858–1937* (1939; rpt., New York: Russell & Russell, 1968) (note the limits of this work, which considers only novels in which a divorce takes place, not those in which divorce is argued against, e.g., Augusta Jane Evans, *Vashti: or, "Until Death Us Do Part"* [London: Milner, 1869]). For those novels in which the possibility of free divorce is the background of the narrative, see, e.g., Edith Wharton, *The Glimpses of the Moon* (New York: Appleton, 1922) (assuming the free-divorce contract can be acted upon).

51. Chapman, "An Account of the Conduct of the Shakers, in the Case of Eunice Chapman and Her Children," in *The Other Side of the Question.*

52. See Blake, "Eunice against the Shakers," 360 (citing Eunice Chapman).

53. His own version stresses that "in order to find my union with these people, I must first fulfill every lawful contract that I had ever made . . . and especially the marriage contract." He then said he considered it right that he should "make one more effort to live with her in peace, and to give her a fair offer of removing with myself and children, to live near these people" (Chapman, *The Other Side of the Question*).

54. Blake, *Road to Reno.* See also Mary Dyer, *The Rise and Progress of the Serpent from the Garden of Eden to the Present Day* (Concord, N.H.: n.p., 1847), 119–25 (extracts from Mrs. Chapman's narrative).

55. The legislature's version of the story stresses the aspects of desertion and nonsupport.

An Act For the Relief of Eunice Chapman, And For Other Purposes, Passed on March 14, 1818

Whereas Eunice Chapman, in the year one thousand eight hundred and four, was lawfully married to James Chapman, by whom she had three children, and with whom she lived until the year one thousand eight hundred and eleven, when the said James Chapman abandoned his said wife, without leaving her any means of support, and soon after joined the society of Shakers in Niskeyuna, in the county of Albany: And whereas, the said James Chapman, since joining the society of Shakers, has taken from his wife her children, and now keeps them concealed from her, and insists that the marriage contract between him and his said wife is annulled, and that he is not bound to support her, and has publicly forbid all persons from harboring her, and declared that he would not be responsible for her debts: Therefore, Be it enacted by the People of the State of New York, represented in Senate and Assembly, That the marriage contract between the said Eunice Chapman and her said husband, James Chapman, be, and the same is hereby declared to be dissolved, and the said Eunice Chapman entirely freed from the same: Provided, That the dissolution of such marriage shall, in no wise, effect the legitimacy of the children thereof.

Quoted in Dyer, *Rise and Progress*, 118–19.

56. Blake notes the heavy gothic atmosphere ("Eunice against the Shakers," 374). In 1818 Eunice Chapman described herself as a widow, a women bereaved of her husband and children while still living.

57. On Mary Dyer's difficulties with the Shakers, see Dyer, *Rise and Progress*, 223–25.

58. Ibid., 119–20.

59. The Dyer/Chapman narratives are in the form of complaint.

60. At one stage in the proceeding, New York's Council of Revision rejected the divorce, finding that separation would provide an adequate remedy and that the anti-Shaker provisions of the bill were objectionable (Blake, *Road to Reno*, 68ff.).

61. See discussion of divorce legislation in several states in Carol Weisbrod, *The Boundaries of Utopia* (New York: Pantheon, 1980), 46.

62. Bailey Memoirs, cited by Cott, "Divorce," 586. Cott reports that Mrs. Bailey did ultimately obtain a divorce. Separation was once one of the legal solutions available. See also Hendrik Hartog, "Abigail Bailey's Coverture: Law in a Married Woman's Consciousness," in *Law in Everyday Life*, ed. Austin Sarat and Thomas R. Kearns (Ann Arbor: University of Michigan Press, 1993). The consequences of separation in the nineteenth century were seen, by Annie Besant at least, to be quite destructive: "A technical tie is kept up, which retains on the wife the mass of disabilities which flow from marriage, while depriving her of all the privileges, and which widows both man and women, exiling them from home life and bearing them from love . . . the semi-divorced wife . . . is compelled to live on, without the freedom of the spinster or the widow, or the

social consideration of the married woman" (*Marriage As It Was, As It Is, and As It Should Be* [1879], 40). A fictional Vashti chose separation (Evans, *Vashti*). See also Mary Killey, *Private Woman, Public Stage* (New York: Oxford University Press, 1984), 237 (quoting novel as calling divorce "sacrilegious trifling").

63. Elizabeth Cady Stanton, in *A History of the National Woman's Rights Movement,* ed. Paulina Wright Davis (New York: Journeymen Printers' Cooperative Association, 1871), 63–64. Stanton sometimes invoked a highly romantic view of marriage; at other times, her view seems more functional. See also the discussion of the drunkard and marriage in *History of Woman Suffrage,* ed. Elizabeth Cady Stanton, Susan B. Anthony, and Matilda Joslyn Gage, vol. 1 (New York: Fowler and Wells, 1887), 482. On Stanton and marriage and divorce, see particularly Elizabeth Clark, "Self-Ownership and the Political Theory of Elizabeth Cady Stanton," *Connecticut Law Review* 21 (1989): 905. Stanton may have seen romantic love in marriage as a solution. She also, however, invoked an image of intellectual women, from the remote past, such as the hetaerae: "Among the Greeks there was a class of women that possessed absolute freedom, surrounded by the wisest men of their day. They devoted themselves to study and thought, which enabled them to add to their other charms an intense intellectual fascination, and to make themselves the center of a literary society of matchless splendor. . . . In the society of this remarkable type of Grecian womanhood the most brilliant artists, poets, historians, and philosophers found their highest inspiration" ("Has Christianity Benefitted Women?" *North American Review* 140 [1885]: 393–94). Stanton knew that "the position of these women was questionable" but was still able to raise the question: "Does the same class in Christian civilization enjoy as high culture and equal governmental protection?" On the heterae see William Sanger, *History of Prostitution* (New York: Medical Publishing, 1921), 53–63; Eva Canterella, *Pandora's Daughters* (Baltimore: Johns Hopkins University Press, 1987), 49–50. Demosthenes said that Athenian men had three women: the wife for legitimate children; concubines for care of the body, and the hetaerae for pleasure (Cantarella, 48). If we say that all three are now in one, "the wife," we might also say that it is possible to classify marriages in terms of whether, and when, the mother or the servant/concubine or consort/companion role dominates the constellation of female roles.

64. Elizabeth Cady Stanton, "Are Homogenous Divorce Laws in all The States Desirable?" *North American Review* 138 (1884): 405. See also "Divorce v. Domestic Warfare," *Arena* 1 (1890): 560 (advancing individual sovereignty in divorce as in marriage). This is of course a familiar argument for federalism generally. Stanton was responding to proposals that would have restricted divorce on the national level.

65. This theme continues to be a major one in feminist writing: "Unless they work, and their work is usually as valuable as their husbands', married women have not even the chance of gaining real power over their own lives which means the power over their own lives which means the power to change their lives. The arts of psychological coercion and reconciliation for which women are notorious—flattery, charm, wheedling, glamour, tears—are a servile substi-

tute for real influence and real autonomy" (Sontag, "Third World of Women," 187).

66. For a contemporary use of horror stories, see Martha Fineman, "Implementary Equality: Ideology, Contraction, and Social Change: A Study of Rhetoric and Results in the Regulation of the Consequences of Divorce," *Wisconsin Law Review* 1983:789.

67. Ellen Carol DuBois, *Feminism and Suffrage: The Emergence of an Independent Women's Movement in America, 1848–1869* (Ithaca: Cornell University Press, 1978), 148 (woman who divorced after hearing Mrs. Stanton speak on divorce).

68. Historians can respond to this issue in a particular individual's case. On Stanton, see Clark, "Self-Ownership." The narrative itself supports both broad and narrow normative implications. Clark notes that Stanton and Anthony had both urged that "wives of chronic inebriates had a 'duty to seek a separation, to sever conjugal relationship, so as not to be the agent of breeding a drunkard's child'" (26). Clark also notes that in general, early feminists invoked ideas of duty rather than right in dealing with the divorce issue (28).

69. Other Stanton ideas go further, focusing on free divorce and self sovereignty.

70. Elizabeth Griffith, "Elizabeth Cady Stanton on Marriage and Divorce: Feminist Theory and Domestic Experience," in *Woman's Being, Woman's Place: Female Identity and Vocation in American History*, ed. Mary Kelley (Boston: Hall, 1979), 236.

71. Ibid., 233.

72. See Martha Minow, "Rights of One's Own," *Harvard Law Review* 98 (1985): 1088 n. 15, reviewing E. Griffith, *In Her Own Right: The Life of Elizabeth Cady Stanton* (New York: Oxford University Press, 1984): "Griffith offers no comment on whether Stanton's passion for divorce reform reflected in any way her own marital experience. Such a connection in not implausible, given the course of Stanton's marriage: she and her husband had frequent personal and political disagreements, and maintained separate residences for many years. Her husband slipped from prominence in the abolition movement after he became the subject of a minor scandal concerning bonds illegally taken from the customs house he directed. Stanton appeared to want independence from him as well as a separate identity for herself, although she never sought a divorce."

73. Elizabeth Cady Stanton, *Eighty Years and More* (New York: Schocken, 1971), 71–72.

74. That is, she was economically independent in that she neither needed his money nor feared his misuse of her money.

75. The aspiration aspects of marriage may be evidenced by the language of William O. Douglas (married four times): "We deal with a right of privacy older than the Bill of Rights—older than our political parties, older than our school system. Marriage is coming together for better or worse, hopefully enduring, and intimate to the degree of being sacred. It is an association that promotes a way of life, not causes; a harmony in living, not political faiths; a bilateral loyalty, not commercial or social projects. Yet it is an association for as

noble a purpose as any involved in our prior decisions" (*Griswold v. Connecti-cut*, 381 U.S. 479, 486 [1965]).

76. William Goode, "The Theoretical Importance of Love," *American Socio-logical Review* 24 (1956): 40–41. Walter Lippmann, quoting Santayana, makes the point that love has largely to do with the lover rather than the love-object (*A Preface to Morals* [New York: Macmillan, 1931], 310). That love has altogether to do with the lover, see Goethe's *Wilhelm Meister*, trans. Thomas Carlyle (London: J.M. Dent, 1930), 1:202: "[I]f I have a touch of kindness for thee, what has thou to do with it?"

77. Herbert Jacobs, *The Silent Revolution: Transformation of Divorce Law in the United States* (Chicago: University of Chicago Press. 1988), 25.

78. Ernest R. Mowrer, "The Variance between Legal and Natural Causes for Divorce," *Journal of Social Forces* 1 (1924): 389. See also Ross, "The Significance of Increasing Divorce," in *Women and Children First*, ed. David Rothman and Sheila Rothman.

79. The statutory enumeration of legal grounds may, of course, increase the possibility that these factors will become actual grounds, as the law communi-cates that these things justify divorce. It also communicates that certain things may be forgiven, condoned, or ignored (no rule forces a divorce for grounds).

80. Riessman, *Divorce Talk.*

81. However, Mowrer notes that "the cycle of events in the diary of Miriam Donaven is a group phenomenon rather than an individual experience" (*Fam-ily Disorganization*, 230). Mowrer prints the diary in full. A reviewer noted that the lay reader would find the diary a "bit of life hot with living." Zorbaugh, "Book Review," *New Republic* 50 (1927): 281.

82. Mowrer, *Family Disorganization*, 231.

83. Ibid., 231–34.

84. Ibid., 257.

85. Ibid., 259.

86. Ibid., 250.

87. William Goode, *Women in Divorce* (Westport, Conn.: Greenwood Press, 1965), 209.

88. Ibid.

89. See discussions of friendship in C. S. Lewis, *The Four Loves* (London: Fontana, 1960). See also Simmel: "For, friendship is a relation entirely based on the individualities of its elements, more so perhaps even than marriage: because of its traditional forms, its social rules, its real interests, marriage con-tains many super-individual elements that are independent of the specific char-acters of the personalities involved. The fundamental differentiation on which marriage is based, as over against friendship, is in itself not an individual, but a species, differentiation. . . . The modern, highly differentiated woman shows a strikingly increased capacity for friendship and an inclination toward it, both with men and with women" (*Sociology of Georg Simmel*, 138).

90. See *Hyde v. Hyde*, 1 L.R.-P. and D. 130, 133 (D. 1866): "[M]arriage . . . may . . . be defined as the voluntary union for life of one man and one woman, to the exclusion of all others."

91. Doris Lessing, "To Room Nineteen," in *Stories* (New York: Vintage, 1980).

92. The history of modern marriage suggests two contrasts, one between marriages considered patriarchal and those considered companionate, another between marriages understood as romantic, or total, and those that are (merely) convertible or companionable. As to the second pair, where it was once thought that romantic marriages could properly mellow into companionable ones, it is now possible to see that the companionable marriage, which exists as a background and may not be the largest part of the life of either of the couple, can easily be judged a poor second to a real or even hypothetical romantic alternative.

93. Lessing, "To Room Nineteen," 411.

94. Ibid., 397–98. The story can be read as an account of individual mental breakdown. (Perhaps, following Laing, insanity is an appropriate response to insane situations?) But it can also be read as an account of an individual unable to find justification in and through institutions. There is some discussion of why the wife's experiences of bondage to the collective is so painful while the husband, who is equally bound in a way, does not experience it that way.

95. Elizabeth Cady Stanton, Susan B. Anthony, *Correspondence, Writings, Speeches,* 247–48.

96. Ibid., 248.

97. The point of divorce, according to the current view, is supposed to be minimized so that divorces are simply messy now, no longer painful. Thus Carl Schneider describes no-fault divorce: "There ought to be no sense of guilt when a marriage doesn't work, because there was simply a technical dysfunction" ("Moral Discourse and the Transformation of American Family Law," *Michigan Law Review* 83 [1985]: 1853).

98. Teitelbaum, "Family in Context."

99. As this book goes to press, Louisiana has become the first state to offer, though a contractual mechanism, a choice of marital dissolution options, the tighter one called "covenant marriage."

Chapter Three

1. Though perhaps notice was needed for an effective divorce under the 1898 statutes. See Bailey-Harris, "Conflict of Laws," 167. The marriage itself might have been a formal marriage in 1898 or, if it failed those tests, might have been an informal union—*naien* (lacking notification.) It was said (in 1956) that *naien* marriages, created by delaying registration, meant that the head of the home retained the traditional power to reject the spouse. See note: "Japanese Family Law," *Stanford Law Review* 9 (1956): 138.

2. Recognized as such in Japan? In the United States? This would depend on the status of the first marriage. See Bailey-Harris, "Conflict of Laws."

3. Although a lawyer, Long may not have focused on or researched the legal issues in *Madame Butterfly*.

4. For an overview of many of the complex themes involved in the ques-

tion of contracts and the family, see Carl E. Schneider and Margaret F. Brinig, *Invitation to Family Law: Principles, Process and Perspectives* (St. Paul: West Publishing, 1996).

5. There is much writing on this subject. See, e.g., June Carbone and Margaret F. Brinig, "Rethinking Marriage: Feminist Ideology, Economic Change, and Divorce Reform," *Tulane Law Review* 65 (1991): 977–79; Scott, "Rational Decision-Making"; Jeffrey E. Stake, "Mandatory Planning for Divorce," *Vanderbilt Law Review* 45 (1992): 415–53. For earlier relevant writings, see Robert H. Mnookin and Lewis Kornhauser, "Bargaining in the Shadow of the Law: The Case of Divorce," *Yale Law Journal* 88 (1979): 950; Marjorie M. Shultz, "Contractual Ordering of Marriage: A New Model for State Policy," *California Law Review* 70 (1982): 291–334; Lenore J. Weitzman, "Legal Regulation of Marriage: Tradition and Change, *California Law Review* 62 (1974): 1249–78. The current discussions, often derived from law-and-economics perspectives, focus heavily on a discussion of incentives in individual bargaining. By contrast, this chapter, in its treatment of Llewellyn and Isaacs, focuses on issues of the relationship of law to the changing social institutions.

6. For one critique, see Ira M. Ellman, "The Theory of Alimony," *California Law Review* 77 (1989): 13–33. Some writing on mandatory planning for divorce stresses that the idea of a premarital contract governing the economics of divorce would have no application to behavior during the marriage. See, e.g., Banks McDowell, "Contracts in the Family," *B.U. Law Review* 45 (1965): 47–54.

7. George B. Shaw, *Man and Superman: A Comedy and a Philosophy*, in *The Bodley Head: Bernard Shaw*, ed. Max Reinhardt (London: Bodley Head, 1971), 2:746–47 ("The Revolutionist's Handbook").

8. This view is perhaps derived from the well-known comment of Oliver Wendell Holmes: "The duty to keep a contract at common law means a prediction that you must pay damages if you do not keep it—and nothing else." "The Path of the Law," *Harvard Law Review* 10 (1897): 462.

9. This reliance interest is not limited to domestic arrangements. See, for example, the discussion of plant closings in Joseph W. Singer, "The Reliance Interest in Property," *Stanford Law Review* 40 (1988): 701–6.

10. See *Ferdinand Tönnies on Sociology: Pure, Applied, and Empirical*, ed. Werner J. Cahnman and Rudolf Heberle (Chicago: University of Chicago Press, 1971), 65, 160–69; and Georg W. F. Hegel, *Philosophy of Right*, trans. Thomas M. Knox (London: Oxford University Press, 1949), 58: "The right which the individual enjoys on the strength of the family unity and which is in the first place simply the individual's life within this unity, takes on the *form* of right . . . only when the family begins to dissolve."

11. 125 U.S. 190 (1888).

12. Ibid., 210–11.

13. Ibid., 211.

14. Ibid.

15. Ibid. The marriage contract was subject to variation even at the time the Supreme Court wrote its description.

It is also clear, as one looks at proposals for reform of marriage, that the facts underlying the word *marriage* can be enormously different from country to country and time to time. Thus, Leon Blum's *Marriage* suggests equal sexual experience as a remedy in a world in which, whatever the theory, the facts usually involved an experienced husband and an inexperienced wife (Blum, *Marriage*, trans. Warre B. Wells [Philadelphia: J.B. Lippincott, 1937], 102–64). Compare this to the American ideology of the romantic marriage of virgins for life, controlling in theory and perhaps in fact, until fairly recently.

16. See Lee E. Teitelbaum, "Family History and Family Law," *Wisconsin Law Review* 1985:1144–58.

17. See Joel P. Bishop, *Commentaries on the Law of Marriage and Divorce* (Boston: Little, Brown, 1881), vol. 1, sec. 2, p. 2, which concludes that the contract ended upon marriage: "Actual marriage, in any form which makes the parties in law husband and wife, is performance. Nothing short is." At marriage, therefore, the contract ceased, and thereafter it was appropriate to think of marriage as a status. But the ideas of status and contract also involve issues of degree and not kind.

18. See Ellman, "The Theory of Alimony," 18, 28–32.

19. Note the difference between readjustments in a context assumed to be stable, on which there is considerable reliance, and readjustments that include the destruction of the context.

20. See Martha Minow, "All in the Family and in All Families: Membership, Loving, and Owing," *West Virginia Law Review* 95 (1992–93): 310–25. See also Mary Ann Glendon, *Rights Talk: The Impoverishment of Political Discourse* (New York: Free Press, 1991), 109–44; and Lee E. Teitelbaum, "Intergenerational Responsibility and Family Obligations: On Sharing," *Utah Law Review* 1992:765.

21. Max Radin, "The Common Law of the Family," in *Legal Relations*, ed. Roscoe Pound et al. (New York: Collier, 1939), 6:169.

22. Ibid., 161.

23. Ibid., 169. These "are created by the status of being husband and wife. The contract of marriage does not establish them. That merely creates the status." The first four of these, Radin continues, "are so inseparably connected with the status of husband and wife that they cannot be altered by any agreement between the parties nor waived by non-insistence or disease." The last two can, however, be "regulated to a limited extent by agreement."

24. See Ian Macneil, "Relational Contract: What We Do and Do Not Know," *Wisconsin Law Review* 1985:483.

25. See Elizabeth S. Scott, "Rehabilitating Liberalism in Modern Divorce Law," *Utah Law Review* 1994:687.

26. See Weisbrod, *The Boundaries of Utopia*, 59–79. In all contexts, there is the issue in contract law of oppression or unfair bargaining. See Peter Gabel and Jay M. Feinman, "Contract Law as Ideology," in *The Politics of Law: A Progressive Critique*, ed. David Kairys (1982), 172–84. See also note the "choices" offered the slave, Betty, in the discussion by Aviam Soifer, "Status, Contract, and Promises Unkept," *Yale Law Journal* 96 (1987): 1921–28, 1931.

27. Henry David Thoreau, *Walden* (Boston: Ticknor and Fields, 1862).

28. Martin Buber, *Tales of the Hasidim: Early Masters* (New York: Schocken, 1947), 251.

29. Note also a distinction between "personalism" and "individualism." "Personalism gives priority to the person and not the individual self. To give priority to the *person* means respecting the unique and inalienable value of the other person, as well as one's own, for a respect that is centered only on one's individual self to the exclusion of others proves itself to be fraudulent." Thomas Merton, *The Way of Chuang Tzu* (1965), 17.

30. At times the law (for example, the Uniform Commercial Code) provides a presumptive contract, or a default contract, for parties in particular conventional relationships. The parties may vary the terms of the contract—"unless otherwise agreed" is one typical formula suggesting the possibility—but contract terms will be supplied if the parties fail to do so. In certain situations, the parties are assumed to have intended a contract of some sort.

31. Domestic arrangement is used here rather than *marriage* because some of the examples relate to nonmarital negotiations. In general, the issues raised in the current discussion relate both to marital and nonmarital contracting, and, in fact, we see much less difference in the relationships than we used to, though—as will be suggested in the second part of this chapter—the default contracts of the two may still be different.

32. The point applies with particular force to women in relationships with men.

33. See, e.g., Shultz, "Contractual Ordering of Marriage," 248.

34. Llewellyn, "Behind Law of Divorce," pt. 1, 1295 n. 36.

35. Grant Gilmore, *The Death of Contract* (Columbus: Ohio State University Press, 1974), 8. The commercial-law and family law approaches may not be as removed from one another as we think. There is, for example, a similarity between the fraud ground for annulment in early English law (fraud as to the person involved, later fraud in the essentials of the marriage) and the idea of a real defense based on fraud (fraud in the factum, not knowing the nature of the document signed) available even against a holder in due course in the field of negotiable instruments. The conclusion here is not somehow that marriage "is" a negotiable instrument. Rather marriage and negotiable instruments both involve contracts viewed as more binding than ordinary contracts. Everyday fraud is not enough to avoid the contract. So, too, *Hochster v. De La Tour*, 118 Eng. Rep. 922 (1853), discusses the idea of anticipatory repudiation in the context of marriage contracts, leases, and the sale of goods. See also *Taylor v. Caldwell*, 122 Eng. Rep. 309 (K.B. 1863).

36. While questions can be raised concerning the wisdom of such contracts in times of economic uncertainty, and their relation to particular feminist objectives, I assume that such contracts could be made within a broad scheme of pluralist contracting.

37. On realism and the realists, see Morton J. Horwitz, *The Transformation of American Law, 1870–1960* (1992), 193–212; Laura Kalman, *Legal Realism at Yale, 1927–1960* (Chapel Hill: University of North Carolina Press, 1986), 190–91; and William Fischer et al., eds., *American Legal Realism* (1993).

38. Karl N. Llewellyn, "What Price Contract?—an Essay in Perspective," *Yale Law Journal* 40 (1931): 705.

39. See Llewellyn, "Behind Law of Divorce," pt. 1; and pt. 2, 249.

40. Nathan Isaacs (1886–1941) made his career as a legal academic, albeit one who spent most of his life on the faculty of Harvard Business School. Isaac's first professional work, entitled "The Merchant and His Law," was published in the *Journal of Political Economy* in 1915. It was a subject he worked on until his death. His early work also was heavily focused on legal history.

41. Isaacs's work on commercial law was cited with approval, and even enthusiasm, by Karl Llewellyn in the 1930s, and his 1917 piece on adhesion contracts is still the first citation on the subject in the Friedrich Kessler and Grant Gilmore casebook of the 1970s, *Contracts: Cases and Materials*, 2d ed. (Boston: Little, Brown, 1970), 11 (citing Nathan Isaacs, "The Standardizing of Contracts," *Yale Law Journal* 27 [1917]: 34). See also Horwitz, *Transformation of American Law* (containing references to Isaacs's works); Howard O. Hunter, "Essay on Contract and Status, Race, Marriage, and the Meretricious Spouse," *Virginia Law Review* 64 (1978): 1039 (containing discussions of Isaacs's works); and Manfred Rehbinder, "Status, Contract, and the Welfare State," *Stanford Law Review* 23 (1971): 941 (same).

42. Isaacs, "The Standardizing of Contracts," 39–40.

43. Ibid., 40.

44. Ibid., 47. Isaacs's papers are at the Baker Library, Harvard Business School. I thank the library for its courtesy in permitting use of these materials.

Isaacs's doctrinal writing through the 1920s and 1930s considered various aspects of business and commercial law. Throughout his work there is a descriptive or analytic rather than prescriptive quality. One of the marks of Isaacs's writing is his historical point of view. Another is his insistence on seeing problems from the point of view of the businessman or the layman. See Nathan Isaacs, *The Law in Business Problems* (New York: Macmillan, 1921).

45. Isaacs, "The Standardizing of Contracts," 34 (citing Henry Maine, *Ancient Law* [1861]).

46. Ibid., 39.

47. Ibid., 39–40.

48. Ibid.

49. Ibid., 45–46.

50. Nathan Isaacs, "Contracts, Torts, and Trusts," in *Legal Relations*, ed. Roscoe Pound et al. (1939), 6:34. Surrogacy contracts provide an example of the odd—if not outlandish—relation for which there is no single clear legal analogue, although several are possible.

51. See Nathan Isaacs, "The Sale in Legal Theory and in Practice," *Virginia Law Review* 26 (1940): 651.

52. See Zipporah Batshaw Wiseman, "The Limits of Vision: Karl Llewellyn and the Merchant Rules," *Harvard Law Review* 100 (1987): 477 n. 43. Wiseman suggest that Llewellyn's two articles of 1939 on sales and society ("Across Sales on Horseback" and "The First Struggle to Unhorse Sales") were titled to

acknowledge Isaacs's criticism of the Uniform Sales Act of 1906, in which a commercial transaction was typified by a horseman purchasing a saddle.

53. See Llewellyn, "Behind Law of Divorce," pt. 1, 1281–84; pt. 2, 249–51. The unpublished third part of the divorce study, "Behind the Law of Divorce," is a seventeen-page typescript (dated 1932–34 and typed in 1965) in the Llewellyn papers at the University of Chicago. I am grateful to the University of Chicago law library for making this material available to me.

Llewellyn begins the third part by reviewing what he had already said: Pair marriage would continue; the desire for relatively permanent relationships was at the base of it, interlocked with matters of sex, child rearing, and economics; expectations of the institution were rising and experiments being made; and divorce was simply the next step in this process. He also speaks of the "neglect-in-action," of the official theories that called for state participation in divorce proceedings, and for strict attention to defenses in order to demonstrate a practice of consent divorce (2).

54. Llewellyn, "Behind Law of Divorce," pt. 1, 1281n; see also Twining, *Llewellyn and Realist Movement*, 194: "[I]nstead of confining himself to testing rigorously and in detail some precisely formulated hypotheses, Llewellyn ended up with a general disquisition on marriage and divorce, a *pot-pourri* of general theory, statistical data and personal impressions."

55. For a summary, in English, of Llewellyn's treatment of marriage in his German work, see Michael Ansaldi, "The German Llewellyn," *Brooklyn Law Review* 58 (1992): 767–70, discussing Llewellyn's *Recht, Rechtsleben und Gesellschaft,* ed. Manfred Rehbinder (1977).

56. Llewellyn, "Behind Law of Divorce," pt. 1, 1285.

57. Llewellyn, "Behind Law of Divorce," pt. 2, 260.

58. Llewellyn, "Behind Law of Divorce," pt. 1, 1291.

59. Ibid., 1281n.

60. Ibid., 1283.

61. Grant Gilmore, "In Memoriam: Karl Llewellyn," *Yale Law Journal* 71 (1962): 814.

62. See Ansaldi, "The German Llewellyn," 717 n. 44, describing Llewellyn's "What Price Contract?" as "fantasmagorical" and "wildly undisciplined."

63. Certainly Llewellyn continues to be interesting to scholars. Recent work includes Ansaldi, "The German Llewellyn"; N. E. H. Hull, "Reconstructing the Origins of Realistic Jurisprudence: A Prequel to the Llewellyn-Pound Exchange over Legal Realism," *Duke Law Journal* 1989:1302; James Whitman, "Commercial and the American Volk: A Note on Llewellyn's German Sources for the Uniform Commercial Code," *Yale Law Journal* 97 (1987): 165.

64. Llewellyn, "Behind Law of Divorce," pt. 2, 262.

65. Llewellyn, "Behind Law of Divorce," pt. 1, 1287.

66. Ibid., 1290.

67. Ibid., 1292 n. 26.

68. Ibid., 1281.

69. Llewellyn, "What Price Contract?" 711–12; see Margaret F. Brinig, "Rings and Promises," *J.L. Econ. and Org.* 6 (1990): 204 (suggesting a possible

relation between use of engagement ring and abandonment of actions for breach of promise to marry).

70. This is particularly evident in the neglect of issues relating to consumers.

71. Karl N. Llewellyn, "Our Case Law of Contract: Offer and Acceptance II," *Yale Law Journal* 48 (1938): 785. The critiques of offer-and-acceptance rules in those articles also found their way into the article 2 provisions on formation of contracts.

72. See, e.g., Noonan, *Persons and Masks*, 3–4, 43–50.

73. See, e.g., references to aging women in Llewellyn, "Behind Law of Divorce," pt. 2, 280.

74. Ibid., 260.

75. Llewellyn was, by this time, generally interested in groups. In 1925, he published an article that contained material on group control. In "The Effect of Legal Institutions upon Economics," *American Economic Review* 15 (1925): 672, he asserted, "Increasingly, associations are forming which adopt their own rules of action and even settle their own disputes." This was not limited to an observation about sales, and the buyers and sellers of goods: "Corporation, labor union, manufacturers' association, farmers' cooperative—their number, size and experience increase. And the rules which, by permission of the state, and within limits which the state prescribes, such associations lay down and apply, are part of the body of our law. They are working rules; the working rules of a technical activity; the very type of working rules which the official legal institutions are unable to construct" (672). By analogy, these rules, in the context of marriage, could be seen as the ways of family life or the ways of wedlock. Llewellyn's ideas about groups are explored in Allen Kamp, "Between-the-Wars Social Thought: Karl Llewellyn, Legal Realism, and the Uniform Commercial Code in Context," 59 *Albany Law Review* 325 (1995).

76. Williston's Uniform Sales Act (1906) was ultimately adopted by thirty-seven states.

77. UCC, sec. 2–104, cmt. 1 (1989): "This Article assumes that transactions between professionals in a given field require special and clear rules which may not apply to a casual or inexperienced seller or buyer."

78. Karl N. Llewellyn, "On Warranty of Quality, and Society," *Columbia Law Review* 36 (1936): 707, citing *Ronaasen and Son v. Arcos Ltd.*, 43 L.1. L. Rep. 1, 5 (1932).

79. Karl N. Llewellyn, *Cases and Materials on the Law of Sales* (Chicago: Callahan, 1930), 1073–77.

80. Llewellyn, "On Warranty of Quality," 706.

81. Llewellyn, "Behind Law of Divorce," pt. 1, 1307. For Llewellyn, the family exists as an image in the background of other discussions of other institutions. He saw the family and family issues as connected to the central inquiries of law, including contract law, and society. The family was also in his mind when he thought about public law. Llewellyn begins his discussion of the Constitution with a section called "the private law background." Karl N. Llewellyn, "The Constitution as an Institution," *Columbia Law Review* 34 (1934): 6. He sees

that "[a]s an institution of major size, then, our working Constitution embraces the interlocking ways and attitudes of different groups and classes in the community—*different* ways and attitudes of *different* groups and classes, but all cogging together into a fairly well organized whole" (18). At that point Llewellyn offers a long description of a family in which the husband goes out to work and provides for the payment of bills. The husband leaves a house that has been organized so that he will be able to leave for work quickly, knowing that there are things he has to pick up on his way home. This pattern essentially carries through, in different details, to other members of the family so that, in their very diverse ways, they all contribute to the whole (18–19).

In considering the interaction of individuals in the smallest unit of society, Llewellyn sees the family unit as the basic model for the structure of society as a whole. The family is not on the "private" side in the sense that it is apart from all the rest of the world. Rather, in Llewellyn's mind, the family is always a part of the map of the world.

82. Llewellyn, "What Price Contract?" 742.

83. Ibid., 748–49.

84. Llewellyn, "Behind Law of Divorce," pt. 2, 278.

85. Llewellyn, "What Price Contract?" 734.

86. Llewellyn, "Behind Law of Divorce," pt. 2, 260: "The work of building marriages, whatever the conditions, is individual work." "To generalize existent ways into such a pattern, or even into a fixed number of typical patterns, is to lose sight precisely of that *rôle* of individual action which we are seeking to explore" ("Behind Law of Divorce," pt. 1, 1285).

87. See Horwitz, *Transformation of American Law*, 210–12; see also Karl N. Llewellyn, "On What Is Wrong with Legal Education," *Columbia Law Review* 35 (1935): 662.

88. Llewellyn, "Behind Law of Divorce," pt. 1, 1290, 1306; pt. 2, 280.

89. See the discussions of "earned and vested rights" and "sense of security" on partners in Llewellyn, "Behind Law of Divorce," pt. 2, 279–80. He also remarks, "There is some point in making the established concern more difficult to dissolve" (284).

90. Ibid., 284.

91. Llewellyn, "Behind Law of Divorce," pt. 1, 1296.

92. Llewellyn, "What Price Contract?" 729; cf. UCC, sec. 1–102(lb) (3) and cmt. 2 (1989) (discussing freedom of contract and UCC).

93. Llewellyn, "What Price Contract?" 729 n. 54.

94. Karl N. Llewellyn, "The Normative, the Legal, and the Law-Jobs: The Problem of Juristic Method," *Yale Law Journal* 49 (1940): 1376–83.

95. Llewellyn, "Behind Law of Divorce," pt. 1, 1298. Llewellyn also commented on problems of duration in this context. "Chance passions do not so often outlast a year. Passions which do outlast that period raise claims of their own" ("Behind Law of Divorce," pt. 2, 283).

96. Holmes, "Path of the Law," 466.

97. Anthony Trollope, *Ralph the Heir*, ed. John Sutherland (New York: Oxford University Press, 1990), 328.

98. The UCC defines agreement as the "bargain in fact" as found in language or by implication. UCC, sec. 1–201(3) (1989). Whether the "agreement" is a "contract" is separately determined. In the commercial-law discussion, it is plain that "law" and "practice" relate to each other. Thus Llewellyn emphasized the issues of custom, leeways, tolerances, and the like, all tending to the point that the contract itself was only the beginning of the inquiry of what a contract meant. Many factors went into what a contract meant. Some implied terms, for example, would be assumed from the situation and in other cases custom or trade usage. Flexibility and readjustments were assumed as desirable and normal, and dispute settlement outside the courts was also considered normal.

These are not necessarily the views of present writers on family and contract, who may assume, for example, a rigidity on the contractual arrangement and a necessary emphasis on litigation as a remedy that Llewellyn would not have assumed.

99. See, e.g., Edward Gibbon, *Memoirs of My Life,* ed. Betty Radice (1990), 146: "A matrimonial alliance, has ever been the object of my terror rather than of my wishes. I was not very strongly pressed by my family or my passions to propagate the name and race of Gibbons, and if some reasonable temptations occurred in the neighborhood, the vague idea never proceeded to the length of a serious negotiation."

100. Bernard, *The Future of Marriage,* suggests that a marriage contract is actually two contracts: his and hers.

101. Stone, *Family, Sex, and Marriage,* 86, 87.

102. Ibid., 87.

103. Ibid., 87–88.

104. Georg Simmel, *The Philosophy of Money,* ed. David Frisby, trans. Tom Bottomore and David Frisby, 2d ed. (Boston: Routledge and Kegan Paul, 1990), 380.

105. See Trollope, *Ralph the Heir.* Trollope simply portrayed the man as ordinary and not particularly sensitive. Note also the contrast between revocable and irrevocable love in Trollope's *Orley Farm,* ed. David Skilten (New York: Oxford University Press, 1985), 270.

106. *Maynard v. Hill,* 125 U.S. 190, 205–16 (1888); *Hyde v. Hyde,* 1 L.R.-P. and D. 130 (1866).

107. One might also note the existence of a general and academic interest in Trollope. See Louise Weinberg, "Is It All Right to Read Trollope?" *American Scholar* 62 (1993): 447–51.

108. Anthony Trollope, *Is He Popenjoy?* ed. John Sutherland (New York: Oxford University Press, 1986), 13. Compare the character in Israel Zangwill's *King of the Schnorrers* (1894), who says, in effect: "I have always wanted to be your son-in-law."

109. Trollope, *Ralph the Heir,* 101.

110. In the modern American context, this type of control is not what we mean by male dominance within a marriage. Instead, the modern idea of marital control has more to do with subordination of a wife's independent interest

to her husband's career and comfort. The husband's life ultimately defines family life. Additionally, there is sometimes an issue of physical abuse.

111. For discussion, see N. John Hall, *Trollope: A Biography* (New York: Oxford University Press, 1991), 339–44.

112. Anthony Trollope, *An Autobiography* (Oxford: Oxford University Press, 1992, 144 (quoting Hawthorne's letter to James Fields).

113. John Sutherland, introduction to Anthony Trollope, *Phineas Finn: The Irish Member*, ed. Sutherland (Harmondsworth, Middlesex: Penguin, 1972), 7, 25. See Anthony Trollope, *An Old Man's Love*, ed. John Sutherland (New York: Oxford University Press, 1991), 245–65.

114. Trollope described his own marriage as essentially happy and successful. He wrote in his autobiography, "My marriage was like the marriage of other people, and of no special interest to any one except my wife and me" (64–65). In fact, his marriage has been of considerable interest to biographers and the subject of some speculation, though very little is actually known about his marriage or his wife. See, e.g., Victoria Glendinning, *Anthony Trollope* (London: Hutchinson, 1992), 143–53. See also *An Autobiography*, 288, in which he records the significance in his life of his friendship with an American woman whom he does not identify (Kate Field, whom he met in 1860).

115. Trollope, *Phineas Finn*, 132. Also see Trollope, *Orley Farm*, which contrasts the method of "moulding a wife" with the "ordinary plan": "Dance with the girl three times and if you like the light of her eye and the tone of her voice with which she, breathless, answers your little questions about horseflesh and music—about affairs masculine and feminine—then take the leap in the dark" (328–29).

On certain models of marriage, the spousal relationships involves economic cooperation and the raising of children. In relation to each other, spouses may have secondary roles. A familiar expression of this view of marriage (if not a worse one) is found in Plato's description of the penultimate encounter of Socrates and Xanthippe. *Phaedo*, ed. Frederick J. Church (1951). For discussion of changing conceptions of, and demands on, marriage, see Barbara Ehrenreich, "Burt, Loni, and Our Way of Life," *Time*, September 20, 1993, 92; and Margaret Mead, "What Does the American Man Expect of a Wife?" *Redbook*, May 1962, 28, 30.

116. Anthony Trollope, *Mr. Scarborough's Family*, ed. Geoffrey Harvey (New York: Oxford University Press, 1989), 240–60.

117. Anthony Trollope, *Doctor Thorne*, ed. Ruth Kendell (Harmondsworth, Middlesex: Penguin, 1991), 87–88. See Hall, *Trollope*, 88–89, 167–68, who concludes that Trollope was recounting his own history.

118. Bishop, *Commentaries*, vol. 1, sec. 1.

119. Ibid., secs. 2110–13.

120. Hall, *Trollope*, 89, quoting Trollope, *An Eye for an Eye*.

121. Jean L. Flandrin, *Families in Former Times*, trans. Richard Southern (London: Cambridge University Press, 1979), 39.

122. See Stake, "Mandatory Planning for Divorce," 441, discussing "romantic intoxication." But in other contexts there may be a demand for prudence. See

generally Harry W. Vanneman, "Annulment of Marriage for Fraud," *Minnesota Law Review* 9 (1925): 500–517. A quite deliberate and rational approach to marital decision-making, to the extent that it involves children, is suggested by the idea that genetic counseling is useful premaritally as a factor influencing the decision whether or not to marry.

123. Llewellyn, "What Price Contract?" 728 n. 49.

124. Ibid.

125. Ibid., 728; see *Standard Fin. Co. v. Ellis*, 657 P.2d 1056, 1061 (Haw. Ct. App. 1983) (refusing to allow abused wife to avoid obligation based on claim of duress); Clare Dalton, "An Essay in the Deconstruction of Contract Doctrine," *Yale Law Journal* 94 (1986): 1024–36.

126. Despite the familiar comment that "necessitous men are not, truly speaking, free men." *Vernon v. Bethell*, 28 Eng. Rep. 838, 839 (1762).

127. Trollope's *Ralph the Heir* (2:329) and *Orley Farm* (329) use this language.

128. In some contexts, however, they may have met through arrangement, an intermediate form.

129. Trollope makes clear the generally powerful role of families in arranging marriages. See, e.g., *Can You Forgive Her?* ed. Andrew Swarbricke (New York: Oxford University Press, 1982), 13–34, describing the arranged marriage between Glencora and Duke.

130. For example, an agreed-upon childless marriage would have been such a case before the public acceptance and legalization of contraception.

131. Anita Brookner, *Hotel du Lac* (London: Jonathan Cape, 1984), 166–67. On open marriage contracts, see Shultz, "Contractual Ordering of Marriage," 221–23.

132. The proposal, with its agreed-upon tolerances explicitly on the table, also is suggestive of a comment of Trollope's to the effect that when he was a child a distinction was made between games in which cheating was allowed, agreed upon in advance, and games in which cheating was not allowed. Anthony Trollope, *North America* (New York: St. Martin's Press, 1986), 1:144.

133. Brookner, *Hotel du Lac*, 167. Historically, love-based deals have also fallen through because of parental refusal to give consent. For example, Edward Gibbon recounts his early love, his father's refusal to approve, and his subsequent life as an unmarried man of letters. Gibbon, Memoirs of My Life, 104–5.

134. See the proposals, first nonmarital and then marital, of the duke of Omnium to Madame Max Goesler. Trollope, *Phineas Finn*, 548, 710. See also Anthony Trollope, *The Way We Live Now* (New York: Random House, 1984).

135. "The baron knows what is expected of him," Colette wrote in *Gigi* (Colette, *Gigi and Selected Writings* [New York: New American Library, 1963], 132). Presumably, liaisons outside of marriage that were *not* economically based could also be, in this sense, conventional.

136. While nonmarital arrangements may vary widely, all might be called cohabitation and be analyzed in terms of contract. These would include cases in which marriage is desired but not possible and also cases in which marriage is

not desired and not necessarily relevant as a model (for example, sibling domestic arrangements).

137. Dick Francis, *Comeback* (Crest, 1991), 184–85.

138. Ross Thomas [Oliver Bleeck, pseud.], *No Questions Asked* (New York: Mysterious Press, 1976), 112.

139. William Congreve, *The Way of the World,* ed. Henry T. E. Perry (Appleton-Century-Crofts, 1951). See also Katha Pollitt, "Bothered and Bewildered," *New York Times,* July 22, 1993, A23. Pollitt notes that when women are economically self-sufficient, they are willing to take care of children, but not willing to care for husbands, although "most men still seem to expect it."

140. Trollope, *Is He Popenjoy?* 1:161. The combination of marriage for interest and conventional feminine behavior can be presented as comic. Thus in a novel by Wodehouse, a father insists on a show of sentiment and enthusiasm from his daughter, who is more direct about the central aspect of the (ultimately failed) arrangement. P. G. Wodehouse, *If I Were You* (1931; reprint, London: Penguin, 1991). The daughter tells her father, "[Y]ou know and I know that it's simply a business deal. I provide the money, Tony supplies the title. . . . You brought me down here to land Tony. And I've landed him" (17). Finally, she responds to her father's insistence on affect and role-playing and displays some appropriate enthusiasm: " 'Oh, Father dear,' said Violet girlishly, 'when Tony asked me to be his wife, I was so taken aback and so completely flabbergasted to think that he should feel that way about me that I simply gasped' " (18).

141. Anthony Trollope, *Linda Tressel,* ed. Robert Tracy (New York: Oxford University Press, 1991), 253.

142. Ibid.

143. Alfred Tennyson, "Locksley Hall," in *Locksley Hall, Daydream, and Other Poems* (New York: T. Y. Crowell, 1892), 38. Trollope, too, invoked the dog image in a speech by Laura. "You cannot make a woman subject to you as a dog is so. You may have all the outside and as much of the inside as you can master. With a dog you may be sure of both" (*Phineas Finn,* 398).

144. Trollope, *Mr. Scarborough's Family,* 498.

145. 83 U.S. (16 Wall.) 130 (1872). The Court held that the Fourteenth Amendment does not prevent the state from limiting admission to the bar to men. Id., 138–39. For another discussion of *Bradwell,* see chapter 7.

146. Ibid., 139 (Bradley, Swain, and Field, J.J., concurring).

147. Ibid., 141–42 (Bradley, Swain and Field, J.J., concurring). See Simmel, *The Philosophy of Money,* 378 n. 121: "The significance and the consequence that society attaches to the sexual relations between man and woman are correspondingly based on the presupposition that the woman gives her total self, with all its worth, whereas the man gives only a part of his personality in the exchange."

148. *Bradwell,* 83 U.S. at 141–42 (Bradley, Swain, and Field, J.J., concurring).

149. Isaacs, "Contracts, Torts, and Trusts."

150. See, e.g., Diana T. Meyers, introduction to *Kindred Matters: Rethinking the Philosophy of the Family,* ed. Diana T. Meyers et. al. (Ithaca: Cornell Univer-

sity Press, 1993), 14 (suggesting child's acceptance of benefits as possibly creating contractual relationship). Perhaps even involuntary relationships—for example, in-laws—can be understood as ancillary to the primary choice to marry.

151. This section does not deny the point that, in general, there is an overemphasis on the legal and remedial aspects of contract law, and inadequate stress on contract as ongoing framework.

152. See Shultz, "Contractual Ordering of Marriage," 226–28.

153. Thus people choose to marry rather than to negotiate special or individualized contracts covering some of the same ground. There are overriding issues of knowledge of the law that are involved here. Lynn A. Baker argues that people should know more about the economic aspects relating to the law of marriage, in "Promulgating the Marriage Contract," *University of Michigan Journal of Law Reform* 23 (1990): 2224–37. For example, people may be particularly ignorant of the tax consequences of the marriage contract or the economic issues of divorce. The argument for default contracts assumes that the central expectations of marriage are generally known.

154. See previous discussion and Isaacs, "Sale in Legal Theory," 667.

155. Llewellyn, "What Price Contract?" 736–37. The framework was not rigid. Llewellyn observed that contracts were so overlaid with unrecorded adjustments and further factual agreements that in the end "the initial contract [is] a wholly misleading guide to what occurs" (731).

156. 2 K.B. 571 (1919).

157. Ibid., 579–80. The court believed that the parties "never intended to make a bargain which could be enforced in law." Id., 575. On intention in Balfour, see Kessler and Gilmore, *Contracts*, 100.

158. See UCC, sec. 2–302. Even aside from such a direct policing doctrine, results can be achieved by manipulation of technical doctrines, although "[c]overt tools are never reliable tools." Karl N. Llewellyn, "Book Review," *Harvard Law Review* 52 (1939): 703.

159. For examples of the law reinforcing traditional societal views of marriage, see *Maynard v. Hill*, 125 U.S. 190, 203–16 (1888); *Reynolds v. United States*, 98 U.S. 145, 161–68 (1878); *Bradwell v. Illinois*, 83 U.S. (16 Wall.) 130, 137–39 (1872); id., at 139–42 (Bradley, Swain, and Field, J.J., concurring).

160. See John K. Galbraith, *Economics and the Public Purpose* (1973), 30–37, 59–60 (describing wives as "crypto-servants" doing menial labor even where husband is highly paid), quoted in Harris, Teitelbaum, Weisbrod, *Family Law*, (Boston: Little, Brown, 1996), 43.

161. The idea that the parties provided information about the standards by which performance is judged is one of the ideas of article 2. "Article 2, then, judges performance, and provides remedies, principally by standards within the control of the parties. Indeed, the Code recurrently invites the parties to state in the contract of sale who shall do what, where and how, and with what consequences, subject only to an inhibition against unconscionability." Ellen A. Peters, "Remedies for Breach of Contracts Relating to the Sale of Goods under

the Uniform Commercial Code: A Roadmap for Article Two," *Yale Law Journal* 73 (1963): 202.

162. Llewellyn, "What Price Contract?" 734 n. 63.

163. Note the current controversy in India over support/maintenance orders under Islamic law. See P. Jagonmohan Reddy, "Shah Bano Verdict and Muslim Law," in *The Shah Bano Controversy*, ed. Asghar Ali Engineer (1987), 41–45; Anika Rahmun, "Religious Rights versus Women's Rights in India: A Test Case for International Human Rights Law," *Columbia Journal of Transnational Law* 28 (1990): 473–82. The use of religious options in the menu raises complex issues, some of them arising simply from the concept of separation of church and state. The constitutional problem is not addressed here.

164. Under Jewish law, rabbis do not grant the divorce. The husband must supply the document of divorce called a "get." At present, the state will be reluctant to use physical sanctions against a recalcitrant husband, although historically the religious authorities were not so reluctant. See generally Leo Pfeffer and Alan Pfeffer, "The Agunah in American Secular Law," *Church and State* 31 (1989): 487–525.

165. Default options could be fact specific. Examples include divorce for marriages with minor children; summary divorce for short no-assets, no-debts marriages; and special rules on divorce for older couples without children of the marriage.

166. See Scott, "Rational Decision-Making," 38–70; Stake, "Mandatory Planning for Divorce," 429–44 (suggesting framework of options).

167. By contrast, in the support-after-divorce context, it is a monetary award that is desired.

168. Sometimes, in family cases, the point seems to be something about *de minimis*, not the difficulty of finding a suitable remedy. For example, Bishop trivialized the problem of the enforceable contract between husband and wife. See *Commentaries*, vol. 2, sec. 192. Classic examples of cases that did not create enforceable obligations (the broken date; the babysitter who didn't follow instructions) are now in fact litigated.

169. It may be noted that contracts to perform operas were another context in which specific performance gave difficulties to contracts. A New York judge wrote in 1833, "I am not aware that any officer of this court has that perfect knowledge of the Italian language, or possesses that exquisite sensibility in the auricular nerve, which is necessary to understand and to enjoy, with a proper zest, the peculiar beauties of the Italian opera, so fascinating to the fashionable world. There might be some difficulty, therefore, even if the defendant was compelled to sing under the direction and in the presence of a master in chancery, in ascertaining whether he performed his engagement according to its spirit and intent. It would also be very difficult for the master to determine what effect coercion might produce upon the defendant's singing, especially in the livelier airs; although the fear of imprisonment would unquestionably deepen his seriousness in the graver parts of the drama." *DeRivafinoli v. Forsetti*, New York (1833) 534.

170. Bishop, *Commentaries*, sec. 29 ("Over England, but not over this country, walks also that other spawn of a dark age, whose mission it was to keep unconjugal sinners in the strait performance of holy matrimonial duties."). Bishop explained that restitution of conjugal rights was an action in which an individual was "thrust back again to the bliss which had been too lightly prized." Id. (See also chapter 6, note 80.)

171. Some writers used specific performance to mean performance of the obligations of marriage; for example, enforcement of the support obligation assumed at marriage. Specific performance could also mean continuance of the marital status by denying a divorce. Of course, the perception of a marital relationship in law says little about the existence of a domestic relationship in fact.

172. Conjugal affection, Llewellyn notes, can only develop "out of lasting life together." Llewellyn, "Behind Law of Divorce," pt. 1, 1293. Note that the romantic drive is not itself conjugal affection, though it produces it. "The romantic ideal is itself the most potent drive conceivable toward producing conjugal affection, if it can be freed from its even greater drive toward impatience, and from mankind's yearning for magic: that things which need work, self-restraint, thought, shall just happen of themselves" (1293 n. 29). See generally Raj Kumari Agarwala, "Restitution of Conjugal Rights under Hindu Law: A Plea for the Abolition of the Remedy," *Journal of the Indian Law Institute* 12 (1970): 257–68. See also *Kaur v. Harmander Singh*, 1984 A.I.R. (S.C.) 66, 66 (India) (upholding restitution of conjugal rights action).

173. Kessler and Gilmore, *Contracts*, 1060 n. 4.

174. For a discussion of the no-fault idiom as one conveying the message that marital breakdown is never anyone's fault, see Mary Ann Glendon, *Abortion and Divorce in Western Law* (Cambridge: Harvard University Press, 1987), 107–8.

175. The most difficult agreed-upon remedies seem to be those that provide for an automatic award, or shift, of custody as a remedy for breach of a contractual promise. In this situation, however, a review of the child's interest is necessary, as it is with all other bargaining concerning children.

176. Anton Chekhov, "Marriage in Ten or Fifteen Years," in *Selected Stories*, trans. Ann Dunnigan (New York: New American Library, 1960), 74–77.

177. Ibid., 76–77.

178. Corbin made the central point in the context of a discussion of offer and acceptance: "The legal relations consequent upon offer and acceptance are not wholly dependent, even upon the reasonable meaning of the words and acts of the parties. The law determines these relations in the light of subsequent circumstances, these often being totally unforeseen by the parties. In such cases it is sometimes said that the law will create that relation which the parties would have intended had they foreseen. The fact is, however, that the decision will depend upon the notions of the court as to policy, welfare, justice, right and wrong, such notions often being inarticulate and subconscious." Arthur Corbin, "Offer and Acceptance and Some of the Resulting Legal Relations," *Yale Law Journal* 26 (1917): 206.

Chapter Four

1. "Japanese Family Law," *Stanford Law Review* 9 (1956): 132. See also Nobushige Hozumi, *Ancestor Worship and Japanese Law*, 2d ed. (Plainview: Books for Libraries Press, 1973).

2. "Japanese Family Law," 153.

3. Ibid., 154.

4. Yogo Watenabe, assisted by Max Rheinstein, "The Family and the Law: The Individualistic Premise and Modern Japanese Family Law," in *Law in Japan: The Legal Order in a Changing Society*, ed. Arthur T. Von Mehren (Cambridge: Harvard University Press, 1963), 364.

5. Captured by the use of the bass as the singing voice of the mother in the Brecht-Weill *Seven Deadly Sins*.

6. See Weisbrod, "Family, Church, and State," 741.

7. Edmund Wilson, *Classics and Commercials: A Literary Chronicle of the Forties* (New York: Farrar, Strauss, and Giroux, 1950), 385–87.

8. The letter was published in English in 1954 as "Letter to His Father," in *Dearest Father; Stories and Other Writings*, trans. Ernest Kaiser and Eithne Wilkins (New York: Schocken, 1954).

9. Wilson, *Classics and Commercials*, 385–87.

10. Ibid., 391.

11. Letter from Max Brod to Felice Bauer (November 22, 1912), in Franz Kafka, *Letters to Felice*, ed. Erich Heller and Jürgen Born, trans. James Stern and Elisabeth Duckworth (New York: Schocken, 1973), 57.

12. "My writing was all about you . . ." Kafka, "Letter to His Father."

13. See Kafka in *Dearest Father*, 405. Brod referred to the letter as "the most comprehensive attempt at an autobiography [Kafka] ever made."

14. Max Brod, *Franz Kafka: A Biography*, trans. G. Humphreys Roberts and Richard Winston, 2d ed. (New York: Schocken, 1967), 15–16.

15. Letter from Franz Kafka to Milena Jesenská (July 4–5, 1920), *Letters to Milena*, trans. Philip Boehm (New York: Schocken, 1990), 63.

16. *Dearest Father*, see note 13.

17. See Christina Crawford, *Mommie Dearest* (New York: W. Morrow, 1978).

18. J. P. Stern argues that *The Trial* was a prophetic or anticipatory account of "both the concepts underlying national socialist legislation and the practice of its law courts." See "The Law of *The Trial*," in *On Kafka: Semi-Centenary Perspectives*, ed. Franz Kuna (New York: Barnes and Noble, 1976), 30. See generally George Steiner, *"K"* in *Language and Silence* (New York: Atheneum, 1970), and "Introduction" in Franz Kafka, *The Trial*, (New York: Knopf, 1992).

19. Alice Miller, *Thou Shalt Not Be Aware: Society's Betrayal of the Child* (New York: Farrar, Straus and Giroux, 1984), 253–56.

20. Ibid., 275.

21. For Miller, the test of pathology is basically whether the child is ever able to confront the parent directly with his or her grievance.

22. William Wordsworth, "Intimations of Immortality from Recollections of Early Childhood."

23. For Kafka's analytic approach to his own life, see his list of arguments on the possibility of marriage. Franz Kafka, *The Diaries, 1910–23,* ed. Max Brod, trans. Joseph Kresh et al. (New York: Schocken, 1976), 225–26.

24. Kafka, "Letter to His Father," 131.

25. Ibid., 133.

26. Miller, *Thou Shalt Not,* 289.

27. Kafka, "Letter to His Father," 133.

28. See David Magarshack, introduction to *The Best Short Stories of Dostoevsky,* trans. David Magarshack (New York: Random House, 1963), vii, xii–xiii.

29. Kafka, *Letters to Milena,* 63.

30. Kafka, "Letter to His Father," 117.

31. Robin West, "Authority, Autonomy, and Choice: The Role of Consent in the Moral and Political Vision of Franz Kafka and Richard A. Posner," *Harvard Law Review* 99 (1985): 384, 386 n. 8 (citing Ernst Pawel, *The Nightmare of Reason: A Life of Franz Kafka* [New York: Vintage, 1984], 3117–22).

32. Richard Posner, "The Ethical Significance of Free Choice: A Reply to Professor West," *Harvard Law Review* 99 (1986): 1431, 1432 n. 8.

33. Lida Kirchberger, *Franz Kafka's Use of Law in Fiction* (New York: P. Lang, 1986), 191. Kirchberger sees the issue of two jurisdictions in *The Trial.*

34. Letter from Franz Kafka to Milena Jesenská (August 9, 1920), *Letters to Milena,* 146, describing his sexual encounter with a shopgirl: "I kept stopping in front of the window, my mouth full of disgusting Roman law; finally we came to an understanding."

35. See, e.g., *Letters to Milena,* 301.

36. See William W. Buckland and Arnold D. McNair, *Roman Law and Common Law* (Cambridge: Cambridge University Press, 1936), 158.

37. See Lon L. Fuller, *Legal Fictions* (Stanford: Stanford University Press, 1967), 59–63 (discussing Rudolf von Ihering).

38. Kirchberger, *Kafka's Use of Law,* 194.

39. As he expressed it in "On Parables," in *The Basic Kafka,* trans. Willa Muir and Edwin Muir (New York: Washington Square Press, 1979), 158.

40. Kafka, *The Diaries,* 321.

41. See Melvin Eisenberg, "Donative Promises," *University of Chicago Law Review* 47 (1979): 1.

42. Kafka, "Letter to His Father," 152.

43. Posner, "Ethical Significance," 1439.

44. Kafka, "Letter to His Father." See also *The Diaries,* 154.

45. Kafka, *The Diaries,* 98.

46. Ibid., 317.

47. Walter H. Sokel, "Language and Truth in the Two Worlds of Franz Kafka," in *Franz Kafka: Modern Critical Views,* ed. Harold Bloom (New York: Chelsea House, 1986), 180. In the same volume see Erich Heller, *"The Castle,"* 141 (for Kafka, "Truth and existence are mutually exclusive"), and Alwin L. Baum, "Parable as Paradox in Kafka's Stories," 151 ("language itself is the archliar," quoting Heinz Politzer).

48. Kafka, *Letters to Friends*, 281 ("I can't help entangling myself in lies when I write about her").

49. See *The Diaries*, 329.

50. Philip Shuchman, *Problems of Knowledge in Legal Scholarship* (Hartford: University of Connecticut Press, 1979), 58. "Somewhere I read that a 'trial is about as much a search for truth as physics is a quest for justice.'"

51. Kurt Wolff, "Franz Kafka," in *Kurt Wolff: A Portrait in Essays and Letters,* ed. Michael Ermarth, trans. Deborah Lucas Schneider (Chicago: University of Chicago Press, 1991), 56. Wolff notes Kafka's interest in a fraud trial in Prague in 1909.

52. Kafka, *Letters to Friends*, 387.

53. Kafka, *The Diaries*, 177.

54. Ibid., 384.

55. Franz Kafka, *The Trial*, trans. Willa Muir et al. (New York: Schocken, 1984), 220.

56. Kafka, "Letter to His Father," 136.

57. Letter from Kafka to Milena Jesenská (September 15, 1920), *Letters to Milena*, 196.

58. Letter from Franz Kafka to Felice Bauer (September 30 or October 1, 1917), in *Letters to Felice*, 544–45.

59. Roman law, with its emphasis on the law of the Roman citizen and rules of *jus gentium*, may have a role here.

60. Clayton Koelb, "The Deletions from Kafka's Novels," *Monatshefte* 68 (1976): 365. See also Posner, "Ethical Significance," 1447 n. 42 (*The Trial* is not about positive law and government). Whatever it is, the court "seems nothing so worldly as an organ of state power." See also Martha S. Robinson, "The Law of the State in Kafka's *The Trial*," *Alsa Forum* 6 (1982): 127.

61. Here arise issues of translation from German and what the negation of a term means. If we say, "It is not an ordinary state trial," is it a nonstate trial or an extraordinary state trial?

62. Petrazycki, *Law and Morality*, 68. For Petrazycki, law exists in the mind of the individual.

63. See Frederick Karl, *Franz Kafka: Representative Man* (New York: Ticknor & Field, 1991), 17; Pawel, *The Nightmare of Reason.*

64. Cf. Kafka, *The Trial*, 59–60, 103.

65. Kafka, "Letter to His Father." Cf. Ernst Freund, "The Study of Law in Germany," *Counsellor* 1 (1892): 131 (discussing "negative reasons," meaning that nothing interests the student more).

66. Kafka, "Letter to His Father," 154.

67. Ibid. See Karl, *Franz Kafka*, on Kafka's studies at the German University of Prague. See generally Pawel, *The Nightmare of Reason.*

68. Kafka, *The Diaries*, 264.

69. Kafka, *Letters to Milena*, 59.

70. Kafka, "Letter to His Father," 124. Compare an anthropologist's account of table rules in Jules Henry, *Pathways to Madness* (New York: Random House, 1971), 89–91, 415.

71. See Kafka, "Before the Law" (law for one person only) in *The Trial*, 234–36.

72. Kafka, "Letter to His Father," 124–25.

73. On expulsion and boycott, see Carol Weisbrod, "Emblems of Federalism," *University of Michigan Journal of Law Reform* 25 (1992): 795.

74. "*Pavlatche* is the Czech word for the long balcony in the inner courtyard of old houses in Prague." Editor's note in Kafka, 119.

75. Not really. But who is? "Where was the Judge whom he had never seen? Where was the high Court, to which he had never penetrated?" Kafka, *The Trial*, 228.

76. Kafka, "Letter to His Father," 119–20. The letter is discussed, inter alia, by Max Brod, Richard Sennett, Alice Miller, Edmund Wilson, and Stanley Corngold. See, e.g., Stanley Corngold, *Franz Kafa: The Necessity of Form* (Ithaca: Cornell University Press, 1988), 88 (referring to the father letter as Kafka's "most deluded work").

77. See Edgar Z. Friedenberg, "Truth: Upper, Middle, and Lower," *Commentary* 30 (1960): 516 (discussing objectivity as associated with the middle class).

78. In 1915, he had left his parents' home for a rented room, but the family power remains obvious in the letter to his father of 1919. The year before his death (1924), he lived with Dora Dymant in Berlin.

79. Kafka, "Letter to His Father," 151. See generally Gerhard Neumann, "The Judgment," "Letter to His Father," and "The Bourgeois Family," in *Reading Kafka*, ed. Mark Anderson (New York: Schocken, 1989), 215. See also Mark Anderson, "Unsigned Letters to Milena Jesenská," in *Reading Kafka*, 241.

80. While the religious-social is used as one category, these can diverge so that as to divorce, for example, a religious code might forbid divorce while a social code allows it or a religious code might allow it while a social code encourages it. A "social" code can, of course, be a street code as well as an upper-middle-class code. A religious code may operate unofficially or officially. Marriage may be "mixed" and involve negotiations over codes of culture. See Gabrielle Varro, *The Transplanted Woman: A Study of French-American Marriages in France* (New York: Praeger, 1988).

81. Letter from Franz Kafka to a sister of Julie Wohryzek (November 24, 1919), *Letters to Friends*, 218.

82. Ibid.

83. Letter from Franz Kafka to Max Brod (July 1922), *Letters to Friends*, 347–48 (emphasis added).

84. Kafka, "Letter to His Father," 142.

85. Note Milena's obituary of Kafka referring to his obsession with the "guilty/innocent" in *Letters to Milena*, 271. On the complexity of the question of fault, see Kafka's two versions of his father's view of the father-son relationship in "Letter to His Father," 115, 165.

86. Letter from Julia Kafka, Franz's mother, to Felice Bauer (November 16, 1912), in Kafka, *Letters to Felice*, 46 (referring to writing as a "pastime").

87. Letter from Franz Kafka to Felice Bauer (November 21, 1912), *Letters to Felice*, 55.

88. See *Diaries*, 163.

89. Brod, *Franz Kafka*, 242.

90. See Kafka, "Letter to His Father," 114–67.

91. Is this to be read as rejection of marital contraception?

92. Kafka, "Letter to His Father," 156. See also *Letters to Friends*, 218 (discussing marriage).

93. Alexis de Tocqueville, *Democracy in America* (New York: Vintage, 1960), 2:216–17.

94. Kafka, "Letter to His Father," 162. On shame: "He is afraid the shame will outlive him" (229); "it was as if the shame of it must outlive him" (145).

95. See John T. Noonan Jr., *Contraception: A History of Its Treatment by the Catholic Theologians and Canonists* (Cambridge: Belknap of Harvard University Press, 1966). For a recent historical account, see Angus McLaren, *A History of Contraception: From Antiquity to the Present Day* (Oxford: Blackwell, 1990).

96. But see Erik H. Erikson, *Childhood and Society* (New York: Norton, 1963), 311: "Generations will depend on the ability of every procreating individual to face his children with the feeling that he was able to save some vital enthusiasm from the conflicts of his childhood."

97. This response can be called punishment whether it is a response of family or state. See generally Nigel Walker, *Why Punish?* (Oxford: Oxford University Press, 1991).

98. Benedict, *Patterns of Culture*, 244–45.

99. Kafka, "Letter to His Father," 164.

100. Lionel Trilling, *The Opposing Self: Nine Essays in Criticism* (New York: Viking, 1955), 38. For a discussion of Trilling, see Carolyn G. Heilbrun, *Reinventing Womanhood* (New York: Norton, 1979), 125–37. Feminist perspectives on the issues deserve separate treatment. Daniel Bell reads Erik Erikson as describing (in 1950) a situation in which equality in the family, including equality between husbands and wives, was largely a fact. Daniel Bell, *The End of Ideology: On the Exhaustion of Political Ideas in the Fifties*, rev. ed. (New York: Free Press, 1967), 92. The second women's movement was upon them and must have come as a particular shock to those who were focusing on the openness and egalitarianism of the American family situation.

101. *Diaries*, 15–17. These are drafts of work, to be narrated by someone in his forties. Kafka was then twenty-eight.

102. Joel Feinberg, "The Child's Right to an Open Future," in *Whose Child? Children's Rights, Parental Authority, and State Power*, ed. William Aiken and Hugh LaFollette (Totowa, N.J.: Rowman and Littlefield, 1980), 125.

103. Kafka to Brod (July 22, 1912), *Letters to Friends*, 81.

104. See letter of Franz Kafka to his sister (fall 1921), *Letters to Friends*, 294–97.

105. Letter to Milena Jesenská (August 13, 1920), *Letters to Milena*, 161.

106. See Walter Benjamin, "Some Reflections on Kafka," in Bloom, *Franz Kafka*, 17.

Chapter Five

1. Long, "Madame Butterfly," 397.
2. Ibid., 384.
3. Watenabe in "Family and Law" connects this to an ideology of unconditional obedience and filial piety resulting in a sense (i.e., the parents) that the children are property.
4. Leti Volpp, "(Mis) Identifying Culture: Asian Women as the Cultural Defense," *Harvard Women's Law Journal* (1994): 48–50.
5. Bailey-Harris, "Conflict of Laws," discusses custody after the death of Cho-Cho-San.
6. E.g., Steve Winter, "On Building Houses," *Texas Law Review* 69 (1991): 1616; Marie Ashe, "The Bad Mother in Law and Literature: A Problem of Representation," *Hastings Law Journal* 43 (1992): 1017.
7. Thus, we have recently been reminded that the works that have provided the "authoritative narratives of particular myths," Euripides' *Medea*, for example, are in reality "just a single link in a chain of narrative transmission": in a line of other versions (21). "Moreover, many of these versions not only refer to the episode treated in the authoritative literary work but also include other details, which help to round out a mythic biography" (21). Fritz Graf, "Medea, the Enchantress from Afar: Remarks on a Well-Known Myth," in *Essays on Medea*, ed. James Clauss and Sarah Johnston (Princeton: Princeton University Press, 1996). Graf continues: "Tensions exist between individual narratives of the same episode, as well as between each of these existing narratives and what might be called the imaginary core narrative, although whether there really ever was such a thing is one question that must be considered. How severe the tensions and differences are between this 'core' narrative and existing narratives is another important question: how great is the plasticity of myth?" (21) See also W. J. T. Mitchell, ed., *On Narrative* (Chicago: University of Chicago Press, 1981) and particularly Barbara Herrnstein Smith's article, "Narrative Versions, Narrative Theories," on Cinderella (212) and its 345 variants, challenging the idea of a single basic story (217). For a version of the Medea story included in a collection of parodies (though described by the editor as "strictly speaking" a travesty), see Maurie Baring, *Jason and Medea*, in *Parodies: An Anthology*, ed. Dwight Macdonald (New York: Da Capo, 1985), 302.
8. For discussion of text, sources, etc., see Clauss and Johnston, *Essays on Medea*.
9. See Phyllis Goldfarb, "A Theory-Practice Spiral: The Ethics of Feminism and Clinical Education," *Minnesota Law Review* 75 (1991): 1599.
10. See discussion in Minow and Spelman, "In Context," *Southern California Law Review* 63:1597. See also Minow, *Making All the Difference* (on Benhabib, "the concrete other").
11. See Clauss and Johnston, *Essays on Medea*, 4, 299.
12. This is the theme of Martha Nussbaum's reading of Seneca's version of Medea in *The Therapy of Desire* (Princeton: Princeton University Press, 1994). As many have suggested, it is not sensible to assume that the child-rearing prac-

tices of any particular culture are universal. Some practices, however, are more alike across particular cultures than are others. Thus, Philip Slater has suggested that there are similarities between the overinvolvement of mothers with their sons in contemporary American culture and in ancient Greece. See discussion in Adrienne Rich, *Of Woman Born* (New York: Norton).

13. The issue was raised in the Nussbaum/Steinberg case, in which a child died at the hands of an abusive man without resistance from an abused woman. "Systematic battering combined with misguided, though culturally inculcated, notions of love is not a sufficient excuse to exonerate Hedda Nussbaum from her share of culpability in Lisa Steinberg's death." Susan Brownmiller, "Hedda Nussbaum Hardly a Heroine," *New York Times*, February 2, 1989, A25. If this argument on culpability can be made about Nussbaum, it can be made about Medea, who is not a battered woman, but a betrayed woman. No one challenges Medea's culpability (except, perhaps Medea). The issue is not whether she is a murderess—or would not be if we were thinking about a trial.

14. Thus we have references to Susan Smith as a Medea figure. See Gillespie, "The Good/Bad Mother," *Ms.*, March 1995; and Clauss and Johnston, *Essays on Medea*. A familiar and difficult aspect of the problem is that violence, particularly against children, is a feature of the description of women in this culture. Indeed, to the extent that violence by women against children is seen as a passing on to the (yet) weaker a violence experienced by women at the hands of men, we may say that women, restricted to the household sphere, have more opportunity than men to engage in this particular form of violence. This is true despite the equally valid point that female socialization disposes women against physical violence in some ways, particularly in relation to men. Goldfarb, "The Theory-Practice Spiral."

15. Christine de Pizan, *The Book of the City of Ladies*, trans. Earl Jeffrey Richards (New York: Persea Books, 1982), 69. Christine attempted to reconstruct a history of women more favorable to them than the accounts conventionally offered by men. This point is anticipated by the chorus in Euripides' *Medea*. See discussion in B. M. W. Knox, "The Medea of Euripides," in T. F. Gould and C. J. Herington, eds., *Greek Tragedy*, Yale Classical Studies (Cambridge: Cambridge University Press, 1977),l 271.

16. Marie Ashe and Naomi Kahn, "Child Abuse: A Problem for Feminist Theory," in *The Public Nature of Private Violence: The Discovery of Domestic Abuse*, ed. Fineman and Mykitiuk (New York: Routledge, 1994), 171.

17. Bartlett, "Feminist Methodologies."

18. Minow (1990): 1682–83.

19. If one accepts male ownership of women as a description.

20. Note that Christine de Pizan indicated that Medea would not have abandoned Jason: "However, Jason lied about his promise, for after everything went just as he wanted, he left Medea for another woman. For this reason, Medea, who would rather have destroyed herself than do anything of this kind to him, turned despondent, nor did her heart ever again feel goodness or joy" (190). One might suggest that if this is true, it is only because she still loved him.

21. She provides an example of the tension between sexuality and maternalism. See Carol Sanger, "Seasoned to the Use," *Michigan Law Review* 87 (1989): 1338.

22. The exchange aspects of this material are described by Winter, "On Building Houses," 616.

23. Euripides, *Medea*, 927–28.

24. Mary Lefkowitz suggests that it is only evil women, attackers of the family, who express criticisms of their roles (including Medea) but notes that female authors, as against the actual male authors, might have been more critical (*Woman in Greek Myth* [Baltimore: Johns Hopkins University Press, 1986]). Women would not, however, have condoned the evil. As Lefkowitz points out, while Antigone is a woman who breaks the law, she is also a defender of the family (84).

25. Emily A. McDermott, *Euripedes' Medea: The Incarnation of Disorder* (University Park: Pennsylvania State University Press, 1989), 40. McDermott also comments on Sophocles *Tereus* and the counterpart of Procne, who murdered her child. On family in Greece, McDermott writes: "Beyond the ties of affection normally presumed between parent and child, the family as an institution was capable of perpetuating itself in classical Greece because of the reciprocal nature of the duties it enjoined upon its members. The parent was expected to nurture *(trephein)* the child during the latter's period of helplessness, on the understanding that, at such a point as the parent was himself again reduced to *aporia* by the onslaught of senility, the child would take over familial responsibility and would in turn provide nurture *(trophe)* for the parent in his old age. The cornerstone from which this fundamental societal construct was erected was the parent's natural love for his or her offspring and concomitant automatic assumption of a nurturing role toward that offspring; such parental response was seen as innate to the race—as, in effect, a *sine qua non* of orderly human behavior. Onto this base was added the prescript that, by having received life and nurture from the parent, the child had involuntarily (but necessarily) incurred a debt which he or she was obligated to pay back in the parent's time of need" (81).

26. Finkelstein, *Legends of the Jews*. Also see Aviva Cantor, "The Lilith Question," in *On Being a Jewish Feminist*, ed. Susannah Heschel (New York: Schocken, 1995).

27. Marina Warner, *Managing Monsters: Six Myths of Our Time* (New York: Vintage, 1994).

28. Euripides, *Medea*. Cf. speech of Procne in Sophocles' *Tereus* (as noted in McDermott, *Euripedes' Medea*). Knox refers to reports that *Medea* was used at suffragists' meetings ("The Medea of Euripedes," 211).

29. Cf. Jacques Presser, *The Night of the Girondists*, trans. Barrows Mussey (London: Harvill, 1992), 21.

30. Robinson Jeffers, *Medea* (New York: Random House, 1946), 96.

31. Rich, *Of Woman Born*, 276–77.

32. See discussion in Knox on Euripides' Medea as on the side of the gods. ("The Medea of Euripedes," 205). See introduction to Seneca's *Medea* in *Three*

Tragedies, trans. Frederick M. Ahl (Ithaca: Cornell University Press, 1986), suggesting that Medea might be a God, but noting also that this would give problems in relation to the last line of the Seneca play. (Her presence is evidence that the gods do not exist.)

If Medea is not only a sorceress, but also somehow divine, then her insistence on the sacrifice of children connects to another tradition involving the death of children. On the commands and love of the command to Abraham to offer Isaac as a sacrifice, the Akedah, see Shalom Spiegel, *The Last Trial,* trans. Judah Goldin (New York: Schocken, 1969); see also Weisbrod, "Charles Guiteau and the Christian Nation," *Journal of Law and Religion* (1989) on arguments relating to the sacrifice of Isaac. Easterling, "The Infanticide in Euripides' *Medea,*" *Yale Classical Studies* 25 (1997): 187, suggests in general that the parental argument that one is saving the children from a worse fate may be the rationalizing impulse at work.

33. See Nussbaum, *The Therapy of Desire.* Stressing these aspects of Medea, we reach the idea that Medea is in ways a mature Antigone.

34. Gardner uses this in his poem several times, first in a treatment of Creon. In a discussion of charity toward Medea, Creon raises his posture in the earlier case involving the daughter of Oedipus. *Jason and Medeia* (New York: Vintage, 1986).

35. Ibid., 457.

36. See Weisbrod, "Images of Woman Juror," 59.

37. On the problem of agency and control in relation to women and violence, see particularly Martha Mahoney, "Women's Lives: Violence and Agency," in Fineman and Mykitiuk, *Public Nature.*

38. Ibid., 45, quoting bell hooks, *Outlaw Culture: Resisting Representation* (New York: Routledge, 1994).

39. De Pizan, *Othea,* in *The Writings of Christine de Pizan,* ed. Charity Ann Willard (New York: Persea Books, 1994), 98.

40. Jason, for example, is a hero and explorer, moving into middle age.

41. See Ashe and Kahn, "Child Abuse."

42. The phrase "vase children" is William Marshall's, *Faces in the Crowd* (New York: Mysterious Press, 1991), 157. For an earlier description of children formed and deformed by a surrounding ceramic shell, see Victor Hugo, *The Man Who Laughs* (Miltipas, Calif.: Atlantean Press, 1991). Questions here would relate both to the shape of the vase (its substantive aspects) and its strength as a shell.

43. See Nathan Leites, *Rules of the Game in Paris* (Chicago: University of Chicago Press, 1969). Medea's narcissism is indicated by the speech she makes thinking of separation from her children, focusing on aspects of their future lives that she will not see.

> I shall never see your brides,
> Adorn your bridal beds, and hold the torches high.
> My misery is my own heart, which will not relent.
> All was for nothing, then—these years of rearing you,

My care, my aching weariness, and the wild pains
When you were born.

It is signaled no less by her response to their death. The focus of her dialogue with Jason is on his loss and then on her loss. Gardner refers to Medea as a child and a child with childlike needs.

44. For another narrative center, see William Morris, *Life and Death of Jason*.

45. See discussion of contraception as the ultimate injury to future generations in C. S. Lewis, *The Abolition of Man* (New York: Macmillan, 1965), 68. Placing abortion as an injury on a spectrum of (future) injuries to the child does not weigh that injury, or that futureness, against the weight of other injuries.

46. Diodorus continues: "Now during this period, we are informed, Medea was highly approved by her husband, because she not only excelled in beauty but was adorned with modesty and every other virtue; but afterward, as time more and more diminished her natural comeliness, Jason, it is said, became enamoured of Glauce, Creon's daughter, and sought the maiden's hand in marriage. After her father had given his consent and had set a day for the marriage, Jason, they say, at first tried to persuade Medea to withdraw from their wedlock of her free-will; for, he told her, he desired to marry the maiden, not because he felt his relations with Medea were beneath him, but because he was eager to establish a kinship between the king's house and his children. But when his wife was angered and called upon the gods who had been the witnesses of their vows, they say that Jason, disdaining the vows, married the daughter of the king."

Diodorus gives two versions of the deaths of Creon and Glauce: "Thereupon Medea was driven out of the city, and being allowed by Creon but one day to make the preparations for her exile, she entered the palace by night, having altered her appearance by means of drugs, and set fire to the building by applying to it a little root which had been discovered by her sister Circe and had the property that when it was once kindled it was hard to put out. Now when the palace suddenly burst into flames, Jason quickly made his way out of it, but as for Glauce and Creon, the fire hemmed them in on all sides and they were consumed by it. Certain historians, however, say that the sons of Medea brought to the bride gifts which had been anointed with poisons, and that when Glauce took them and put them about her body both she herself met her end and her father, when he ran to help her and embraced her body, likewise perished." Diodorus of Sicily, trans. C. H. Oldfather (Cambridge: Harvard University Press, 1935), 2:517.

47. Ibid., 2:514ff. A later history of Thessalus is also given: "After the Corinthians had performed this command, Thessalus, they say, who had escaped being murdered by his mother, was reared as a youth in Corinth and then removed to Iolcus, which was the native land of Jason; and finding on his arrival that Acastus, the son of Pelias, had recently died, he took over the throne which belonged to him by inheritance and called the people who were subject to himself Thessalians after his own name (2:519)." Acastus was the fig-

ure who expelled Jason and Medea from his kingdom, presumably because Medea had killed his father.

48. This theme can be connected to the idea of a nurturing Jesus. See Carolyn Bynum, *Jesus as Mother*. But it relates also to protective aspects of the father, and God the Father: "He Watching Over Israel slumbers not nor sleeps" (Ps. 121). To the extent that the Old Testament is part of the Christian tradition, the idea of the paternal-nurturing-protective father cannot be excluded.

49. Albert V. Dicey: "protection invariably involves disability." *Lectures on the Relation between Law and Public Opinion in England During the 19th Century* (1905), 150 n. 1.

50. See McDermott, *Medea,* on the comparison between Jason and Medea as loving parents, 67 ff.

51. Seneca, *Medea,* 146, in *Three Tragedies,* trans. Frederick Ahl (Ithaca: Cornell University Press, 1986).

52. Hannah Arendt, "What Is Freedom?" in *Between Past and Future* (New York: Penguin, 1993), 295 n. 14. Arendt's distinction between reason and emotion and her association of women with emotion and men with reason can of course be seen as yet another illustration of Arendt's traditional orientation. On the stereotype of women as emotional, see the summary by Joan Williams: "As the philosophs of the enlightenment celebrated logic and reason, women's intellectual inferiority came to be expressed as an inability to engage in rigorous, abstract thinking. The enlightenment also celebrated reason over emotion and women's pre-modern alliance with the devil was transmuted into the view that women's ability for rational thought meant that they were fundamentally emotional creatures." Joan Williams, "Deconstructing Gender," *Michigan Law Review* 87 (1989): 797.

John Gardner, in *Jason and Medeia,* uses as an anticipatory story the narrative of the women of Lemnos. Here irrationality is initially a quality of both men and women. Those women "became as irrational as men, but fiercer than men— unchecked by the foolish poetry, the stupid ideals of the more romantic part of the two part beast." The women killed their husbands, their husbands' mistresses, and their sons (*Jason and Medeia,* 139). See also Apollonius, *The Voyage of the Argo.*

53. Rich, *Of Woman Born.* And see Sylvia Plath, "Edge," in *Ariel* (New York: Harper and Row, 1965), on Medea, beginning "The Woman is Perfected" (84).

54. Rich, *Of Woman Born.* With this issue in mind, we may note that in the same way that women are not primarily socialized through contact sports, they are also not socialized through poker. Medea's response to Jason's act involves an aspect of her own thinking. It is something that is within her own control. Her response, in the language of Judith Jarvis Thompson, is one in which the harm is somehow mediated by her own mental activity. Thompson, *The Realm of Rights* (Cambridge: Harvard University Press, 1990), 153.

Note the idea that men must be taught to restrain their own violence. If this is true of men, presumably it is equally true of women, whether that violence is verbal or physical. But Jason of course also fails to control his emotion, to the extent that he permits himself to fall in love—if he does—and to the extent (beyond doubt) that he allows his desire for advancement to outweigh a commitment to his first wife.

55. Jane Smiley, "Can Mothers Think?" in *The True Subject: Writers on Life and Craft*, ed. Kurt Brown (St. Paul: Graywolf Press, 1993), 14–15.

56. See comment of Easterling, "Infanticide in Euripides' *Medea*," on Corneille's *Medea* (179).

57. McDermott, *Medea*, 76–77.

58. Nussbaum, *The Therapy of Desire*, 441.

59. Euripides, *Medea*, line 92.

60. The daughter of Creon does not have a name either. (This is added in at least one translation.) If they had been given names, would the very names create or at least shape consciousness? Isn't this an aspect of the power of naming?

61. See *The Invulnerable Child*, ed. E. James Anthony and Bertram Cohler (New York: Guilford, 1987), discussing Piaget, H. C. Anderson, and others. Thessalus might be a child who lives in a psychic castle, like the child who described the castle as "the little space" that she had arranged for herself in the household and into which she could retreat when things were "rough" outside. "She pointed to the most important part of the castle, the iron gate, which she could lift whenever she wanted to escape from the 'enemies' on the outside and make it impossible for them to penetrate behind her defenses and disturb the even tenor of her development. When asked how it felt like to be inside the castle, she laughingly gave a lyrical response: 'It was like being in a world in which everything worked and everyone worked together and where you had a job to do that was the job that you wanted to do and no one could stop you from doing it. I am the queen of this castle and I do not want anyone to enter who can spoil my life.'" The author notes, "The comment has certainly a narcissistic quality about it, but it does indicate how self-protective and self-preventative the egos of these resilient children can be" (E. James Anthony, "Children at High Risk for Psychosis Growing Up Successfully," in *The Invulnerable Child*, 181–82).

62. See Raskolnikov's response to a letter from his mother in Dostoyevsky, *Crime and Punishment*, trans. Richard Pevear and Lorissa Volokhonsky (New York: Vintage, 1992), 40ff. A same-sex identification might be even stronger. Thessalus might be violent himself. This is also true of Jason.

63. "In my plot to kill the princes they must help." *Medea*, line 781.

64. On symbolic murders in which a child is forced to participate see Pamela Painter, "New Family Car," in *Family Matters*, ed. Martha Minow (New York: New Press, 1993), describing the mutilation of family photographs by one parent trying to obliterate the other in the mind and memory of the child.

65. Elias Canetti, *The Human Province*, trans. Joachim Neugroschel (New York: Farrar, Straus and Giroux, 1978), 248.

66. This work is described as a "very significant development in psychological literature," "perhaps the strongest theoretical treatments focusing very directly upon child abuse and its implications for human development and for

human history" (Ashe and Kahn, "Child Abuse"). See Alice Miller, *The Drama of the Gifted Child*, trans. Ruth Ward (New York: Basic Books, 1981). See also bell hooks's comments on Miller in *Outlaw Culture* (New York: Routledge, 1994), 226, noting, as others have, that the damage to children may be in the imposed need to maintain a fiction more than in the fact itself.

67. Miller, *Drama of the Gifted Child*. The theme is developed in subsequent books. For a lighter example, see the *New York Times* regarding a mother who misrepresented her own age and then that of her daughter. Her daughter is diminished by the lie. Sue Hubbel, "A Gift Decade," *NYT Magazine*, Feb. 19, 1995, 25.

68. Doris Lessing, *Under My Skin* (New York: Harper Collins, 1994), 25.

69. McDermott refers to the children as Medea's "tools" in this connection (*Medea*, 85).

70. Medea herself, in Euripides, suggests a conditional aspect to these vows, when she says that she would have understood Jason's looking for a second wife if she had not borne children (31).

71. Gardner, *Jason and Medeia*, 27–28; see also Robinson Jeffers on "barbarian mating," not marriage (4). As Easterling, "Infanticide in Euripides' *Medea*," points out, this is not an argument in Euripides (180).

72. As the chorus says in Euripides. Jason is described by Gardner as a man in effect more sinned against than sinning and described by others as a man simply behaving reasonably in his context.

73. Is his remarriage an example of efficient breach?

> I wanted to ensure
> First—and the most important—that we should live well
> And not be poor; I know how a poor man is shunned
> By all his friends. Next, that I could bring up my sons
> In a manner worthy of my descent; have other sons,
> Perhaps, as brothers to your children; give them all
> An equal place, and so build up a closely-knit
> And prosperous family. *You* need no more children, do you?
> While *I* thought it worth while to ensure advantages
> For those I have, by means of those I hope to have.
> Was such a plan, then, wicked?

74. See Appleby hypothetical in Schneider and Brinig, *Invitation to Family Law*, 60. Can we avoid the murders by insisting that Jason stay with Medea? Should we?

75. If the couple remains all to each other as they were when they started—in the theory of modern romantic marriage—there may be no emotional room for children. If the mother shifts her focus to her children, psychoanalytically interesting tensions are set up between the father and the children. In either case, the woman lacks an independent self-definition, a point largely raised by feminists.

76. See Winter's analysis of her contract arguments. "On Building Houses," 1616.

77. See McDermott, *Medea*, 26 quoting *Nicomachean Ethics*. Aristotle also, however, signals the separateness of the child.

78. Sometimes the child is viewed as an outside "it," as by the English family in E. M. Forster's, *Where Angels Fear to Tread*, in which only the Italian father sees a fully human personality, kicking, laughing, expressing himself as an individual infant consciousness. Perhaps mothers particularly, because they once experienced their children as part of themselves, a distension of themselves, find it natural to see children later as extensions of themselves.

79. For a contemporary statement, see Rich, *Of Woman Born*: "The institution of motherhood must be destroyed. The changes required to make this possible reverberate into every part of the patriarchal system. To destroy the institution is not to abolish motherhood. It is to release the creation and sustenance of life into the same realm of decision, struggle, surprise, imagination, and conscious intelligence, as any other difficult, but freely chosen work" (280).

80. Aldous Huxley, *Brave New World* (New York: Harper and Row, 1969), 36.

81. Ira C. Lupu, "Home Education, Religious Liberty, and the Separation of Powers," *Boston University Law Review* 67 (1987): 971.

82. Something of this perspective is offered in *Hart v. Brown* (child as organ donor): "it has been stated that the donor would enjoy a better future life if her ailing twin sister were kept alive" (*Hart v. Brown*, 289 A2d 396 [Conn Supp 1972]).

83. If the rejection of imposed representation is a major part of the agenda for minorities (see for example, hooks, *Outlaw Culture*), it is equally so in the case of individuals (again, hooks, citing Alice Miller). Peer culture and popular culture, as well as schools, limit and even defeat that monopoly for older children.

84. See Feinberg on rights-in-trust, in "Child's Right," 124.

85. Cf. Bartlett: "Asking the women question does not require a decision in favor of a women, rather, the method requires the decision-maker to search for gender bias and to reach a decision in the case that is defensible in light of that bias. It demands, in other words, special attention to a set of interests and concerns that otherwise may be, and historically have been overlooked" (Feminist Legal Methods, 1846).

86. Warner, *Managing Monsters*.

87. Knox, "The Medea of Euripedes," 195–96.

88. Boccaccio sees her as "the most cruel example of ancient wickedness" (35). Giovanni Boccaccio, *Concerning Famous Women*, trans. Guido Guardino (New Brunswick: Rutgers University Press, 1963), a work described by Guardino as the "first collection of women's biographies ever written" (ix).

89. John Gardner, *Jason and Medeia*. This line is described by one critic as particularly pretentious. For a general defense, see Jeff Henderson, "John Gard-

ner's *Jason and Medeia:* The Resurrection of a Genre," *Papers on Language and Literature* 22 (1986): 76–95.

90. John Gardner, *The Art of Fiction* (New York: Random House, 1993), 143.

91. Easterling, "Infanticide in Euripides' *Medea,*" 177. He adds, "But we accept their inactivity because these women are not at the center of the play: they are peripheral figures whose role is not to do and suffer but to comment, sympathize, support or disapprove."

92. Easterling, "Infanticide in Euripides' *Medea,*" 179.

93. *DeShaney v. Winnebago County Department of Social Services,* 489 U.S. 189 (1989).

94. Aviam Soifer, "Moral Ambition, Formalism, and the 'Free World' of DeShaney" 57 *George Washington Law Review* 1513, 1530.

95. See Martha Minow, "Words and the Door to the Land of Change," 43 *Vanderbilt Law Review* 1665 (1990).

96. Glendon, *Rights Talk,* 95–96.

Chapter Six

1. Long, "Madame Butterfly," 382.

2. Ibid., 379.

3. Ibid., 375, 381.

4. Belasco, *Six Plays,* 21.

5. CBS CD.

6. To the wife? Is this an allusion to a right under the new fault-based system? Another formulation of the idea that desertion equals divorce?

7. Are some domestic institutions officially illegal? Cf. polygamy.

8. See Linda Greenhouse, "Family Law: Battle Ground in Social Revolution," *New York Times,* September 2, 1988, B6, col. 3.

9. Glendon, *Abortion and Divorce,* 9, 142.

10. Gorecki, "Moral Premises," 129. See also Gorecki, "Divorce in Poland—a Socio-Legal Study," in *Sociology of Law,* ed. Vilhelm Aubert (Harmondsworth, Middlesex: Penguin, 1972) (discussing, inter alia, moral and pedagogical purposes of the rule of recrimination).

11. Gorecki, "Moral Premises," 126–28.

12. See Glendon, *Abortion and Divorce,* 78.

13. Ibid., 138.

14. Ibid., 5–9.

15. Plato, *The Laws,* trans. T. Saunders (1978), 503 (translator's enumeration omitted).

16. See e.g., Alasdair MacIntyre, *A Short History of Ethics* (New York: Macmillan, 1966), 55–56.

17. See Glendon, *Abortion and Divorce,* 139.

18. Ibid., 138–39. Glendon cites in this connection Michael Kammen's *The Machine That Would Go of Itself: The Constitution in American Culture* (New York Knopf, 1986), for examples of misinformation regarding the American Constitution. Id., 189 n. 78.

19. Glendon, *Abortion and Divorce*, 139.

20. "'Law' is primarily a great reservoir of emotionally important social symbols." Thurman Arnold, *The Symbols of Government* (New York: York University Press, 1962), 34.

21. Glendon suggests, for example, that a change in the message of the law on abortion might affect how we think about and deal with neonatal issues. See Glendon, *Abortion and Divorce*, 61.

22. For an example of the law's contribution, see Milner Ball, *The Promise of American Law: A Theological, Humanistic View of Legal Process* (Athens: University of Georgia Press, 1981), 42–45 (discussing legal trials and morality plays).

23. Gorecki, "Moral Premises," 128. Gorecki suggests that a prime function of law, particularly family and criminal law, is society's moral education. Another view sees family law increasingly through the optic of contracts. See, e.g., John Eekelaar, *Family Law and Social Policy*, 2d ed. (London: Weidenfeld and Nicolson, 1984), 32–33 (critiquing Gorecki's position, particularly on the law/society issue).

24. Patrick Atiyah, "From Principles to Pragmatism: Changes in the Function of the Judicial Powers and the Law," *Iowa Law Review* 65 (1980): 1272 (questioning whether we have unduly neglected this function).

25. Glendon, *Abortion and Divorce*, 109.

26. Ibid., 66, discussing Max Rheinstein, *Marriage Stability, Divorce, and the Law* (Chicago: University of Chicago Press, 1972), 254 ("With advancing age I have come not only to accept but to admire the compromise").

27. On the symbolism of prohibition, see Joseph Gusfield, *Symbolic Crusade*, 2d ed. (Urbana: University of Illinois Press, 1986).

28. See Glendon, *Abortion and Divorce*, 15. But, to consider France only, how successful has that compromise really been? See *New York Times*, September 24, 1988, p. 1, col. 1 (recounting controversy over abortion pill). On the point that complexity may seem incapacitating, see Martha Minow, "Supreme Court Forward: Justice Engendered," *Harvard Law Review* 101 (1987): 82. This assumption raises the problems reviewed here.

29. Robert Gordon, "Exchange on Critical Legal Studies," *Law and History* 6 (1988): 181 ("The existing order, like past orders, is a teeming jungle of plural, contradictory, orders, struggling for recognition and dominance").

30. Grant Gilmore, *The Ages of American Law* (New Haven: Yale University Press, 1977), 110. See also Ellen Peters, "Grant Gilmore and the Illusion of Certainty," *Yale Law Journal* 92 (1982): 8.

31. See Carl E. Schneider, "The Next Step: Definition, Generalization, and Theory in American Family Law," *University of Michigan Journal of Law Reform* 18 (1985): 1041. His point, in part, is that family law has never achieved the appearance of a system of connected doctrines (id., 1045–47).

32. Ibid., 1048.

33. Judith Areen, "Baby M Reconsidered," *Georgetown Law Journal* 76 (1988): 1942 ("We have never really decided, for example, what obligations a parent owes to a child, when the law should intervene to enforce those obligations, and whether enforcement should be accomplished by punishing the par-

ent or by removing the child"). Surrogacy, of course, exists. Cloning is also real, though limited thus far to animals. The debate as to human cloning continues.

34. Martha Minow, "We, the Family: Constitutional Rights and American Families," *Journal of American History* 74 (1987): 978.

35. "Aylmer's Field," in *The Works of Alfred Lord Tennyson* (1903), 146.

36. 330 U.S. 1 (1947).

37. Ibid., 19. For another example, see *Zapeda v. Zapeda*, 41 Ill. App. 2d 240, 262, 190 N.E. 2d 849, 859 (1963) (holding that wrongful life is a tort but presenting no remedy).

38. 18 Cal. 3d 660, 557 P. 2d 106, 134 Cal. Rptr. 815 (1976).

39. Id., 665, 557 P. 2d at 109, 134 Cal. Rptr. at 818.

40. See *In re* Greene, 45 F. 2d 428 (S.D.N.Y. 1930); see also *Restatement (Second) of Contracts,* sec. 86 comment a, illustration 3 (1981) ("A has immoral relations with B, a woman not his wife, to her injury. A's subsequent promise to reimburse B for her loss is not binding under this Section").

41. However, it did not resurrect common-law marriage.

42. *Marvin v. Marvin,* 18 Cal. 3d at 684, 557 P.2d at 122, 134 Cal. Rptr. at 831.

43. Leonard Bernstein, *Candide,* book by Lillian Hellman, lyrics by Richard Wilbur, with additional lyrics by John Latouche and Dorothy Parker (New York: Random House, 1957), 7–8. I would like to thank Richard Warren, Curator, Yale Collection of Historical Sound Recordings at Yale University Library, for his assistance with this reference.

44. And with *Marvin,* would we here cite cases expanding the rights of illegitimate children? For a discussion of the "confusion and vacillation" of Supreme Court decisions in this area, see Homer Clark, *The Law of Domestic Relations in the United States,* 2d ed. (1988), 155.

45. J. Cohen, R. Robson, and A. Bates, *Parental Authority: The Community and the Law* (1958).

46. See generally Lawrence Friedman and Stewart Macaulay, *Law and the Behavioral Sciences,* 2d ed. (Indianapolis: Bobbs Merrill, 1977), 596–610 (discussing material on the *Parental Authority* study).

47. Cooperrider, review of *Parental Authority, Michigan Law Review* 57 (1959): 1121. Kalven makes the same point in his review of *Parental Authority.* See Kalven, book review, *Rutgers Law Review* 14 (1960): 846.

48. Cohen, Robson, and Bates, *Parental Authority,* 14.

49. J. Cohen, R. Robson, and A. Bates, "Ascertaining the Moral Sense of the Community: A Preliminary Report in an Experiment in Interdisciplinary Research," *Journal of Legal Education* 8 (1955): 143.

50. Cooperrider, review, 1123.

51. Kalven, review, 846.

52. Saunders, "Collective Ignorance: Public Knowledge of Family Law," *Family Co-ordinator* 24 (1975): 70.

53. Milner, book review, *University of Pittsburgh Law Review* 21 (1959): 148 (quoting Cohen, Robson, and Bates, *Parental Authority,* 14), 147.

54. See Gilmore, *The Death of Contract,* 59–85 (discussing Restatement of

Contracts); see also *Restatement (Second) of Contracts*, sec. 89A, illustrations 1, 6 (1981).

55. See Tennessee Williams, *A Streetcar Named Desire* (1947), 40.

56. For references on legal knowledge, see Cortese, "A Study in Knowledge and Attitudes toward the Law: The Legal Knowledge Inventory," *Rocky Mountain Social Science Journal* 3 (1966): 192; Dwyer, "Law Actual and Perceived: Sexual Politics of Law in Morocco," *Law and Society Review* 13 (1979): 739; Greg, "Popular Perceptions of Supreme Court Rulings," *Am. Pol. Q.* 4 (1976): 3; Williams and Hall, "Knowledge of Law in Texas: Socio-economic and Ethnic Differences," *Law and Society Review* 7 (1972): 99; Note, "Legal Knowledge of Michigan Citizens," *Michigan Law Review* 71 (1973): 1463.

57. See, e.g., Macaulay, "Private Government," in *Law and the Social Sciences*, ed. Leon Lipson and Stanton Wheeler (New York: Russell Sage, 1987), 445.

58. Saunders, "Collective Ignorance," 72.

59. Lawrence Friedman, book review, *Law and History Review* 6 (1988): 195, reviewing Kammen, *A Machine That Would Go of Itself: The Constitution in American Culture*.

60. Fineman, "Implementary Equality," 854 (discussing use of legal "horror stories"); see also Givelber, Bowers, and Blitch, "Tarasoff, Myth and Reality: An Empirical Study of Private Law in Action," *Wisconsin Law Review* 1984:443.

61. Arnold, *The Symbols of Government*, 35.

62. See generally Chase, "Toward a Legal Theory of Popular Culture," *Wisconsin Law Review* 1986:527 (discussing popular culture's images of law and lawyers).

63. See La Rou, "The Portrayal of Law in Literature: Weisberg's Failure of the Word," *American Bar Foundation Research Journal* 1986:313 (reviewing R. Weisberg, *The Failure of the Word* [1984]).

64. Ibid., 317.

65. Ibid. For Sherlock Holmes on solemnization and duress, see Arthur Conan Doyle, "The Solitary Cyclist," in *The Return of Sherlock Holmes* (1974), 99–100.

66. Ed McBain, *Blood Relatives: An 87th Precinct Mystery* (1975), 134 (distinguishing "real law" and "religious law").

67. Arthur Upfield, *Sinister Stones* (1954), chap. 20.

68. P. Woodruff [Philip Mason], *Call the Next Witness* (1945; reprint, Chicago: University of Chicago Press, 1986); see also Vrooman, "British Justice, and the Indian Mind," *New York Times*, March 10, 1946. Mason was a member of the Indian Civil Service who was serving as a joint magistrate when the episode on which the book is based occurred.

69. R. Austin Freeman, *The Red Thumb Mark* (1986), 89. This is reminiscent of the Gypsy curse: "May you be in a lawsuit in which you are in the right" (*Viking Book of Aphorisms*, ed. W. H. Auden and Louis Kronenberger [New York: Viking, 1962], 210). Cf. Learned Hand's view of litigation: "After now some dozen years of experience I must say that as a litigant I should dread a lawsuit beyond almost anything else short of sickness and death." Learned Hand, in "Lectures on Legal Topics," *Association of the Bar of the City of New*

York, 1921–22, 105 ("The Deficiencies of Trials to Reach the Heart of the Matter").

70. See J. Symons, *Bloody Murder* 144 (1972).

71. Stephen Wizner, "The Child and the State: Adversaries in the Juvenile Justice System," *Columbia Human Rights Law Review* 4 (1972): 389.

72. Ibid., 399. See also O'Barr and Conley, "Litigant Satisfaction Versus Legal Adequacy in Small Claims Court Narratives," *Law and Society Review* 19 (1985): 694 (reporting different perceptions by magistrate and litigants of conversational agenda in small claims courts).

73. 77 Ill. 2d 49, 394 N.E. 2d 1204 (1979).

74. Id. at 53, 394 N.E. 2d at 1205.

75. So that a man might come home and say, "I went downtown and got us married" and be believed.

76. See Anita Brookner, *A Friend from England* (London: Grafton, 1988), 118: "And did one return wedding presents in the case of annulment, or were they just thrown in, as if the recipient probably needed or deserved some sort of consolation prize?"

77. Petrazycki, *Law and Morality,* 68.

78. On Petrazycki, see Jan Gorecki, *Sociology and Jurisprudence of Leon Petrazycki* (Urbana: University of Illinois Press, 1975); see also Adam Podgorecki, "Unrecognized Father of Sociology of Law: Leon Petrazycki," *Law and Society Review* 15 (1980–81): 184. Also see chapter 4, p. 81ff.

79. Barbara Ehrenreich, *The Hearts of Men* (Garden City, N.Y.: Anchor Press/Doubleday, 1983), 11 ("[C]onsidering the absence of legal coercion, the surprising thing is that men have for so long, and, on the whole, so reliably, adhered to what we might call the 'breadwinner ethic'").

80. As to which, consider the interesting linkage in Gage's *Women, Church, and State* (390), between American efforts to recapture runaway wives and the English writ of restitution of conjugal rights, enforceable originally by excommunication, then by contempt, and after 1884, not at all. For a discussion on the action, defenses, and meaning of a breach of duty to cohabit, see Peter Bromley, *Family Law,* 3d ed. (London: Butterworth, 1966), 164. Note the parallel Scottish writ of adherence, which still exists but is unenforceable. See E. M. Clive, "Marriage: An Unnecessary Legal Concept?" in Eekelaar and Katz, *Marriage and Cohabitation,* 71 n. 8. See also W. Blackstone, *Commentaries* (1899), 3:94; and A. Herbert, *Uncommon Law* (London: Methuen, 1969), 95–99 (*Marrowfat v. Marrowfat:* "Is marriage legal"; action for restitution of conjugal rights). (Cf. chap. 3, note 170.)

81. See Ehrenreich, *The Hearts of Men,* 146.

82. See Anthony Lewis, "The Limits of Law," *New York Times,* December 22, 1988, p. 23, col. 1. The point in general is not new. See generally Pound, "Limits of Effective Legal Action," *American Bar Association Journal* 55 (1917). On the efficacy of law, see Charles Black, "Paths to Desegregation," *New Republic,* October 21, 1957, 11 ("beyond all question, law does shape attitude").

83. See Atiyah, "From Principles to Pragmatism," *Iowa Law Review* 65 (1980): 1249; Schneider, "Moral Discourse," 1803. See *Reynolds v. United States,*

98 U.S. 145 (1879); *Marvin v. Marvin*, 18 Cal. 3d 660, 557 P.2d 106, 134 Cal. Rptr. 815 (1976). *Reynolds* is a case in which instrumental and expressive functions work in the same direction. *Marvin* is a case in which they diverge to some degree. The instrumental function of *Reynolds*, as has often been noted, was not entirely fulfilled.

84. C. Neustadt, *Presidential Power* (1960), 9, quoted in T. Schelling, *Choice and Consequence* (Cambridge: Harvard University Press, 1984), 27. See also Alexander Bickel, *The Least Dangerous Branch*, 2d ed. (Indianapolis: Bobbs Merrill, 1986), 258 ("the Supreme Court is a court of last resort presumptively only").

85. See Glendon, *Abortion and Divorce*, 106–7, for consequences of no-fault divorce.

86. See Schneider, "Moral Discourse," 1056.

87. Rheinstein, *Marriage Stability*, 406.

88. Richard Abel, "Law Books and Books about Law," *Stanford Law Review* 26 (1973): 183. "[L]egal professionals, with their strong and obvious commitment to the importance of law, are clearly the last people likely to accept its irrelevance. Instead of doing so, they will make that *irrelevance* the central problem." Id.

89. Glendon, *Abortion and Divorce*, 60. Again, her basic point concerns the impact that law may have in the formation of ideas, attitudes, and ultimately the social consensus (58–59).

90. See generally material on the impact of law on society in Friedman and Macaulay, *Law and Behavioral Sciences*, 197–492; see also John Griffiths, "Is Law Important?" *New York University Law Review* 54 (1979): 339; Martha Fineman, "Illusive Equality: On Weitzman's Divorce Revolution," *American Bar Foundation Research Journal* 1986:781; Lenore Weitzman, "Bringing the Law Back In," *American Bar Foundation Research Journal* 1986:791.

91. Clive, "Marriage," 78.

92. Ibid.

93. Lee E. Teitelbaum, "Moral Discourse and Family Law," *Michigan Law Review* 84 (1985): 439. See generally Arthur Leff, "Unspeakable Ethics, Unnatural Law," *Duke Law Journal* (1979); Richard Kay, "Moral Knowledge and Constitutional Adjudication," *Tulane Law Review*.

94. Teitelbaum, "Moral Discourse," 439.

95. Clifford Geertz, *Local Knowledge: Further Essays in Interpretive Anthropology* (1983), 217.

96. Grant Gilmore, review of Karl N. Llewellyn, *The Bramble Bush, Yale Law Journal* 60 (1951): 1252.

97. Grant Gilmore, "Anarchy and History," *University of Chicago Law School Rec.* 14 (1966): 7. See also Gilmore, 111 ("In Heaven there will be no law. . . . In Hell there will be nothing but law"). For recent discussions of legal realism, see Laura Kalman, *Legal Realism at Yale*; Joseph Singer, "Legal Realism Now," *California Law Review* 76 (1988): 465.

98. Grant Gilmore, "What Is a Law School?" *Connecticut Law Review* 15 (1982): 4.

99. Anthony Trollope, *Kept in the Dark* (1978), 50.

100. Jeremy Bentham, *Theory of Legislation* (1840), 248, quoted in Joseph Goldstein, Anna Freud, and Albert Solnit, *Beyond the Best Interests of the Child* (New York: Free Press, 1979), 7.

101. Goldstein, Freud, and Solnit, *Beyond the Best Interests,* 7. When do parents forfeit this authority? Here, views differ.

102. *Matarese v. Matarese,* 131 A. 198, 199 (R.I. 1925).

103. Horace Bushnell, *Christian Nurture* (Grand Rapids, Mich.: Baker Book House, 1991), 315. Family government was thus placed in relation to official government.

104. John Locke, *Two Treatises on Government.*

105. Roscoe Pound, "Individual Interests in the Domestic Relations," *Michigan Law Review* 14 (1916): 180.

106. Ibid., 180–81.

107. Ibid., 186.

108. Jay Fliegelman, *Prodigals and Pilgrims: The American Revolution against Patriarchal Authority, 1750–1800* (1982), 1.

109. Some of these issues are the background for Martha Fineman, "Intimacy outside of the Natural Family: The Limits of Privacy," *Connecticut Law Review* 23 (1991): 955; Frances E. Olsen, "The Myth of State Intervention in the Family," *University of Michigan Journal of Law Reform* 18 (1985): 835.

110. See W. Michael Reisman, "Looking, Staring, and Glaring: Micro Legal Systems and the Public Order," *Denver Journal International and Pol'y* 12 (1983): 165.

111. W. Michael Reisman, "Sanctions and Enforcement," in *International Law Essays: A Supplement to International Law in Contemporary Perspective,* ed. Myres S. McDougal and W. Michael Reisman (1981), 385 n. 12.

112. Heman Humphrey, *Domestic Education* (1840), in *Children and Youth in America: A Documentary History,* ed. Robert H. Bremner (Cambridge: Harvard University Press, 1970), 1: 351–52.

113. Tocqueville, *Democracy in America,* 1:292.

114. *Reynolds v. United States,* 98 U.S. 145, 165 (1878).

115. See, e.g., Jean Bethke Elshtain, "The Family and Civic Life," in *Rebuilding the Nest: A New Commitment to the American Family,* ed. David Blankenhorn et al. (1990).

116. Antony Allott, *The Limits of Law* (London: Butterworth, 1980), 173.

117. Ibid.

118. Teitelbaum, "Placing Family in Context," 813.

119. Ibid., 825.

120. Ibid.

121. Ibid.

122. "Missouri Couple Sentenced to Die in Murder of Their Daughter," *New York Times,* December 20, 1991, A33.

123. See Richard Ewald, "Building Bridges at Island Pond," *Vermont Maga-*

zine, March–April 1991, 45. See generally Philip Greven, *Spare the Child* (New York: Vintage, 1992), 32.

124. See Olsen, "Myth of State Intervention," 843. Martha Fineman, "Intimacy outside the Family," 957 n. 1, remarks about Olsen's view that in effect inaction qualifies as intervention: "While I recognize that Professor Olsen is attempting in her analysis to provide protection for women and children within the context of the traditional patriarchal family, I find this line of reasoning disturbing as it leaves the impression that there are no qualitative distinctions to be made between intervention and nonintervention."

125. See Anne Dailey, "Constitutional Privacy and the Just Family," *Tulane Law Review* 67 (1993); Kathleen Sullivan, "Rainbow Republicanism," *Yale Law Journal* 97 (1988): 1713.

126. See Christopher Lasch, *Haven in a Heartless World: The Family Besieged* (1979).

127. Henry Maine, *Ancient Law* (London: J. M. Dent and Sons, 1977), 81. See also William V. Harris, "The Roman Father's Power of Life and Death," in *Studies in Roman Law: In Memory of A. Arthur Schiller*, ed. Roger S. Bagnall and William V. Harris (1986), 81.

128. See Edmund S. Morgan, *The Puritan Family*, rev. ed. (1966), 144–46.

129. Humphrey, *Domestic Education*, 352 (citing statutes).

130. See Jacques Donzelot, *The Policing of Families*, trans. Robert Hurley (New York: Pantheon, 1979), 85. Cf. Hendrick Hartog, "Mrs. Packard on Dependency," *Yale Journal of Journal and Humanities* 1 (1988): 79; *Parham v. J.R.*, 422 U.S. 584 (1979). In Kafka's world, this issue was raised by Milena and by the son of the criminologist Hans Gross.

131. See, e.g., *Mass Gen. Laws Ann.* (St. Paul: West Publishing, 1990), chap. 191, sec. 20.

132. Ibid. (emphasis added).

133. *Matarese v. Matarese*, 131 A. 198, 199 (R.I. 1925).

134. See generally Carl E. Schneider, "The Channeling Function in Family Law," *Hofstra Law Review* 20 (1992): 495.

135. But see *DeShaney* (discussing the constitutional grounding of such a right).

136. For a discussion of *DeShaney*, see chapter 5. Some rights are classified as "common to adults and children." Feinberg, "Child's Right," 124–25.

137. Ibid., 125–26.

138. How can we find out about this? For an example of small group research, see Walter O. Weyrauch, "The 'Basic Law' or 'Constitution' of a Small Group," *Journal of Social Issues* 27 (1971): 49.

139. See, e.g., Plato, *The Republic*, trans. Benjamin Jowett (New York: Vintage, n.d.).

140. Ibid., 37. Note the emphasis on the relationship to mother. See Dorothy Dinnerstein, *The Mermaid and the Minotaur: Sexual Arrangements and Human Malaise* (New York: Harper and Row, 1976).

141. Laing, *The Facts of Life*, 23.

142. See Miller, 10.

143. Philip Larkin, "This Be the Verse," in *High Windows* (New York: Farrar, Straus and Giroux, 1974), 30.

144. Compare G. Brandes's characterization of Goethe's approach to his own life in his autobiography: "This is the way a genius has slowly been evolved from within and by favorable surroundings." Introduction to Peter Kropotkin, *Memoirs of a Revolutionist* (New York: Horizon Press, 1968), xxxi.

145. Elshtain, "Family and Civic Life," 119.

146. Carl Jung, "Marriage as a Psychological Relationship," in *The Basic Writings of C. G. Jung*, ed. Violet Staub De Laszlo (New York: Random House, 1959), 531.

147. An issue that has been traditionally worthy of comment.

148. Kafka, *The Trial*, 263 (app. 2) (passages deleted by author).

149. Brod, *Franz Kafka*, 23.

150. *Seneca Falls Declaration of Sentiments* (1848), reprinted in Barbara Babcock, Ann Freedman, Eleanor Norton, and Susan Ross, *Sex Discrimination and the Law* (Boston: Little, Brown, 1971), 1–2.

151. Lawrence M. Friedman, *Total Justice* (New York: Russell Sage, 1985), 43.

152. See Susan Moller Okin, *Justice, Gender and the Family* (New York: Basic Books, 1989); Dailey, "Constitutional Privacy."

153. Llewellyn, "Behind Law of Divorce," pt. 1, 1293–94.

154. Michael Walzer, *Spheres of Justice: A Defense of Pluralism and Equality* (New York: Basic Books, 1983).

155. Trilling, *The Opposing Self*, 59.

156. See Benjamin Franklin, *The Autobiography of Benjamin Franklin* (New Haven: Yale University Press, 1964), 23 (referring to beatings by his brother).

157. See Nomi M. Stolzenberg, "He Drew a Circle That Shut Me Out: Assimilation, Indoctrination, and the Paradox of a Liberal Education," *Harvard Law Review* 106 (1993): 581; Martha Minow, "The Free Exercise of Families," *University of Illinois Law Review* 1991:925; Minow, "All in the Family," 275.

158. Erikson, *Childhood and Society*, 2d ed. (New York: Norton, 1963), 317.

159. Ibid., 316–17. We can stipulate that there are difficulties involved in Erikson's view of the mother as someone largely without individual interests. The point here is to see Erikson's adaptation of the idea of interest group politics to the inner life of families. On Erikson and women's "inner space," see Susan Moller Okin, *Women in Western Political Thought* (Princeton: Princeton University Press, 1979), 239ff.

160. Sigmund Freud, *Civilization and its Discontents* (1961), 60–61.

161. *Mercein v. People*, 25 Wend. 64 (N.Y. 1840).

162. *Alison v. Bryan*, 97 P. 282 (Okla. 1908).

163. Sullivan, "Rainbow Republicanism," 1713.

164. See Jean Bethke Elshtain, *Power Trips and Other Journeys: Essays in Feminism as Civic Discourse* (Madison: University of Wisconsin Press, 1990), 82–83.

165. Teitelbaum, "Placing Family in Context," 815 n. 58.

166. Ira Mark Ellman et al., *Family Law* (1986).

167. See Diana T. Meyers, *Self, Society, and Personal Choice* (New York:

Columbia University Press, 1989), 202 (noting however, that parents also have a role here).

168. Okin, *Women in Political Thought*, 286–87.

Chapter Seven

This chapter title is used also by Robert Skloot, "Breaking the Butterfly: The Politics of David Huang," *Modern Drama* 33 (1990): 59–66.

1. Michael Kennedy, *Concise Oxford Dictionary of Music*, 3d ed., 389.

2. Edith Wharton, *Age of Innocence* (New York: Ivy Classics, 1996). The meeting does not happen. Newland Archer goes back to his hotel alone without seeing her. The images in his mind are, finally, more real than the meeting itself would be. Ellen Olenska is, apparently, prepared to contemplate a joint future.

3. Joan Mellen, *The Waves at the Genji's Door: Japan through Its Cinema* (New York: Pantheon, 1976), on stereotypes of women in Japanese film (esp. p. 47).

4. Long, "Madame Butterfly."

5. B. F. Pinkerton (in Belasco's *Madame Butterfly*), 23.

6. See John Wigmore, "The Legal System of Old Japan," in *Green Bag* (1897), 407: "Many of us can testify to promises made with full knowledge of inability to perform."

7. In Ryunosuke Akutagawa's short story "In a Grove," one of the two stories on which the film is based, the bride is nineteen. *Rashomon and Other Stories*, trans. Takashi Kojima (New York: Liveright, 1952), 22.

8. See Thomas Morawetz, "Law and Literature," in *Companion to the Philosophy of Law and Legal Theory* (Cambridge: Blackwell, 1996).

9. James Fitzjames Stephen wrote with relative comfort of the wise and good guiding the foolish and bad (*Liberty, Equality, Fraternity*, [London: Cambridge University Press, 1967], 213). Do we wish that Stephen were less comfortable with conventional categories of morality?

10. It is worth noting perhaps that Freud had some interest in telepathy. Peter Gay, *A Godless Jew* (New Haven: Yale University Press, 1987), 22, 148. See, in general, Thomas Morawetz, *The Philosophy of Law: An Introduction* (New York: Macmillan, 1980).

11. The issue of insider and outsider is seen here to be contextual so that an "outsider" narrative in one community is an "insider" account in another.

12. This distinction between acknowledgment and credence is captured in the expression "I hear you."

13. E.g., Anthony Lewis, "At Home Abroad," *New York Times*, Dec. 22, 1988, quoting Joseph Goldstein on the Morgan case. Among law journal articles discussing *Rashomon* is David Sokolow, "From Kurosawa to Duncan Kennedy: The Lessons of *Rashomon* for Current Legal Education," *Wisconsin Law Review* 1991:969.

14. In Kyoto, built in 789. Akutagawa, "In a Grove," 34.

15. E.g., as "the Japanese film *Roshomon* [sic] teaches us, the eyewitnesses to any event often have sincere but quite different views of the event depending

upon their position and motivation." *In re the Public Service Co. of New Hampshire* 99 Bankruptcy Reporter (1989), 170.

16. Ethan Coen's introduction to *Fargo*, by Ethan Coen and Joel Coen (London: Faber and Faber, 1996), x. *Fargo* begins with a text that says, "This is a true story."

17. Howard Hibbitt, introduction to Akutagawa, *Rashomon and Other Stories*.

18. Donald Richie, *The Films of Kurosawa* (Berkeley and Los Angeles: University of California Press, 1965), apparently done on Kurosawa's instruction. See also Stanley Kauffmann, *"Rashomon,"* in *Perspectives on Kurosawa*, ed. James Godwin (New York: G. K. Hall, 1994), 97–98.

19. This discussion draws on Carol Weisbrod, "Groups in Perspective: A Comment on Soifer," *Washington and Lee Law Review* (1991), 437–46.

20. *Michael H. v. Gerald D.*, 491 U.S. 110 (1989) (discussion of which level of generality should be used when courts look for relevant traditions and forms).

21. Friedrich Nietzsche, *Human, All Too Human* (Lincoln: University of Nebraska Press, 1984). If one does not have a good father, he should acquire one (381). Fathers have much to do to make amends for the fact that they have sons (382). So, even the good father one has acquired, standing in the (social) role of father, has much to be sorry about. The critical point being not the biological (natural) but the social role?

22. Laurence Sterne, *The Life and Opinions of Tristram Shandy* (New York: Modern Library, 1950).

23. Ibid., 339. Uncle Toby and the vulgar remain of the opinion, however, that there is "some sort of consanguinity between the mother and her son." This suggests that the learned, including the judges, are not the final authorities on such questions.

24. See Pamela Sheingorn, "Appropriating the Holy Kinship," in *Interpreting Cultural Symbols: Saint Anne in Late Medieval Society*, ed. Katherine Ashley and Pamela Sheingorn (Athens: University of Georgia Press, 1990), 173.

25. Lawrence Friedman, *The Republic of Choice* (Cambridge: Harvard University Press, 1990).

26. Ibid., 89–90 (noting that immutability is "not so obvious a concept as it seems at first glance").

27. Cf. Karl N. Llewellyn, *The Bramble Bush* (1951; reprint, New York: Oceana, 1975), 59: "Courts sometimes look directly at society, sometimes at the work of other courts."

28. For one description of that social construction, see Peter Berger and Thomas Luckmann, *The Social Construction of Reality* (1967), 76–77.

29. See Peter Ouspensky, *Strange Life of Ivan Osokin* (London: Arkana, 1987) (for the same theme in another idiom, see also Morris Bishop, "We Have Been Here Before," in *The Best of Bishop* [Ithaca: Cornell University Press, 1980], 39); Philip Dick, *Blade Runner (Do Androids Dream of Electric Sheep?)* (New York: Ballantine, 1968); Brian Aldiss, *Cryptozoic!* (New York: Avon, 1967).

30. Except, for example, as they are implicated in our law and morality. See Weisbrod, "Charles Guiteau."

31. Hart and McNaughton, *Evidence and Inference in the Law* (extract in John Waltz, and Roger Park, 65–66, *Cases and Materials on Evidence* [Westbury, N.Y.: Foundation Press, 1991]).

32. See Robert Cover, "Violence and the Word," 95 *Yale Law Journal* 1601–29, quoted in Sarat and Kearns, *Law's Violence*, 216.

33. Sarat and Kearns, *Law's Violence*, 228.

34. Ibid.

35. Cover, "Nomos and Narrative," 53, quoted in Sarat and Kearns, *Law's Violence*, 229.

36. Sarat and Kearns, *Law's Violence*, 231.

37. The custody case *Quiner v. Quiner* (59 Cal. Rep. 503 (1969)), is discussed in Carl E. Schneider, "Religion in the Custody of Children," *Michigan Journal of Law Reform* (1989). Edmund Gosse, whose *Father and Son* was published anonymously, was among other things an early commentator on English biography. Gosse, "Custom of Biography," *Anglo Saxon Review* 1901:195–208. As to *Father and Son*, Roger Scruton has written: "The economy, objectivity and evocative power of this book are sufficient reason to admire it. Yet more impressive, however, is the self-therapy that Gosse conducts through its pages. His father, a biblical fundamentalist, famous for arguing against the Darwinists that the earth was created 7,000 years ago with all the fossils implanted in it by God, was the archetypal Victorian authority-figure, whose love for his son took the form of a remorseless interrogation of young Edmund's thoughts and emotions. . . . Torment after torment is imposed upon the helpless boy; but the prose in which it is recalled has the tone of forgiveness. *Father and Son* is one of the most poignant testimonies that I know, to the redeeming power of literature." "Books I Wish I'd Written," *Guardian*, October 17, 1996. Gosse included a striking account of the development of his dual nature. "I had found a companion in myself. There were two of us, and we could talk to each other." (*Father and Son* [London: Penguin], 58). On Philip Henry Gosse, see Stephen Jay Gould, "Adam's Navel," *Natural History* 93 (1984): 6.

38. Garrison Keillor, *We Are Still Married* (New York: Penguin, 1990); Paul Boyer, *When Time Shall Be No More* (Cambridge: Harvard University Press, 1993).

39. Keillor, *We Are Still Married*.

40. Garrison Keillor, *Lake Wobegon Days* (New York: Penguin, 1986), 253ff.

41. A recent law review article quotes the line as meaning spending too much to realize too little. Peter A. Alces, "Commentary on Professor White's Lopucki's Article: Abolish the Article 9 Filing System," *Minnesota Law Review* (1995).

42. Jeffrey Shamans, "Constitutional Fact: The Perception of Reality by the Supreme Court," *Florida Law Review* 35 (1913): 241.

43. For a general sense of the issues, see Daniel Farber and Susanna Sherry, "Telling Stories Out of School: An Essay on Legal Narrative," 45 *Stanford Law Review* 807 (1993); see also Richard Delgado, "On Telling Stories in School: A Reply to Farber and Sherry" 46 *Vanderbilt Law Review* 665 (1995).

44. Oscar Wilde, *The Decay of Lying* (London: Syrens, 1995), 38. See also Peter Brooks in *Law's Stories* (New Haven: Yale University Press, 1996), 19.

45. Smiley, "Can Mothers Think," 7.

46. Milner Ball, "Minority Scholarship," *Harvard Law Review* 102 (1989): 1745. Also on law and outsiders, see Milner Ball, *The Word and the Law* (Chicago: University of Chicago Press, 1993).

47. Georg Simmel, *On Individuality and Social Forms* (1971), 314. Simmel noted the connection between law and fashion.

48. Llewellyn, *The Bramble Bush*, 38.

49. Leon Lipson, letter to the editor on a proposal for a science court, *Science*, November 26, 1976.

50. Cf. George Orwell: " 'Who controls the past,' ran the party slogan, 'Controls the future: Who controls the present controls the past.' " *Nineteen Eighty-Four* (New York: Harcourt Brace, 1949), 35.

51. Constitutional facts, *Florida Law Review* 35 (1983).

52. See Richie, *The Films of Kurosawa*.

53. Thus the debate over Patricia Williams's discussion of Tawana Brawley's allegations. See Kathryn Abrams, "How to Have a Culture War" 65 *Chicago Law Review* 1091, 1104–5 (1998), reviewing Daniel Farber and Susanna Sherry, *Beyond All Reason*.

54. William L. Twining, *Rethinking Evidence* (Evanston, Ill.: Northwestern University Press, 1990), 261.

55. A history told by Schneider, in "Moral Discourse."

56. Cf. Goethe's maxim on analogic reason, as thinking that does not even aim at finality (*Maxims and Reflections*, trans. Bailey Saunders [New York: Macmillan, 1893], 70).

57. Richard Rorty, *Objectivity, Relativism, and Truth*, 207. See also Morawetz on the inevitability of generalizing. Thomas Morawetz, "Law's Essence: Lawyers as Tellers of Tales," 29 *Connecticut Law Review* 899 (1997), reviewing "Law's Stories" (some laws are a kind of generalizing in "an imperative mode").

58. This draws on Carol Weisbrod, "Building Community in Sarastro's Dungeon," *Yale Journal of Law and Humanities* 9, no. 2 (1997): 443–59, reviewing David Damrosch, *We Scholars* (1995).

59. Fuller, *Legal Fictions*, 136, quoted in Minow, *Making All the Difference*, 371.

60. Morawetz, "Law's Essence."

61. Schneider, "Channeling Function," quotes Whitehead to the effect that civilization proceeds because of things we can take for granted. Assuming that everyone agrees that change is, nonetheless, sometimes needed, the problem becomes: "how can we know that change is needed?" One way is by listening to the accounts of those who find that civilization and the values it takes for granted contain highly problematic elements. See also the discussion of Isaacs on adhesion contracts in chapter 3.

62. In theory this might be true for all words, and we would be close to the orientation to language described in discussion of Kafka in chapter 4.

63. Gustave Flaubert, *The Dictionary of Accepted Ideas*, trans. Jacques Barzun (New York: New Directions, 1968), 58.

Conclusion

1. Robert Ferguson, *Law and Letters in American Culture* (Cambridge: Harvard University Press, 1984).

2. Martha Minow notes that the "incompleteness of storytelling as a mode of decision-making may be both a defect and a virtue." The incompleteness is a defect if one seeks articulated norms to guide future for the decision-makers, "but it is a virtue if one knows that prevailing articulated norms are not the right ones." Martha Minow, "Stories in Law," in *Law's Stories: Narrative and Rhetoric in the Law*, ed. Peter Brooks and Paul Gewirtz (New Haven: Yale University Press, 1996).

3. Goethe, *Maxims and Reflections*, trans. Bailey Saunders (New York: Macmillan, 1893), 62. The aural rather than visual metaphor is worth noting. Bernard J. Hibbits, "Making Sense of Metaphors: Visuality, Aurality, and the Reconfiguration of American Legal Discourse," *Cardozo Law Review* 16 (1994): 229.

4. Learned Hand, "A Plea for the Open Mind," in *The Spirit of Liberty*, ed. Irving Dillard, 3d ed. (New York: Knopf, 1960), 281.

5. E. M. Cioran, *Anathemas and Admirations*, trans. Richard Howard (New York: Arcade, 1991), 196.

6. Richard Posner, *Overcoming Law* (Cambridge: Harvard University Press, 1995), 131. See also Alexander Bickel, *The Least Dangerous Branch*, 238–40, on passive virtues.

7. Hand, "A Plea for the Open Mind."

8. *Pirke Avot, A Modern Commentary on Jewish Ethics*, ed. and trans. Leonard Kravitz and Kerry M. Olitzsky (New York: UAHC Press, 1993), 56.

Index